AM DOM
(Kea)

Books are to be returned
the last date be

SCOTTISH INDUSTRIAL POLICY

SERIES: 3

Editors: Neil Hood and Stephen Young

realise   pros of comm. enterprises p. 115.
but√   put n= of jobs into perspective   116
           "value of local control over
           social + economic control.
                                              P128
cb   Should not replace policy
                                              P13
      CB - negatives.

REMAKING URBAN SCOTLAND

Strategies for Local Economic Development

Michael Keating and Robin Boyle

———

EDINBURGH

© Michael Keating and
Robin Boyle 1986
Edinburgh University Press
22 George Square, Edinburgh

Set in Linoterm Times by
Speedspools, Edinburgh
Printed in Great Britain by
Redwood Burn Ltd, Trowbridge

British Library Cataloguing
in Publication Data
Keating, Michael, *1950-*
Remaking urban Scotland: strategies for
local economic development. —(Scottish
industrial policy series; 3)
1. Scotland—Economic conditions—
1918-1973   2. Scotland—Economic conditions
—1973-
I. Title   II. Boyle, Robin   III. Series
330.9411'0858   HC257.54

ISBN 0 85224 531 9

CONTENTS

Preface   vii

Glossary of Abbreviations   ix

1. INTRODUCTION   1

   Mapping the Policy Field   1

   The Government of Urban Scotland   13

2. URBAN PLANNING IN SCOTLAND   28

   The Local Planning System   28

   Regional Planning   31

   New Towns   33

   Planning in the 1980s   38

   Changing Direction   41

3. CENTRAL INITIATIVES FOR LOCAL ECONOMIC
   DEVELOPMENT   47

   Regional Policy   47

   Enterprise Zones   55

   European Initiatives   65

4. LOCAL GOVERNMENT AND ECONOMIC
   DEVELOPMENT   69

   Local Government Expenditure   69

   Local Economic Development Policies   76

      Administrative Reorganisation   77

      Bending of Existing Policies   78

      Provision of Land and Factories   79

      Joint Ventures   80

      Promotion of Inward Investment   80

      Direct Aid to Firms   81

Contents

5. SDA INITIATIVES   85
   The Development of the Area Approach   85
   Resources   91
   Working Relationships   101
   Evaluation in Area Projects   109
   The Future of the Area Approach   110

6. COMMUNITY-BASED LOCAL ECONOMIC
   DEVELOPMENT   115
   The Origins of Community Business   115
   The Organisation of Community Business in Scotland   121
   The Potential of Community Business   134

7. PRIVATE STRATEGIES FOR LOCAL ECONOMIC
   DEVELOPMENT: The Role of Enterprise Trusts   137
   Origins   137
   Organisation and Management   145
   Local Enterprise Trusts in Scotland   146
   Assessing Enterprise Trusts   154

8. NEW DIRECTIONS   158

   References   167
   Index   171

PREFACE

Local economic policies have become of increasing importance over the last decade, initially as a development of policies aimed at combatting urban deprivation and, more recently, as a contribution to reversing national economic decline. Our initial interest was stimulated by the distinctive form which these policies have taken in Scotland, where the Scottish Development Agency, a body without parallel in England, has, since 1975, had wide-ranging responsibilities for physical and economic regeneration. Scotland's distinctive administrative structure is sometimes said to provide a greater coherence to spatial development policies than is achieved in England. In the following chapters, we assess this claim, examining six strands of local development policy. After an initial mapping of the policy field, we review the experience of urban and regional planning in Scotland, noting the change in direction of spatial policy in the late 1970s away from regional planning and urban dispersal towards more tightly focussed urban initiatives. Next, we examine central government's spatial policies, in the form of regional policy and the enterprise zone experiment and the attempts by the European Community to forge urban and regional policies. Chapter 4 reviews local government economic initiatives and chapter 5 the area projects of the Scottish Development Agency. We then examine community-based strategies, their goals and achievements and, in chapter 7, assess the recent growth of the private-sector enterprise trust movement. Our conclusion focusses on the new directions which urban economic policies are taking and warns of the danger of a disintegration of the social, physical and economic strands of policy which, in our view, should be considered together.

In a modest way, this book has been its own job-creation project. Juliet Gilchrist, Gary Hughes and Kevin Doran assisted at various times with the research while Peter Taylor was employed on an earlier project on which this draws. Yvonne Macleod typed the tables with her customary accuracy. We are grateful to officials of central and local government and the Scottish Development Agency for their help in collecting material, to Derrick Johnstone and Ivan Turok for helpful comments on draft chapters and to David Heald, Arthur Midwinter and Urlan Wannop for advice. Financial support was provided by the Carnegie Trust for the Universities of Scotland, the

Departments of Administration and Urban and Regional Planning at the University of Strathclyde and the Nuffield Foundation. The earlier project was supported by the Social Science Research Council under its initiative on central-local relations. Finally, our thanks go to the College of Urban Affairs and Public Policy at the University of Delaware, USA, where the book was completed in April 1985.

Michael Keating, Robin Boyle

GLOSSARY OF ABBREVIATIONS

AEI	American Enterprise Institution.
ARC	Action Resource Centre.
ASSET	Ardrossan, Saltcoats and Stevenston Enterprise Trust.
BASE	Bathgate Area Support for Enterprise.
BIC	Business in the Community.
BSC	British Steel Corporation.
BSC(I)	British Steel Corporation (Industry) Ltd.
CADET	Cumnock and Doon Enterprise Trust.
CAP	Community Action Programme.
CBI	Confederation of British Industry.
CBS	Community Business Scotland.
CCP	Comprehensive Community Programme.
CDP	Community Development Project.
CIPFA	Chartered Institute of Public Finance and Accountancy.
COSLA	Convention of Scottish Local Authorities.
DHSS	Department of Health and Social Security.
DI	Department of Industry.
DOE	Department of the Environment.
EC	European Community.
ECSC	European Coal and Steel Community.
EFFY	Enterprise Fund for Youth.
EIB	European Investment Bank.
EPA	Economic Priority Area.
ERDF	European Regional Development Fund.
ESF	European Social Fund.
EVENT	Edinburgh Venture.
EZ	Enterprise Zone.
GEAR	Glasgow Eastern Area Renewal.
GET	Glenrothes Enterprise Trust.
GO	Glasgow Opportunities.
HIDB	Highlands and Islands Development Board.
HPSO	Home Production Sales Organisation.
IIA	Industrial Improvement Area.
IDC	Industrial Development Certificate.

IDO	Integrated Development Operation.
IDS(SEPD)	Industry Department for Scotland (formerly Scottish Economic Planning Department).
IMF	International Monetary Fund.
LEAP	Local Enterprise Advisory Project.
LEDIS	Local Economic Development Information Service.
LEGUP	Local Enterprise Grant for Urban Projects.
LEntA	London Enterprise Agency.
LIFE	Lanarkshire Industrial Field Executive.
LIS	Locate in Scotland.
LISC	Local Initiatives Support Corporation.
MET	Motherwell Enterprise Trust.
MIT	Massachusetts Institute of Technology.
MSC	Manpower Services Commission.
NESDA	North East of Scotland Development Association.
PEGLEG	Port Glasgow Local Enterprise Group.
PPD	Planning and Projects Directorate (of SDA).
PSBR	Public Sector Borrowing Requirement.
RDG	Regional Development Grant.
RSG	Rate Support Grant.
SARC	Scottish Action Resource Centre.
SBD	Small Business Division (of SDA).
SCB	Strathclyde Community Business.
SCDC	Scottish Co-operative Development Committee.
SDA	Scottish Development Agency.
SDD	Scottish Development Department.
SPU	Special Programmes Unit (of CBI).
SSHA	Scottish Special Housing Association.
STUC	Scottish Trades Union Congress.
TCPA	Town and Country Planning Association.
TRIO	Tayside Regional Industrial Office.
TUC	Trades Union Congress.
UP	Urban Programme.
WEA	Workers' Educational Association.
YTS	Youth Training Scheme.

1

INTRODUCTION

Mapping the Policy Field

Urban policy – the subject matter of this book – is a complex term, encompassing a wide range of policies bearing on the cities. To simplify, one can distinguish three main strands – the physical/environmental; the social; and the economic. For much of the post-war period, the 'urban problem' was seen in physical terms, with the emphasis placed on the reconstruction and modernisation of the urban fabric, spatial design and the decanting of surplus urban populations to new towns and other overspill areas. Crash programmes were launched to attack the problem of delapidated and over-crowded housing, commercial redevelopment transformed city centres and ambitious highway programmes were designed and, sometimes, implemented.

By 1964, however, the commitment to physical determinism was on the wane. While two decades of planned reconstruction had extensively rebuilt bomb-damaged town centres, decanted whole communities from inner-city slums to peripheral housing estates, constructed New Towns from industrial Clydeside to rural Hertfordshire, driven multi-lane motorways through major cities and created the conditions for commercial expansion, the economic and especially the social condition of certain major urban areas had barely improved. There was, moreover, disquieting evidence that the best efforts of well-intentioned public policy was having a regressive effect on parts of cities. Instead of solving or eradicating urban problems as promised by planners, their physical solutions were merely shifting the locus of the malaise and not confronting the socio-economic roots of urban decline. Not only was policy failing to deliver urban improvement but the very structure of urban government seemed incapable of managing the scope or pace of change. The wider economic climate, too, was changing. Urban policy in the 1950s and early 1960s was built around technical means for controlling and managing growth; by the late 1960s, economic crisis and the failure of much public intervention led to a different perspective, one focussed on managing first the social and then the economic consequences of urban decline.

The literature on this redirection of urban policy is generally agreed that the initial change came through a review of housing policy. Studies in London, Manchester and Clydeside revealed serious housing stress, particu-

1

larly in the private rented sector, continuing structural decline and a failure of the public sector effectively to replace sub-standard stock. These and other studies also began to record the failure of public sector housing. Highlighted by the Ronan Point disaster in London, the industrialised building techniques that produced high rise and deck-access high density housing were increasingly condemned as structurally unsafe and socially undesirable. Moreover, just as the technical solution to physical renewal was attracting criticism, mechanistic housing management was being seen as socially divisive, acting against rather than in the interests of certain sectors of the population. This reaction against monolithic housing structures – physical and managerial – eventually led to a retreat from the policy of demolition and rebuilding and its replacement by programmes of rehabilitation, initially the improvement of individual dwellings and then of neighbourhoods through, in England and Wales, General Improvement Areas. There was also a shift from the public to the private sector as the dominant mode of improving British housing conditions. Housing associations, too, with finance from the Housing Corporation, were encouraged to undertake improvement programmes, reducing further local government's role.

Housing policy in Scotland moved in a similar direction, if at a slower pace, with the larger urban housing authorities not surprisingly reluctant to reduce their house building programmes. Keating and Midwinter (1983a) demonstrate the importance of housing policy, housing finance and house building in the relationship between central and local government and the connections between housing and other components of urban policy – job opportunities, income levels and the poor social environment of a number of older Scottish cities. So the changes in British housing policy were to have a major influence on the type of urban planning and development that subsequently emerged in Scotland. At the centre of the change was the major shift from new-build to rehabilitation and the activities of community-based housing associations in the improvement of the traditional tenemental stock.

If housing supplied the ignition for the redirection of urban policy and the demise of planned, comprehensive renewal, the rate of policy change was accelerated by the 'rediscovery of poverty' and the identification of a series of social problems spatially concentrated into areas of multiple deprivation. Once again, housing was important and area policies were designed to tackle areas of 'housing stress' but it was an analysis of urban primary school education, conducted by the Plowden Committee, that introduced policies directed at specific problems in selected target areas. It was equally significant that these Education Priority Areas also addressed the educational problems of ethnic minorities.

Growing public concern about immigration and the concentration of certain ethnic groups in a number of English cities is often cited as the 'specific stimulus' (Higgins et al. 1983) for the introduction in 1968 of the

Urban Programme (UP). Folklore has it that the UP was an immediate response by Prime Minister Harold Wilson to Enoch Powell's inflammatory 'rivers of blood' speech but there is evidence that the Government was already considering financial assistance for social and community programmes in areas of racial tension. The UP, administered by the Home Office, was initially concerned mainly with education, welfare services and community development, diverting a small proportion of the Rate Support Grant to local authorities and voluntary organisations in areas having identifiable social problems. In Scotland, UP resources were channelled through the Scottish Office. The Urban Programme has been criticised as being too small, badly directed and aimed at the wrong targets; nevertheless it was the most tangible expression of government policy directed at urban problems and remained largely unaltered from 1969 to 1978.

Another component of the redirected urban policy and perhaps the clearest indicator of its social welfare/neighbourhood focus came in the shape of the Community Development Project (CDP). This was basically an experiment 'ambitious in scope but modest in terms of expenditure' (Higgins et al. 1983) that selected twelve areas in the UK, one being Ferguslie Park in Paisley, where the existing social and, to a lesser extent, economic problems could be addressed through an unusual combination of neighbourhood self-help, improved local social services and community action. In contrast to the UP, which was hurriedly developed as a political expedient, the CDP was conceived by a civil servant in the Home Office on the basis of his experience with the Educational Priority Areas in the Department of Education and Science and some knowledge of the American Community Action Programme. Each CDP was coupled to a research team working from a university or polytechnic with the goal of linking analytical research directly to action research at the community level. As widely reported, the CDP experiment met with considerable hostility in central government and, after the publication of a series of highly critical reports both by individual CDP teams and by the Information and Intelligence Unit, the programme was axed in 1977. Despite its abrupt termination, the CDP was important in the evolution of urban policy in Britain in that it demonstrated the weakness of programmes based on the area concept of poverty and the futility of expecting social improvement without tackling the underlying weaknesses of the local, or even the national, economy. These lessons were to play an important part in the next phase of evolution of urban policy, with the emphasis on economic development.

The Ferguslie Park CDP did not appear to play a significant part in the evolution of urban policy in Scotland. The Scottish Office, for example, did not introduce a series of improved neighbourhood experiments, although subsequent local authority policies aimed at improving living conditions in public sector housing did learn from the analysis of problems found in the Paisley experiment. Nevertheless, the scale of urban deprivation in parts of

Scotland, the ever-present problems of Glasgow's housing and the realisation that the combination of population 'overspill' and urban redevelopment was not solving the problems, gave the Scottish Office the opportunity to examine a range of policy options on urban deprivation. This experience was used by the Home Office when they developed the Comprehensive Community Programme (CCP), a short-lived experiment based on a partnership between central and local government. The CCP was an attempt to apply the techniques of corporate management to areas demonstrating severe multiple deprivation. Glasgow was considered as a contender for the experiment but was rejected because of the scale and severity of its problems. Eventually, Motherwell was chosen as the token Scottish representative, with the council selecting Craigneuk, a public sector housing scheme in the shadow of the Ravenscraig steel works. Like the other CCPs, however, Craigneuk was essentially a still-born experiment in area management, with few additional resources, little sustained interest by central government, suspicion and hostility by the local authority and apathy in the local community.

The CCP marked the end of a phase in urban policy in Scotland as in Britain as a whole in which urban problems were seen as essentially social, spatially constrained and capable of local solution through improved co-ordination between government agencies using limited but tightly targetted sums of money. As this phase was being wound down, the next phase was already under way. In England and Wales, the Inner Area Studies, commissioned by Peter Walker while at the Department of the Environment and accepted by his Labour successor, Peter Shore, refocussed urban policy towards the inner city, towards the weaknesses of the local economy and towards a combination of social, economic and physical solutions to urban decay. With the transfer of the Urban Programme from the Home Office to the DOE, this Policy realignment led first to the 1977 White Paper, Policy for the Inner Cities, then to the Inner Urban Areas Act in 1978. While sticking largely to the 'multiple deprivation' view of urban decline the White Paper recognised the economic dimension and the 1978 Act expanded the urban programme to include economic activities introducing the Partnership and Programme arrangements between central government and 'designated' local authorities to plan integrated schemes for urban regeneration, encompassing physical, social and economic policies. The U-turn in national urban policy was epitomised in England by the instruction to the Location of Offices Bureau to stop encouraging dispersal of office employment from London and devote its efforts to getting it back in again. In Scotland, policy moved again in a similar direction but its implementation took a different course. There were no partnerships established in Scotland but the same policy switch had been made here in 1976, with the cancellation of the plans for Stonehouse new town in favour of the GEAR project for Glasgow's east end. GEAR, too, sought to integrate the three policy strands of physical, social and economic regeneration.

4

In addition to these u k-wide trends, three specific factors were important in the redirection of Scottish urban policy in the mid-1970s and in the approach to urban planning that followed. The results of the 1971 census and the detailed analysis in the West Central Plan graphically illustrated the inner city problems in Glasgow and the traditional industrial areas. This trend was confirmed by the 1981 census. While the population of Scotland remained stable over the period 1961–81, there were significant changes in its distribution, with Strathclyde losing 100,000 people while regions in the North and East, notably Grampian and Central, gained population (tables 1.1 and 1.2).

In order to reverse these demographic trends and to address the economic, social and physical problems of the industrial heartland, policy attempted to reorientate public and private investment away from the suburbs and the New Towns towards areas of severe urban deprivation.

Table 1.1. Population characteristics of the Scottish regions, 1961-81.

	1961	1971	1981	% change 1961-81
SCOTLAND	5,179,344	5,228,963	5,130,735	−0.9
Borders	102,232	98,477	99,784	−2.4
Central	244,620	263,028	273,391	+11.8
Dumfries & Galloway	146,434	143,187	145,139	−0.9
Fife	320,692	327,131	327,362	+2.1
Grampian	440,351	438,630	471,942	+7.2
Highland	163,796	175,473	200,150	+22.2
Lothian	710,163	745,623	738,372	+4.0
Strathclyde	2,584,068	2,575,514	2,404,532	−7.0
Tayside	397,820	397,605	391,846	−1.5
Orkney	18,747	17,077	19,056	+1.6
Shetland	17,812	17,237	27,277	+53.1
Western Isles	32,609	29,891	31,884	−2.2

Source: Census.

Table 1.2. Population characteristics of the cities, 1961-81.

	1961	1971	1981	% change 1961-81
Glasgow	1,140,078	982,315	765,915	−32.8
Edinburgh	483,854	476,531	436,939	−1.5
Aberdeen	206,319	211,848	203,927	−1.6
Dundee	195,258	197,371	179,674	−8.0

Source: Census.

The second factor was the formation by the Scottish Office of an Urban Renewal Unit to formulate broad urban policy based on coordinated, controlled positive discrimination for selected urban renewal schemes, encompassing both socio-economic and physical change. Thirdly, local government reorganisation in 1975 and the requirement to produce Regional Reports gave the new regional councils their first opportunity comprehensively to examine urban conditions and begin the development of policy directed at social and economic deprivation. In the case of Strathclyde Regional Council, the Regional Report contained policies of positive discrimination through what became known as Areas of Priority Treatment. Furthermore, following the recommendations of the West Central Scotland Plan, the Regional Council also called for the de-designation of Stonehouse New Town, then being built some 17 miles south of Glasgow. This recommendation was endorsed by the Scottish Secretary in 1976.

At the same time, the growing recognition that economic change might be at the root of the urban problem received statistical confirmation. Analysis of the 1971 and 1981 census data and academic research confirmed the view that the cities were suffering a loss of jobs as well as population and that the decline of manufacturing industry was particularly pronounced. Along with the rest of the UK, Scotland has experienced rising levels of unemployment since the mid-1970s (figure 1.1). At the same time, the distribution of

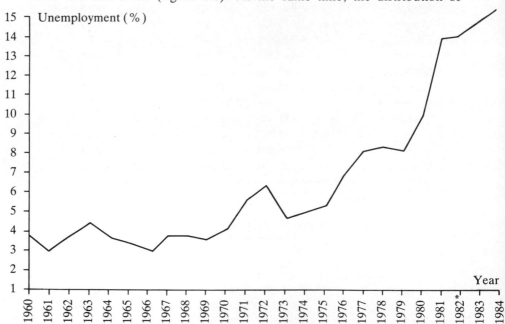

Figure 1.1. Percentage unemployment rate in Scotland 1961-83.
(*In 1982 the method of calculating the number of unemployed was changed.) Source: Scottish Abstract of Statistics.

Table 1.3. Employees by % of workforce employed in industry by SIC (1968) order groupings 1965-82.

Sectors	1965	1966	1967	1968	1969	1970	1971	1972	1973	1974	1975	1976	1977	1978	1979	1980	1981	1982
I	3.7	3.4	3.2	3.1	2.9	2.9	2.7	2.7	2.5	2.4	2.4	2.4	2.4	2.3	2.3	2.2	2.3	2.3
II	2.9	2.6	2.5	2.2	2.0	1.9	1.9	1.9	1.7	1.6	1.7	1.7	1.7	1.9	2.0	2.1	2.2	2.3
III-XIX	34.3	34.2	33.7	33.8	34.4	34.4	33.4	32.3	32.0	32.4	30.7	29.4	29.7	29.2	28.5	26.7	24.9	24.1
XX	8.5	8.8	8.9	9.0	8.8	8.4	7.9	7.9	8.4	8.2	8.3	8.3	7.9	7.7	7.8	7.7	7.1	6.7
XXI	1.6	1.7	1.6	1.6	1.6	1.5	1.5	1.5	1.4	1.3	1.3	1.4	1.4	1.3	1.4	1.4	1.5	1.5
XXII-XXVII	49.0	49.2	50.0	50.3	50.3	50.9	52.4	53.7	53.9	54.0	55.6	56.9	56.9	57.5	58.1	59.9	62.0	63.2

I Agriculture, Forestry and Fishing
II Mining and Quarrying
III-XIX Manufacturing Industries
XX Construction
XXI Gas, Electricity and Water
XXII-XXVII Services

Source: Department of Employment, *Employment Gazette.*

7

employment shifted from manufacturing to the service sector. Between 1965 and 1982, the share of employment in manufacturing fell from 34 to 24 per cent while that of services increased from 49 to 63 per cent of the workforce (table 1.3).

The decline of the traditional industrial areas is confirmed by figure 1.2, which compares the unemployment rates of Strathclyde and Grampian regions between 1971 and 1983, showing the contrast between a declining industrial area and the centre of the oil boom. Regional variation in urban

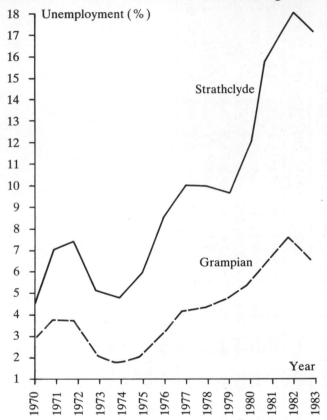

Figure 1.2. Regional unemployment rates in Strathclyde and Grampian 1971-83. Source: Scottish Abstract of Statistics.

economic decline is most clearly seen in table 1.4, where, against the Scottish trend, male unemployment in Aberdeen rose by less than 2 per cent between 1971 and 1981 while, in sharp contrast, it rose by 8 per cent in Dundee and 11 per cent in Glasgow. Tables 1.5 and 1.6 show the differential impact of the economic recession of the late 1970s on Scotland's regions and cities. Of a net loss of 58,000 jobs in manufacturing, 43,000 were in Strathclyde Region, which has just under half the Scottish population and, of that,

Table 1.4. Male unemployment (16-64) in the cities.*

Year	Aberdeen	Dundee	Edinburgh	Glasgow
1971	6.5	9.9	7.6	13.5
1981	8.1	17.7	11.1	24.3

* i.e. men (16-64) out of employment as a % of economically
active men.

22,000 were in the city of Glasgow. Of the 3,900 manufacturing jobs lost in Tayside, 3,400 were in the city of Dundee, which accounts for just half the region's population. The overall picture, then, is one of decline in the traditional industrial areas and the cities of the Industrial Revolution, lending support to the view that it is economic and industrial change which underlies the growth of urban deprivation.

Table 1.5. Openings/closures within major cities 1975-80.

City	Openings		Closures		Net
	No.	Jobs created	No.	Jobs lost	employees
Aberdeen	45	864	81	3,464	−2,600
Dundee	21	470*	50	3,905*	−3,435
Edinburgh	40	1,014*	69	3,173	−2,159
Glasgow	125	2,710	393	24,361	−21,651

* Some data preserved to retain confidentiality and employment figures
do not include estimates for this.
Source: Industry Department for Scotland.

The importance of the GEAR project in shifting the policy focus yet further towards economic objectives and away from the comprehensive approach is traced in chapter 2. One effect which must be noted here is that this new economic emphasis on urban policy has caused further definitional problems, for government continues to pursue not only sectoral economic policies but also spatial ones which may conflict with the new urban focus. Regional policy is based on a quite different rationale, as we shall see, and may even conflict with urban priorities, as happened in the West Midlands in the 1970s and may still happen in inner London, where a declining urban core is located in a relatively prosperous region. In England, the conflict between the 'urban' and 'regional' definitions of the problem is exacerbated by the division between the Departments of the Environment, responsible for urban economic policies and Trade and Industry, responsible for regional and sectoral policies. A revealing glimpse of this was given in the 1977 White Paper on the inner cities, which makes the extraordinary proposal that

Table 1.6. Openings/closures 1975-80 by region.

Region	No. of openings	% of Scottish openings	No. of closures	% of Scottish closures	Work created from openings	Employees lost from closures	Net employees
Scotland	823	100.0	1,747	100.0	22,408*	80,477*	−58,069
Borders	38	4.6	56	3.8	636*	2,054*	−1,418
Central	30	3.6	59	4.0	789*	3,227*	−2,438
Dumfries and Galloway	23	2.8	31	2.1	515*	1,136*	−621
Fife	55	6.7	65	4.4	1,535*	2,612*	−1,077
Grampian	82	10.0	127	8.6	1,436	3,648	−2,212
Highlands and Islands	34	4.1	52	3.5	641*	1,194*	−553
Lothian	115	14.0	161	10.9	3,852*	7,169	−3,317
Strathclyde	399	48.5	853	56.5	10,947	54,151	−43,204
Tayside	47	5.7	90	6.1	995*	4,899	−3,904

* Some data preserved to retain confidentiality and employment figures do not include estimates for this.
Source: Industry Department for Scotland.

henceforth the two departments were going to work closely together (extra-ordinary in that they should not be doing it already). The persistence of the problem is testified in the 1983 White Paper on regional policy which repeats the good resolution in almost identical language.

To this plethora of policies have been added in recent years a series of ad hoc initiatives, some of which have not initially had an explicit spatial focus. Enterprise zones were initially said to be neither urban nor regional policy but soon became a bit of both. The Merseyside Task Force was a one-off initiative but in 1985 City Action Teams were set up to coordinate central government's input to urban renewal in several English cities. In the run-up to the 1983 General Election a minister was appointed to look after the politically crucial West Midlands, suffering from industrial collapse. Urban Development Corporations have been established in Liverpool and London Docklands. In Scotland, Task Forces were sent into Clydebank and Garnock Valley and the Scottish Development Agency has a series of urban area projects. Local authorities have launched their own urban economic initiatives, in some cases with quite elaborate machinery such as the local enterprise boards in the West Midlands and Greater London.

By 1983, the Regional Studies Association could make the harsh judgement that 'spatial economic policy has degenerated into an uncoordinated morass of disparate, often ad hoc and potentially wasteful initiatives' (RSA 1983, 99). We should perhaps be wary of the temptation to excessive tidy-mindedness here. A national hierarchy of spatial policies and priorities may be neither possible nor desirable, given the differing conditions of localities and a lack of 'coordination' may be the result of differing levels of government adopting quite legitimately differing priorities. Overt policy conflict, on the other hand, can be wasteful and damaging. One of our concerns in this book is to test the idea that there is a distinctive spatial policy and one that is better integrated in Scotland than elsewhere in the United Kingdom. This in turn has two dimensions, whether the physical, social and economic strands of policy are integrated and whether the economic elements are consistent among themselves.

Analysing spatial policy objectives is notoriously difficult. The aim of urban economic policies, for example, may be to enhance the economic performance of specific urban areas or to maximise the contribution of the latter to national economic objectives. The former could justify resource discrimination in favour of particular areas while the latter would only permit investment where uniform national criteria were satisfied. At certain times, there may be a consensus on diversionary industrial policies. As we shall see, this was the case for many years with regional policies. In a recession, however, it is difficult to justify intervention where this merely displaces economic activity from one needy area to another (perhaps needier) one.

Economic objectives themselves may be based on maximising produc-

11

tion, contributing to exports or maintaining and increasing employment. As employment is a major means whereby incomes are maintained and community morale sustained, it is a social as well as an economic objective, so that employment-generating schemes may need to be evaluated on both social and economic criteria. At the small area level, externalities create further links among policy fields. Closure of an enterprise on commercial grounds may impose such costs on a local community through multiplier effects on local incomes and added welfare spending as to justify subsidies to keep it going or provide alternative employment. On the other hand, this may have unfavourable repercussions on competing enterprises or areas which would suffer in their turn. It is not only economic collapse which can create spin-offs into other policy arenas. Industrial modernisation, one of the aims of national and regional economic policy, may, in today's circumstances, be employment-destroying, with serious implications for the distribution of income.

In so far as environmental, social and economic policies are targetted on specific areas, there is a question as to whether they are effective in reaching the target clients. It has long been accepted that spatial definitions of social deprivation are inadequate. In the case of economic and employment initiatives, there is nothing to prevent people from outside the target area taking advantage of the new job opportunities.

There are those who argue that this creates too large an agenda for urban economic policy, which should be concerned simply with 'wealth creation', leaving other questions as purely distributional issues, to be solved through social policy measures. This is a point to which we return in the conclusion. In the book we shall note several instances of the conflict between narrowly drawn economic criteria for policy and wider social and environmental concerns. Suffice it to note here that there are policy conflicts and that their reconciliation is a matter for the political system.

There are several reasons to believe that there may be a greater capacity in Scotland to resolve these policy conflicts. One is purely geographical; the 'urban' and regional blackspots tend to coincide in Strathclyde region and one or two other places such as Dundee, so that the tension between 'urban' and 'regional' definitions of the problem is largely absent. Then there is the existence of the Scottish Office, a territorial department of central government, combining in itself the responsibilities of an industrial department with urban policies and most local government functions. It is party to decisions on the boundaries of assisted areas for regional policy (though the lead is taken by the Department of Trade and Industry) and disburses regional development assistance. It is the sponsoring department for the Scottish Development Agency, runs the Urban Programme in Scotland and is responsible for physical planning and infrastructure. At the same time, the Scottish Office covers most of the matters which in England would be the responsibility of the health side of the DHSS. The SDA itself provides a means for drawing together the several strands of spatial and environmental policy under the sponsorship of the Industry Department for Scotland.

The Scottish local government system may lend itself better than the English to the production of coherent urban policies. Regional councils combine planning powers with the responsibility for most infrastructure and the major services except housing and bring together urban and rural areas, so avoiding the weaknesses of the English metropolitan counties. Finally, there is the Scottish tradition of integrated land use and economic development planning, which gave birth to the sub-regional plans of the 1960s and early 1970s and provided much of the impetus for the creation of the regional councils themselves. Before going on to examine urban policy initiatives, it is therefore appropriate to give a brief review of the machinery for framing and delivering urban policies in Scotland.

The Government of Urban Scotland

The Scottish Office. The urban policy arena is characterised by the large number of agencies with overlapping or complementary responsibilities, each bringing its own perspective to the problems of redevelopment and renewal. Central government is represented mainly by the Scottish Office which, as well as a general responsibility for the oversight of local government, deals with nearly all the policy fields administered by local authorities. This contrasts with the position in England where the Department of the Environment has the general responsibility for local government but deals in policy matters only with housing and planning, with other departments looking after education, social services and so on. Whether this makes for a more corporate approach to urban problems by the Scottish Office, is one of our main themes. Within the Scottish Office, there are five departments as follows:

Scottish Development Department (SDD), responsible for local government structure, housing, planning, transport and roads;

Industry Department for Scotland (IDS), formerly known as the Scottish Economic Planning Department, responsible for regional economic development, electricity, selective aid to industry, new towns and sponsorship of the Scottish Development Agency;

Department of Agriculture and Fisheries for Scotland (DAFS), responsible for most agriculture and fisheries matters;

Scottish Education Department (SED), responsible for education outside the universities and for social work services;

Scottish Home and Health Department, responsible for police, prisons, criminal justice, fire services and the National Health Service.

In addition there is a unit called Central Services, which is responsible for finance and personnel and has in recent years assumed greater importance as the Office has sought to unify these functions. It is Central Services which is responsible for local government finance.

The economic responsibilities of the Scottish Office, mainly concentrated in the IDS are largely of a 'promotional' nature, that is they consist in measures to persuade other actors, notably private firms, to do things. Since 1975, selective regional development grants and since 1984 automatic ones as well have been administered by the Scottish Office, within UK guidelines. There is a separate Scottish effort to attract inward investment, centred on Locate in Scotland, a unit run jointly by the Scottish Office and the Scottish Development Agency. As we show later, this is under constant threat from Whitehall interests who want to subordinate it to the larger British effort. The fact that the new towns come under the IDS is an indication of the way they are seen as part of economic policy, particularly with regard to the attraction of inward investment. The other major economic powers available to Scottish bodies are vested in the Scottish Development Agency and the Highlands and Islands Development Board.

Of course, many of the Scottish Office's powers have a major indirect influence on urban economic development. The SDD is responsible for trunk roads and for approving regional councils' transport policies and programmes and structure plans. Increasingly, these have been geared to the needs of economic regeneration. The SED's education responsibilities have economic implications, either in a general sense or, with ventures like the Technical and Vocational Education Initiative, for specific areas.

Administrative responsibility for urban policy is substantially decentralised to the Scottish Office, creating at least the potential for the development of a coherent policy in a field which, in England, is notoriously fragmented. Whether advantage can be taken of this depends on two related factors – the degree of autonomy which the Scottish Office has in making its own policy and the degree of coordination and common purpose among the Scottish Office departments themselves. As far as policy making is concerned, two modes have been identified (Keating and Midwinter 1983b), policy autonomy and policy leadership. Policy autonomy occurs where the Scottish Office is allowed to develop its own policy, consulting other departments and keeping them informed but framing the main measures itself. This is possible in areas where the Scottish Office has the entire administrative responsibility, where there are no major cross-border spillovers and where the Treasury has been satisfied as to the financial implications – this last is a contentious point which we discuss further below. Policy autonomy is most commonly found in environmental and social policy, including local government organisation and education and in the field of private law. Policy leadership occurs when policy is made jointly by the Scottish Office and the corresponding Whitehall departments and is important in matters with an economic impact and in the implementation of party election commitments.

Even where policy is made jointly with Whitehall departments and the substantive content is the same as for England and Wales, implementation may take a different form in Scotland. Indeed, it is arguable that the Scottish

Office's role in implementation is more significant than that in policy making. Given the increasing recognition that policy continues 'to evolve within what is conventionally described as the implementation phase' (Ham and Hill 1984, 11), this is of considerable importance. As the Scottish Office is an example of administrative decentralisation and not of political devolution, its role is, by and large, to deliver UK policies into the distinctive Scottish environment, adapting them to Scottish legal and administrative forms (Ross 1981). In the process, however, it may be that distinctive strategies might emerge, particularly in a complex field like that of urban policy where several policy strands which in England are the responsibility of several functional departments come together under its purview. This brings us to the question of whether the Scottish Office does operate as a coherent entity, rather than as five separate departments. Page (1979) has cast doubt on the ability of the Scottish Office to react in a corporate fashion to local authorities' own plans, yet it does appear that the more overt conflicts observable between, for example, the Departments of Trade and Industry and of the Environment in England are absent in Scotland. Another dimension to the administrative devolution in Scotland is the status of ad hoc agencies, notably the Scottish Development Agency, considered below, the Highlands and Islands Development Board, and the Manpower Services Commission (MSC). The MSC is a UK-wide body sponsored by the Department of Employment, though there is a Scottish Committee with an advisory role and a Scottish plan is prepared, within the national MSC plan, approved jointly by the Secretaries of State for Employment and for Scotland. MSC programmes of job-creation and training notably through the Youth Training Scheme and the Community Programme to provide short-term employment for those who have been out of work for some time, have a role to play in urban policy as we shall see, though they are rarely tailored to the requirements of rebuilding local economies. Indeed, the absence of training policies has often been identified as a missing element of local economic strategies (Booth and Moore 1985). At a more general level, the extent to which coherent spatial policies have emerged in Scotland is one of the themes of this book and we shall return to it in the conclusion.

The ability to make its own policy or adapt common policy to Scottish needs is only one aspect of the Scottish Office's role. Traditionally equally important has been its role as a privileged channel of communication between Scottish interests and the machinery of central government. With its own minister in the Cabinet, membership of key inter-departmental committees and close links with Scottish interest groups, it can take Scottish issues up in the highest levels of government, even in matters beyond its formal functional responsibilities. As early as 1937, the Gilmour Committee commented on the 'increasing tendency to appeal to (the Secretary of State) on all matters that have a Scottish aspect, even if on a strict view they are outside the province of his duties as statutorily defined'. In the 1960s, this was one of the factors leading to the strengthening of the economic responsibilities of the Secretary of State. There is no question here of his pursuing his own economic policies, different to those being pursued in England. But the designation of the Secretary of State as an economic and industrial minister gives him and his civil servants access to interdepartmental discussions on these matters and membership of the appropriate Cabinet and official committees.

There are two aspects to the Secretary of State's role as a lobbyist for Scotland – his role in securing as large a share as possible of public expenditure, and his role in intervening on behalf of Scottish interests across the policy spectrum but especially with regard to economic and industrial matters. Before examining these, it will be useful to sketch in general terms the factors which affect his standing within government and the 'weight' which he is able to throw into Cabinet arguments.

The party balance in Scotland and the standing of the Secretary of State within the party are clearly important. A government dependent on Scotland for its majority will heed Scottish demands more than one for which Scotland is electorally dispensable. A government disposing of a large Scottish majority will also of course find the Scottish influence within its own parliamentary ranks correspondingly great. Such was the case under the Secretaryship of Willie Ross in the 1960s. Electoral pressure on the party, on the other hand, can also have its uses, especially from the nationalist quarter. Tom Johnston (1940–45) was known to use the nationalist threat to great effect in Cabinet battles but it was in the mid-1970s that pork-barrel politics in Scotland reached its peak as Labour sought to buy off the SNP challenge. Few Secretaries of State for Scotland have been major party figures in their own right, ambitious Scottish MPs often choosing to make their names in the wider UK arena, and few have moved on to high office after leaving St Andrew's House. Good relationships with the Prime Minister, though, can be very important as was shown in the tenures of James Stuart (1951–57), a confidant of Churchill and Willie Ross (1964–70, 1974–76) whose tenure coincided with the two premierships of Harold Wilson.

It is also important for a Scottish Secretary to have an organised Scottish lobby behind him. It is the existence of a series of separate Scottish interest groups or Scottish wings of British groups whch has allowed major political questions to be presented as Scottish national issues rather than purely local or sectional matters. The Scottish Trade Union Congress is quite independent of the British TUC, with the major unions affiliating to both. The CBI is more of a unitary body but has a Scottish organisation with its own full-time staff. The Scottish Council (Development and Industry) has a long association with government and brings together a variety of bodies with an interest in industrial development. Consultation between the Scottish Office and both sides of industry also takes place through the Scottish Economic

Council. The political parties in Scotland have their own organisation and the churches have from time to time taken an interest in public affairs. So it has been possible to develop a lobby for industrial development in Scotland cutting across but by no means attenuating the industrial class divide and partisan loyalties. What is striking about this Scottish lobby, however, is its dependence on political channels, notably the Secretary of State and the Scottish MPs. There is little by way of an independent Scottish industrial lobby, though the Scottish Council (Development and Industry), itself the product of government initiative in the days of Tom Johnston, attempts partially to fill this role. This is a reflection of the weakness of Scottish industrial capital since the 1920s, when control of Scottish industry started to move south of the border. The drift, which continued after the Second World War, deprived Scottish business of much of its leadership, creating major problems for attempts at private-sector led regeneration such as those we examine in chapter 7. The need for locally-based and controlled centres of industrial and financial leadership was widely recognised in the early 1980s, with the battles over the bids for the Royal Bank, Scotland's last locally owned clearing bank and Anderson Strathclyde, a major industrial firm. In the Royal Bank case, the argument for retaining control in Scotland was explicitly recognised by the Monopolies Commission (1982), which declared 'We accept that in certain cases the comparative economic diffi-culties of regions such as Scotland have been accentuated by the acquisition of locally managed and controlled businesses by companies from outside, whether elsewhere in the United Kingdom or overseas.' Although the Government accepted this analysis this did not, despite the expectations raised at the time, develop into a policy of protecting Scottish ownership in industry and finance.

The Scottish lobby probably reached its high point in the late 1960s, under the Wilson government and the Secretaryship of Willie Ross. Since then, its power has declined along with the status of the Scottish Office itself. This becomes apparent from an examination of the Scottish Office's role in public expenditure policy making and in economic and industrial lobbying.

At one time, spending on services in the province of the Secretary of State was determined by the Goschen formula giving Scotland $^{11}/_{80}$ of the total. This gradually fell into disuse after the Second World War, by which time, such had been the changes in the relative populations of Scotland and England, it was producing significantly higher per capita spending in the former. Then, up until the mid-1970s, Scottish expenditure was bargained function by function and expressed as subtotals of the relevant functional totals. By allowing the Scottish Office to make a series of special pleas and to protect the inherited Goschen advantage, this produced significantly higher totals per capita in all areas of public spending controlled by the Scottish Secretary. The English backlash to the devolution proposals together with pressure on public spending generally produced a return to a formula in 1978

(Heald 1980).

Spending within the responsibility of the Secretary of State is now divided into two categories. For agriculture, fisheries and food and industry, energy, trade and employment (excluding tourism), where expenditure is said to be influenced to a greater extent than other functions by United Kingdom and European Community policies, finance is allocated to the Scottish Office by function. The remainder of the Secretary of State's expenditure forms a 'block' determined by a procedure which Heald (1980) has christened the 'Barnett formula'. The Scottish Office receives $^{11}/_{85}$ of any changes in English expenditure on the corresponding range of items. The effect is to freeze the relative base expenditures in England and Scotland but to allocate marginal increases or decreases on a rough population basis. The only way the Scottish Secretary can increase his block is to back English ministers in their demands for increases in the appropriate functional totals. He is then, however, free to reallocate expenditure within his block among his various functions.

As nearly all economic policy expenditure lies outside the block, the Secretary of State does not have the ability to increase his expenditure on economic regeneration in Scotland at the expense of other priorities. Nor can he, for example, decide to reduce regional policy expenditure in favour of putting money into the newer urban initiatives. So the capacity of the Secretary of State to frame new policy instruments in the field which is our present concern is very limited.

In practice, the Secretary of State's freedom to reallocate expenditure within his block is also limited. Although the official line in government is to emphasise the Scottish Secretary's wide discretion and his complete control over his own block, there is no evidence of significantly different choices emerging, nor is it likely that Treasury and Cabinet would take kindly to it if they did. Recent public expenditure White Papers show the Scottish Office following very closely the options pursued by English departments in areas such as health, housing, transport and local government (Keating 1985). One recent notable departure from England was the decision not to transfer resources from education authorities to the Manpower Services Commission for vocational training but this was exceptional and concerned less the substance than the mechanisms for delivering policy. In response to the ratepayers' revolt of 1985, the Secretary of State was able to rearrange his plans so as to provide additional domestic rate relief, though the manner and timing of this concession indicate that the Treasury and Cabinet had first to be convinced of its political necessity. The sum, in any case, was only about 0.5 per cent of the expenditure within the Secretary of State's responsibility. Generally, deviations from the English pattern are marginal.

The Barnett formula owes little to political principle or administrative logic, combining, as it does, two principles, neither of them very rational, for determining the base and the marginal expenditure in the Secretary of

State's block. It emerged in the 1970s as a political compromise, a way of holding the line, and has survived since because of the lack of agreement on an alternative. In 1980, the Treasury published its Needs Assessment Study, produced in anticipation of devolution and purporting to show the 'correct' allocation of expenditure in the various parts of the United Kingdom on the basis of need. While many observers have criticised the Study's methodology, few have seriously disputed the main finding, that Scotland's expenditure relativities cannot be entirely justified on the basis of need. Drastic reductions in Scottish expenditure to bring it into line would not be politically feasible. On the other hand, in a return to the old system, the Scottish Office would be hard put to defend its totals, given the new awareness of them among English departments and MPs. So the Barnett formula provides a convenient way out for both Treasury and Scottish Office. As much was conceded by the Scottish Office before the Select Committee on Scottish Affairs in 1980.

The Scottish Office's role in lobbying on economic and industrial matters is more diffuse, less easy to pin down. In the 1960s, as well as pioneering regional planning exercises, it helped to develop the system of regional assistance which we shall examine later. Regional policies in the 1960s, however, were based on a series of assumptions – notably about the existence of 'overheating' in the more prosperous regions – which have become increasingly tenuous in the 1970s and 1980s. The 1980s have seen deindustrialisation become a national phenomenon, the collapse of the economy of the West Midlands and the emergence of severe 'inner city' economic problems even in formerly prosperous regions, making it increasingly difficult for the Scottish Office to get a sympathetic hearing. On the other hand, the Scottish lobby has had more success in defending another of its creations, the Scottish Development Agency.

The final area in which Scottish Office lobbying has been important is in decisions about major industrial developments and closures. In the 1960s, interventions by the Secretary of State succeeded in bringing to Scotland major developments like the Post Office Savings Bank, the steel complex at Ravenscraig, split at the last minute between Scotland and Wales, the vehicle plants at Linwood and Bathgate and the aluminium smelter at Invergordon. Nowadays, however, the issues are the reverse; how to keep open major industrial plants, including some of those brought to Scotland by earlier regional policy initiatives. In 1976, it was the threat to the Linwood plant and the political implications for the besieged Labour Government which led to the state rescue of the Chrysler Corporation in spite of this being contrary to the 'industrial strategy' of backing winners. It was a short-term victory. The plant was gradually run down and in 1982 closed by its French owners without effective opposition. In the same year, the Invergordon smelter was closed despite the efforts of the Scottish Office. More successful was the battle over Ravenscraig, when the Scottish Office was able to mobilise a most impressive lobby, including all the political parties, the churches, trade unions, industrialists and local authorities, backed by a veiled threat from the Secretary of State to resign if closure went ahead. The decision was taken into the Cabinet and at the end of 1982 a reprieve announced. It is not to take credit away from the Ravenscraig campaign to point out that its victory was fragile. The Scottish Office was soon giving its support to the 'American deal' to export semi-finished slabs to the United States, which would have kept Ravenscraig going with a much reduced workforce. The collapse of the deal was followed by warnings from the European Commission that British steel targets were excessive, with the implication that one plant – probably Ravenscraig – would have to go.

The 1984 crisis at the Scott Lithgow yard of British Shipbuilders provides another example of the mobilisation of the Scottish industrial lobby. In that case, a deal was done to sell the yard to a private owner and so save at least some of the jobs.

So the Scottish Office in the 1980s finds itself on the defensive, whether on public expenditure or on industrial policy. Last-ditch campaigns are fought against major closures on ground not of its own choosing; few opportunities have arisen for chasing new investments. When major closures have occurred, it is the Scottish Office which has often had to cope, sending 'fire-brigade' operations into places like Clydebank and Glengarnock, sending an Enterprise Zone to Invergordon, encouraging the SDA to go to Motherwell. This has given a strong element of crisis management to spatial policy initiatives in Scotland, with a conflict rarely far below the surface between defending and replacing employment in the older industrial areas and the traditional industries themselves and, on the other hand, the need to develop forward-looking strategies for industrial development. One of the themes of this book is whether there is in Scotland the capacity for such a forward-looking and strategic response to local economic crises and the extent it is being realised.

Why has Scottish Office influence declined? We have shown that in the present recession it has been increasingly difficult to maintain a consensus on diversionary regional policy measures. Scotland, as a major beneficiary of these, was bound to suffer consequently. We must add to this the changed political climate of the 1980s. The devolution debacle did immense damage to the credibility of the Scottish lobby in Whitehall and Westminster. Scottish politicians had cried wolf too often; now their bluff was called. The demise of the SNP in the 1979 General Election and their failure to revive since has convinced English politicians of the fragility of the nationalism underlying the Scottish lobby and reinforced the view that it is needless to make concessions to it. It is undoubtedly also a weakness that the Conservative Government elected in 1983, with its massive overall majority, holds only a minority of the Scottish seats. Scotland is not central to its electoral strategy in the way in which the West Midlands, for example, are. A resignation by the Secretary of State might be embarrassing but it would not be a political disaster.

The Scottish Development Agency. The idea of a Scottish Development Agency has been around since the 1930s but gained increasing support in the 1960s when the STUC suggested the need for an agency to revitalise the Scottish economy. In 1974, the West Central Scotland Plan had proposed a West of Scotland Development Agency, an idea which gained considerable support from various quarters. In the same year, the Scottish Council Research Institute – attached to the Scottish Council (Development and Industry) – proposed a Scottish Development Corporation as 'a body solely committed to the promotion of industrial growth' (SCRI 1974). Shortly before this, the Labour Party Scottish Council had proposed a Scottish National Enterprise Board as a subsidiary of the National Enterprise Board to which the party was committed, but with a considerable degree of operational independence (Labour Party 1973). Its role would be to intervene to create and preserve industrial employment and reorganise industry in Scotland. There was no suggestion at this stage that it would have a specifically urban role or be concerned with environmental matters.

It was the political pressure on the Labour Party from the advance of the SNP, however, which finally brought the SDA into being. In its October 1974 manifesto, Labour promised a Scottish Development Agency, to be 'the main instrument for the regeneration of the Scottish economy', with responsibilities for tackling industrial decay and unemployment as well as environmental dereliction, paying special attention to those industrial areas which have suffered the worst effects of decline. In 1975, the Agency was duly established, taking over the Scottish Industrial Estates Corporation, the Small Industries Council for the Rural Areas of Scotland and the section of the Scottish Development Department responsible for administering grants to local authorities for derelict land clearance. Further responsibilities were created in investment in industry in the form of money and management services; industrial promotion, particularly the encouragement of investment from overseas; and, reluctantly, the coordination of major comprehensive urban development schemes – which meant, in fact, the Glasgow Eastern Area Renewal (GEAR) project. Some of the Agency's tasks are financed by grant from central government. Investment is financed from borrowing, within a limit set by Parliamentary order. Sponsorship of the Agency rests with the Secretary of State for Scotland, through the Industry Department for Scotland. He issues guidelines, agreed with the other relevant departments, and can issue directions of a specific or general character.

The SDA was born into a difficult political environment and for some years its survival was at issue. Conservatives criticised it as an agent of 'backdoor nationalisation' and predicted that it would merely prop up 'lame duck' industries. The Labour Government replied by pointing to the requirement

21

Finance and Property Management
Finance Division
Funds management; Agency financial control and accounting; development of computerised information systems; central computer operations; internal audit; investment monitoring.
Property Management Division:
General Manager
Development of industrial estates; property marketing; property valuation; estates management and maintenance.

Small Business and Electronics
Small Business Division
Financial assistance and commercial, marketing, technical and manufacturing advice to small businessmen; trade promotion in UK and overseas for small firms; grants and promotional and marketing services to craftsmen.
Electronics Division
Implementation and co-ordination of Agency programme for the Scottish electronics industry.

Area Development
Co-ordination and management of area projects: integrated projects, Task Forces, self help initiatives, Glasgow Eastern Area Renewal Project; preparation of financial programmes and development studies; identification and development of economic initiatives; promotion of private development; programme and performance review; operation of training and manpower initiatives; Training and Employment Grants Scheme; Information Technology Centres.

Planning and Projects
Industrial Programme Development
Area and Enterprise Programme Development
Formulation of Agency Programmes
Health Care and Biotechnology
Engineering
Scottish Industries
Tourism and Leisure
Service Industries
Implementation of programmes
Corporate Services
Technology Transfer
Advisory Services to Industry

Property Development and Environment
Land Engineering Division
Civil Engineering; derelict land clearance; environmental improvement.
Construction and Technical Services Division
New building; property refit and maintenance, special project development, engineering and architectural design team.
Property Development Division
Property development; property investment, LEGUP, PRIDE.
Information and Administration Division
Directorate administration; financial monitoring and budgetary control; property finance and information data bases.

Investment (Scottish Development Finance Limited)
Policy on industrial investment; evaluation of projects, post-investment relationships, advice to invested companies; encouraging private sector involvement.

Aberdeen Office
An all-purpose office of the Agency for the north east of Scotland. A Scotland-wide office to help the oil service industry in the UK and international oil and gas markets.

Marketing
Advertising; press and public relations; information and research services; industrial promotion; special projects; internal communications.

Secretariat
Board servicing; legal services; staff relations and administration; office services.

Associate:
Locate in Scotland
Attraction of industry to Scotland from overseas and from other parts of the UK; associated Industry Act incentives; monitoring existing overseas investment in Scotland.

Figure 1.3. Scottish Development Agency structure. Source: SDA Annual Report 1985.

for a specified rate of return on the Agency's investments, which were to be limited to firms with prospects for moving into profit. The argument came to hinge on the question of whether there was an 'equity gap', an area of business finance in which potentially viable firms were unable to get investment capital because of lack of access to financial markets or the time-scale of their plans. In a gesture of support before the 1979 General Election, Labour increased the Agency's borrowing limit to £800 million; the new Conservative administration promptly reversed the decision. Both gestures were entirely symbolic as, given the strict guidelines on investment, there was no prospect of the SDA being able to spend anything approaching this sum. Further restrictions were placed on the investment activity, with a lowering of the limit above which investments had to gain the approval of the Secretary of State. An attempt to hive off the investment function altogether to a new body run jointly with the banks, however, failed when the banks declared, in effect, that they did not believe in the equity gap. Instead, a new body, Scottish Development Finance Ltd, was set up within the Agency, to involve private businessmen in investment decisions. New guidelines were issued removing the requirement to create jobs and substituting that of providing 'stable and productive employment'.

Generally, then, the SDA survived the change of government little scathed, though its investment function continues to be regarded with some suspicion. A more serious battle has had to be fought over the inward investment function. After the task of attracting overseas investment to Scotland was transferred from the Scottish Council (Development and Industry) to the Agency in 1976, offices were opened in New York, San Francisco and Tokyo, to the intense chagrin of the Department of Trade's Invest in Britain Bureau and the Foreign and Commonwealth Office. At the same time, regional and district councils and new town development corporations began to mount their own inward investment efforts. Further confusion was added after 1979 with a series of trips organised by the Scottish Office minister for industry. The conflicts thus engendered within Scotland and between Scottish interests and Whitehall departments first came to a head in 1980 with an investigation by the Select Committee on Scottish Affairs. Amid intensive lobbying, the committee divided along party lines, with the Conservative majority, still basically hostile to the SDA, voting to close the overseas offices. The Government's decision compromised, with the creation of a new body, Locate in Scotland (LIS), jointly run by the Agency and the Scottish Office, under a Scottish Office civil servant. In the Local Government and Planning (Scotland) Act of 1982, restrictions were placed on local authorities' investment promotion activity, bringing their overseas visits under the control of LIS. This delicate institutional compromise was soon itself under attack, with a renewed assault on LIS by the Department of Trade and Industry in 1984. This time, Scottish interests were more united, with Conservative as well as Labour MPs defending the separate Scottish effort, from which the Secretary of State was now trying to make considerable political capital.

Apart from ensuring its own survival, the Agency had over its early years to develop a positive strategy. It had been given only the vaguest idea when it was created of what its task should be. A series of commitments had been inherited in environmental renewal and industrial estates. Almost immediately it had been established, it was pushed by the Scottish Office into taking the lead role in the GEAR project for the East End of Glasgow. There was a danger that its efforts and resources could be swallowed up, on the one hand, in responding to appeals from firms and local authorities and, on the other, in 'fire-brigade' operations undertaken at the behest of the Scottish Office. So a more purposive, forward-looking strategy was needed to allow the Agency to set its own priorities and seek out opportunities for promising developments. Opportunities soon became the Agency's watchword, with an insistence that it is not in business to deal with the 'problems' of firms or areas. It is in business to encourage internationally competitive industry in Scotland and to exploit the potential of sectors and areas which can contribute to this. Such a hard-nosed approach of course has helped the Agency to survive in the changed political climate since 1979 but has inevitably led to a downgrading of the wider social objectives, including employment creation, envisaged in 1975, a process which we trace in chapter 2.

SDA strategy, as developed over the years, has now come to focus on three concerns, major firms, sectoral initiatives and area development. Sectoral initiatives have been undertaken in electronics, health care industries and energy related industries, including North Sea oil (Hood and Young 1984). Area development is described in detail in chapter 5. As we note there, one of the difficulties facing the Agency is the relationship between the area and the sectoral approach to development, with major sectoral ventures not always being suitable for the urban priority areas. Much publicity has been given to the Agency's investment work and this, with the inward investment effort, have been its most controversial activities. In terms of expenditure, however, they are relatively small. In the year until March 1984, of a total current expenditure of £72 million, some £30 million went on land reclamation and environmental improvements and £18 million on property management. Of £52 million capital expenditure, £37 million went on property and some £13 million on new investment. The main items in the Agency's income were £83 million in government grant-in-aid and £16 million from rents and other property income. In 1984–85, however, the property function was under review, with strong indications emerging that the Agency wished to reduce its commitment in this area.

The SDA has therefore been able to gain a sense of direction for its efforts and a philosophy of action. Perhaps its most significant achievement in its ten years of existence, however, is to have survived intact despite the demise of its sister organisation, the National Enterprise Board and the hostility to it, initially of the Conservative Party and, latterly, of English departments.

Local Government. The present system of local government in Scotland was inspired by the planning needs of the 1960s. As we shall see in chapter 2, the Scottish Office had launched a series of 'sub-regional' plans for the regions of Scotland as a basis for strategic decision-making. Local government reform was to be the means of ensuring that there were authorities in place to implement these plans without the need for detailed intervention from the centre. So the SDD recommended to the Wheatley Commission that its seven planning regions should be the basis for regional councils, which should control all major spending and infrastructure decisions and most local services. Wheatley (1969) duly recommended seven powerful regions, with second-tier districts below them, the latter to be responsible for local plans and development control. Wheatley was clear that the regions' planning responsibilities should extend to the location and encouragement of industry, but the Commission was very cautious about a wider economic role for local government, making no positive recommendation for new powers.

Although Wheatley was accepted by both the Labour Government and the incoming Conservative Government of 1970, its recommendations were considerably altered in the course of enactment (Keating 1975). The Conservative Government decided that housing should go to the district level, ostensibly so that district councils would have something important to do, though political considerations clearly played a part, with rural and suburban Conservatives unwilling to share the burden of urban council housing support. An extra region was created in the Borders and single-tier all-purpose authorities in the Western Isles, Orkney and Shetland. In Parliament, yet another region was created in Fife, and Glasgow district cut back by excluding the peripheral suburbs of Bearsden, Milngavie, Bishopbriggs and Newton Mearns, together with Clydebank. The effect of this was largely to destroy the regional system on the east coast. The Grampian Region, based on Aberdeen, remained, but instead of two large 'estuarial' regions straddling the Forth and the Tay, there are four regions more akin to English counties (map 1.1). Indeed, it is arguable that Strathclyde Region, which survived parliamentary attempts to dismember it, is the only true region in Scotland.

The creation of a two-tier system of local government everywhere except the islands has itself given rise to some difficulties, particularly in the cities. With its boundaries slightly enlarged and a population larger than any region apart from Strathclyde itself, Glasgow District Council regards itself as the lineal descendant of the old Corporation, with the prime responsibility for the planning and development of the city and resents the existence of the Region. There has been a history of poor relationships, despite the fact that both levels are controlled by the Labour Party (Keating and Midwinter 1983b). In the other cities, party divisions reinforce antagonisms about

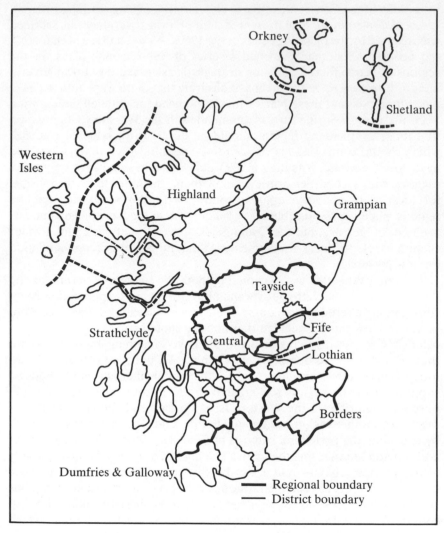

Map 1.1. Local Government (Scotland) Act 1973, regions and districts. Source: Scottish Development Department.

status and functions. Labour Aberdeen faces Conservative Grampian; Labour Dundee faces Conservative Tayside; while Lothian has experienced both a Labour region with a Conservative Edinburgh and, more recently, a Conservative region with a Labour Edinburgh.

Generally, however, local government structure has been much less of a contentious issue than in England. Neither of the major parties has any plans to abolish any authority, in contrast to England, where the Conservatives are pledged to the abolition of the metropolitan counties and the Greater

London Council and the Labour Party to the abolition of the shire counties. The Stodart Committee (1981) found no need for a radical redistribution of functions, though it did comment that the question of single-tier local government might have to be brought back into discussion at some future time.

The main local government responsibilities are as follows:

Nine Regional Councils
Strategic Planning (including structure plans);
Transportation and roads;
Water and sewage;
Industrial development;
Education;
Social Work;
Police and Fire.

Fifty-three District Councils
Local planning (including local plans and development control);
Housing;
Industrial development;
Building control;
Environmental Health;
Cleansing;
Leisure and recreation;
Libraries;
Licensing.

In the rural regions of Highland, Borders and Dumfries and Galloway, local planning and libraries are a regional function. The three islands councils are all-purpose authorities, though sharing some services with Highland Region.

2

URBAN PLANNING IN
SCOTLAND

The Local Planning System

The modern urban planning system dates from the Town and Country Planning Act of 1947. This laid down that all counties, counties of cities and large burghs in Scotland should submit a development plan to the Secretary of State. As revised every five years, this would lay down what types of development would be permitted and where. All development would require planning permission from the relevant planning authority, with appeal to the Secretary of State in the case of refusal.

At the time, it was assumed that most development would be undertaken by the public sector and that economic and population growth would be modest. These assumptions proved unfounded and by the 1960s the system, in Scotland as in England and Wales, had come under a great deal of criticism. Preparation of plans was too slow and the plans themselves tended to be too detailed and rigid. Planning applications were overwhelming councils and appeals were piling up in central government. Immersed in planning detail, neither the central departments nor local authorities had the opportunity to consider the main strategic issues. In West-Central Scotland, the multiplicity of planning authorities made it difficult to arrive at agreed population projections or to get the right local response to such central initiatives as the attraction of the Rootes car plant to Linwood.

The defects which we have noted in the old town and country planning system, notably the lack of strategic focus, the lack of coordination and the overwhelming detail leading to congestion of the system, led the Government to establish the Planning Advisory Group in 1964. It is on their 1965 report that the present system is based. The main legislation was the 1969 Town and Country Planning (Scotland) Act (closely based on the 1968 Act for England and Wales) and the Local Government (Scotland) Act, modifying the 1969 Act to fit the new system of local government.

Three levels of planning were established, structure plans, local plans and development control. Structure plans are general statements of policy with regard to the physical development of an area, taking account of demographic, economic and social trends and forces. As the structure plan is a vehicle for general policy decisions and not a precise blue print for development, it is accompanied not by a map but by a diagram illustrating the relationship of its elements but not their precise location. This is intended to allow a focus on policy issues separately from their local impact – though whether this was ever realistic is perhaps debatable. The structure plan is preceded by a survey, leading to a draft plan upon which public comment is invited. The plan, amended as appropriate, is then submitted to the Secretary of State for Scotland who sets up an Examination in Public, at which selected elements of the plan can be challenged before a Reporter. Taking the Reporter's recommendations into account, the Secretary of State then discusses any changes he wants with the local authority before giving the modified plan his approval.

Local plans were initially intended to be the detailed elaboration on the ground of the policies of structure plans (Cullingworth 1976). There is both a written statement and a map on an ordnance survey base showing precise details of proposals and zonings. Three types of local plan exist, district plans, the most common, covering eventually the whole country and laying down general planning policies; subject plans for some aspect of planning such as conservation or features such as the Forth and Clyde Canal; and action area plans for areas subject to intensive or comprehensive redevelopment. Local plans are subject to public participation but do not require the approval of the Secretary of State. It was thought at the time of the original proposals that both structure and local plans would be produced by the same authorities, with the latter flowing from the former. So, in line with contemporary thinking on planning systems, central government would be able to withdraw from detailed concern with the implementation of planning policies while retaining ultimate control of the broad lines of policy. Local government reform, establishing two tiers throughout mainland Britain, required major modifications in the system and the thinking which underlay it.

Development control is the process whereby prospective developers need to obtain planning permission from the local authority. As local plans are prepared and enacted, development control decisions should come to be based largely on these, though here again local government reform has raised complications. Refusal of planning permission by the local authority can be the subject of an appeal to the Secretary of State.

Under the reformed system of local government, planning was split, in Scotland as in England, with structure plans going to the regions and local plans and development control to the districts. At the same time, the requirement for structure plan authorities to prepare a plan for the whole of their areas was dropped and replaced by a duty for local planning authorities to achieve such comprehensive coverage. Because of this and the anticipated delays in drawing up structure plans, districts were allowed to start producing local plans in advance of an approved structure plan. This raises serious problems about how structure plans are to be implemented, given that district councils are separate and independent authorities. There are some safeguards. Where a structure plan exists, local plans must conform to it. Regions also have power to 'call in' and decide themselves planning applications where a proposed new development does not conform to the approved structure plan or raises a major planning issue of general concern to the region. This is a more general power than was contained in the corresponding English legislation (which has itself since been further limited) but, as we shall see, it has given rise to a series of problems in region-district relations.

The final element in the new planning system was regional reports. These are wide-ranging corporate planning documents prepared by regional councils and setting out their priorities. They were seen as more flexible than structure plans, less tied to land use and with potential as a vehicle for central-local dialogue on a broad front. However, after the first round of regional reports on reorganisation, the system fell into disuse.

In the Scottish Office, planning is dealt with by the Scottish Development Department, which advises the minister on planning appeals, approval of structure plans and the drawing up of the national Planning Guidelines. The latter lay down some general principles to be followed by planning authorities but in practice are more important in the rural than in the urban areas. The Department of Industry for Scotland (formerly the Scottish Economic Planning Department) is responsible for economic policy matters, sponsorship of the Scottish Development Agency and the new towns. The separation within the Scottish Office of economic planning and physical/land use planning reflects a longstanding and much-criticised British tradition, though the problem is made less severe by the fact that IDS does not now produce a Scottish economic plan; in any case, liaison is close and the split is by no means comparable to the division of responsibilities in England. Nevertheless, the Select Committee on Scottish Affairs, examining the matter in 1972, did criticise the fact that not enough was being made of Scotland's potential for integrated planning and suggested that a national structure plan could usefully be produced. Since then, as planning generally has gone into decline, this idea has not found much favour.

Since local government reform effectively inaugurated the new planning system, progress in producing plans has been disappointingly slow. Coon (1981) calculated that, in Strathclyde Region, by the end of 1980, only 14 per cent of local plans had been finalised, covering 8 per cent of the population; this compared with a population coverage of 83 per cent in the corresponding five years after the 1948 Act. So the aim of speeding up plan preparation has clearly not been achieved, despite a five-fold increase in the planning profession in the meantime. Thomson (1983) similarly found that there was an inordinate delay in the production of local plans, though this did not always cause problems, as it is only in the changing urban areas that a plan is of crucial importance. Very little use has been made in Scotland of local plans other than the district type. There have been no action area plans and only two subject plans, for Loch Lomond and the Forth and Clyde Canal, where recreational and amenity features straddle regional and district boundaries, requiring joint planning (Coon 1983).

Structure plans have made more progress, all the regions having decided to go for a comprehensive coverage. In some cases, including Strathclyde, councils have decided to produce a single structure plan. In Strathclyde's case, political reasons are probably at the root of this decision, the council leadership wishing to emphasise the unity of the region, though in practical terms the plan concentrates on the Glasgow conurbation. Grampian have adopted two plans, the first to cope with the pressures of oil-related development in the Aberdeen area, the second, and later, one for the rural area. Central Region have produced three structure plans, but have persisted with an annual regional report. All the plans contain general statements about future economic development policy. In Strathclyde, priority is given to the conurbation and the needs of the urban areas. In Grampian, the emphasis is on the needs of the rural areas, where the impact of oil has not been felt. Highland Region has begun, with its revised plan, to shift the emphasis away from industrial development in the Moray Firth area towards the needs of the rural periphery. Nowhere, however, except perhaps around Aberdeen, where development pressure still exists, is the structure plan seen as a major instrument of developing policy. Rather, councils are increasingly glad to get whatever development they can and to accommodate it accordingly.

Regional Planning

Scotland in the post-war period saw a series of regional planning exercises which were to influence the development of regional planning in Britain as a whole as well as the contemporary planning system in Scotland itself. Much of the initiative was taken by the Scottish Office and it has been suggested (Grieve 1980) that the weakness of many of the old county planning departments both made necessary and facilitated this central role, focussing on areas larger than the then existing local authorities. The main planning priority was seen as relieving congestion in the Glasgow conurbation and combatting the city's appalling housing conditions. The first and most important regional plan was the Clyde Valley Plan of 1946, produced by a consultant team working for the region's local authorities in conjunction with the Scottish Office (Carter 1980). It was followed by plans for the Forth and Tay valleys in 1947 and 1950. The Clyde Valley Plan, much influenced by Sir Patrick Abercrombie who was one of the consultants, went for a policy of reducing Glasgow's population through overspill and the creation of satellite communities beyond a green belt. Four new towns were recommended, of which East Kilbride was designated immediately under the 1946 New Towns Act. Glasgow Corporation, however, opposed the strategy, maintaining that it could solve its housing problems within its own boundaries and refused to sign an overspill agreement with East Kilbride. The Plan did touch on questions of industrial policy though it was stressed that economic policy 'was the responsibility of the government and it was felt inappropriate for the town planner to enter the field of industrial planning' (Randall 1980). However, as Carter (1980) points out, there was a large degree of coincidence between government economic policy aims and the priorities of the Plan. In the event, the Plan survived despite the hostility of Glasgow and the Conservatives' move away from regional planning in the 1950s partly because of the movement of several of its progenitors into the Scottish Office and the planning departments of local authorities (McDonald 1983). The Forth valley plan, Plan for Central and South East Scotland, was largely concerned with the expected movement of the mining industry from Lanarkshire to the Fife coalfields and resulted in the designation of Glenrothes new town. In the event, the failure of the Rothes colliery led to the town becoming instead a recipient of Glasgow overspill and centre for more general regional development (Cullingworth 1976). The Tay Plan was concerned with Dundee and Glasgow overspill and with some issues of rural development.

During the 1950s, Glasgow came to reverse its policy on overspill to the extent of signing an overspill agreement with East Kilbride and agreeing to the designation of another new town at Cumbernauld – the only British new town to be designated at this time. By 1959 Glasgow was encouraging the dispersal of both industry and population (Carter 1980) and in the late 1950s and early 1960s made a series of overspill agreements accepting a share of rehousing costs with a large number of local authorities in Scotland. In 1962, a further new town was designated at Livingston, again linked to Glasgow overspill.

In the early 1960s, the emphasis began to be put on economic development as the decline in Scotland's heavy industries and rising unemployment began to be felt. So began a series of ambitious attempts at integrated planning, bringing together land use and industrial considerations. In 1962, the Scottish Council (Development and Industry) published the semi-official Toothill Report on the Scottish Economy, prepared with Scottish Office help. At the same time, there was a move towards a diversionary regional policy to steer new industry to areas like Central Scotland; notable successes were the vehicle plants at Linwood and Bathgate and the steel plant at Ravenscraig. In 1962, the Scottish Development Department was created and, though its remit was largely concerned with land use, there was an increasing awareness of the need for more economic intelligence.

The first integrated plan was the 1963 White Paper on Central Scotland, produced by the SDD in response to the Toothill Report. It emphasised the need for 'growth poles' and stressed the links between infrastructure provision and industrial development. The following year, a Regional Development Division was established, which was eventually to grow into the Scottish Economic Planning Department. Further machinery was established under the Labour Government after 1964 in the form of the Scottish Economic Planning Board and Scottish Economic Planning Council, counterparts to machinery being set up at the same time in the English regions to implement the regional aspects of the 1965 National Plan. The Scottish Plan, in the form of the White Paper on The Scottish Economy, 1965–70, again brought together physical and economic planning but its realisation was frustrated by the failure of the National Plan in 1966–67.

Regional planning continued in the form of 'sub-regional' plans for eight regions which bear a striking (though hardly coincidental) similarity to those identified by the Wheatley Commission for the purposes of local government reform. The plans, undertaken by the Scottish Office with the help of consultants and consultative groups of people involved in economic life, covered both physical and economic planning questions (Carter 1980). Their weakness, however, was the lack of means for their implementation, partly because of the fragmented local government system, partly because of rapidly changing events. It was for this reason above all that the Scottish Office recommended to the Wheatley Commission the creation of regional councils which would combine responsibility for planning with control of the main investment and service responsibilities.

The last of the 'subregional' plans was for West-Central Scotland and was prepared in 1970–74. As local government reform was by this time under way, it was presented as laying the ground for the structure plan which the new Strathclyde Regional Council would have to prepare. Its influence was indeed strong on both Regional Report and Structure Plan priorities, pinpointing unemployment and urban deprivation as the key issues. Reflecting the changing emphasis in urban policy away from overspill and towards the 'inner city' problem, the plan questioned the need for the proposed new town at Stonehouse. Given the success of the new towns in attracting investment and industry, Carter (1980) sees a choice between the desirable social and physical renewal of inner Glasgow and the economic logic of new town development in the interests of Scottish development as a whole; so that the decision against Stonehouse may have represented the parting of the ways for physical and economic planning at the regional scale. As we shall see, this dilemma still presents government with problems in new town policy; we shall also see that the integrated planning of the 1960s has all but disappeared for a variety of reasons, though Scotland still provides examples of more integrated approaches to the urban and regional initiatives of the 1980s.

New Towns

The idea of new towns originated with late nineteenth-century utopian planners like Ebenezer Howard. Between the wars, it was pursued by the Town and Country Planning Association and endorsed by the Committee on Garden Cities and Satellite Towns (1930) and the Barlow Committee on the distribution of the industrial population which reported in 1940 (Culling-worth 1976). After the war, the Reith Committee on New Towns gave birth to the 1946 New Towns Act applying both to England and Wales and to Scotland [though the relevant legislation currently is the New Towns (Scotland) Act, 1968]. This provided for the establishment of new towns to be financed by central government and run by special development corporations separate from local government. As we have seen, the first Scottish new towns grew from regional planning exercises in the 1940s and were primarily aimed at accommodating Glasgow overspill. The third new town, Cumbernauld, was designated in 1955 despite the policy of the then government not to go for more new towns but to concentrate on the planned expansion of existing towns. This was partly because the necessary Town Development legislation did not apply to Scotland, so making the new town mechanism the most appropriate available way of coping with Glasgow's new enthusiasm for co-operating with overspill. Livingston and Irvine, designated in the 1960s along with 'Mark II' new towns in England, were more closely related to the 'growth pole' strategy of regional development, though it was still expected that Livingston would play a part in Glasgow overspill. The final new town to be named was Stonehouse, designated in 1973 for Glasgow overspill and as a regional growth centre.

New towns are run by appointed development corporations as recommended by the Reith Committee which saw such machinery as essential to give development the impetus and priority needed and to allow the creation of balanced communities. They are financed by loans from central government, giving the Scottish Office a determinant say in policy matters. This machinery was largely endorsed by the Wheatley (1969) Commission which, in a rather ambiguous passage, implied that the creation of further new towns should be a matter for regional councils but that the existing development corporations were doing a good job and should be left to run their term. The legislation provides that when a new town is complete the corporation should be wound up and the local authorities should resume their normal functions. As it is, local authorities do retain many functions within new towns. The development corporation is responsible, in agreement with the Secretary of State, for planning matters and it is the corporation, not the district council which is the housing authority; but the regional council retains its functions in education, highways, social work, police and other matters.

Some 222,000 people have been housed in Scottish new towns and, up until 1981, 76,000 jobs, 43,000 of them in industry, had been created. However, only East Kilbride was anywhere near its target population (table 2.1).

New towns came under increasing attack in the 1970s. Critics pointed to the lack of social balance in the new communities, with a predominance of skilled and white collar workers and socially upwardly mobile people; and there is evidence that the new towns can often have a very different age and

Table 2.1 Scottish new towns: population

	Designated population	Present population	Glasgow overspill (households) 1959-78
East Kilbride	82,500	70,600	6,696
Glenrothes	55,000	36,700	662
Cumbernauld	70,000	49,500	10,555
Livingston	70,000	39,200	1,406
Irvine	95,000	56,400	—
Total	372,500	252,450	20,295

class structure to the older settlements (Randall 1980). The 1981 Census data shows that this is true of Cumbernauld and East Kilbride which have only 16.5 per cent and 16.9 per cent respectively of their workforces in semi-skilled and unskilled manual occupations, compared with 23.6 per cent for Glasgow and 20.3 per cent for Strathclyde Region as a whole. Glenrothes, Livingston and Irvine, however, were shown as having an occupational class structure very similar to Glasgow's. In the view of their critics, new towns were bleeding older towns and cities of jobs, dynamic populations and resources; local authorities were beginning to complain about the cost of infrastructure and services which they were obliged to put into new towns. Relationships between local authorities and new towns were sometimes strained and complaints about the unaccountable and undemocratic structure of the development corporations were common.

Against this, defenders of the new towns, notably the Town and Country Planning Association, continued to argue for dispersal, albeit with a better social mix in the new towns. It was pointed out that the new towns were not responsible for the increasing city centre blight, which was mainly the result of unplanned migration. According to Lock (1977), only 10 per cent of those leaving large cities in the UK went to new towns and only 7 per cent of city jobs lost were restarted in new towns. In the case of Glasgow, annual net emigration in the 1960s averaged nearly 25,000, of whom only 6,300 were part of planned overspill (Randall 1980). This compared with projections of 10,000 planned and 6,000 unplanned migrations annually in the 1960 review of Glasgow's Development Plan (Randall 1980). While Glasgow was also losing jobs in this period, it appears that here, too, there was little direct transfer of industry to the new towns. Henderson (1974) found that only 58.8 per cent of jobs transferring out of Glasgow between 1958 and 1968 had gone to planned overspill areas, the new towns' share being 20.1 per cent. In 1968, only 3.4 per cent of manufacturing employees in Cumbernauld and 7.5 per cent in East Kilbride worked in establishments which had transferred from Glasgow (Henderson 1974). Other research (SEPD 1978) shows that the new towns were particularly successful in attracting industry from out-with Scotland. On the other hand, it is not possible to say where jobs coming into new towns would have been located in the absence of sites there and so whether they were inhibiting the growth and redevelopment of the city's industrial base. So, according to the TCPA and other defenders of the new towns, they cannot be accused of taking jobs directly away from the cities and, as far as population dispersal is concerned, new towns still have a vital role in planning and focussing an otherwise unplanned but inevitable flight.

By the late 1970s, in Glasgow and elsewhere, dispersal, both planned and unplanned had gone so far as to undermine the case for further encourage-ment. The 1981 census showed the city on its present boundaries as having declined from 1,140,078 to 765,915 between 1961 and 1981. This provides a sharp contrast with the 1960 projection of 997,000 by 1970 for the smaller area of the former burgh. So the new towns came to be seen more in terms of their potential for stimulating economic development and, in particular, for attracting investment from abroad. By 1975, the Government saw this as the main objective of new towns. Significantly, responsibility was vested in the Scottish Economic Planning Department when this was created in 1973 and shortly afterwards a reassessment of the objectives of Stonehouse was made with this in mind (SEPD 1975). By the mid-1970s, the tide was flowing so strongly against the new towns that the West-Central Scotland Plan team recommended the de-designation of Stonehouse and, when the new Strath-clyde Regional Council repeated this in its first Regional Report, the Government abandoned the whole project in favour of the inner-city GEAR project. In its Regional Report, Lothian expressed some concern over the priority for industrial development as between Livingston and the rest of the region. Both Fife and Lothian expressed worries over the cost of infra-structure provision for new towns and asked for extra money to cope with this (McDonald 1978).

Central government, however, has continued to see the new towns as having a vital role in the economic development of Scotland. This was emphasised in the 1975 Consultative Document (SEPD 1975) issued by the Labour Government, which proposed the continuation of existing new towns and suggested that the powers of the corporations and skills of the staffs could be kept in being after the completion of towns, to help in the regeneration of older urban areas, a proposal pursued in the transfer of Stonehouse staff to the GEAR project. Apart from this, the document emphasised the commitment to building houses for rent and to policies for creating more balanced communities.

The Conservative Government after 1979 took a cautious line on Scottish new towns, in contrast to its attitude in England, where development corporations were to be wound up as quickly as possible. The Secretary of State's approval with modifications of the Strathclyde Structure Plan expressed the view that the new towns' power of attracting jobs will continue to be an important asset during the 1980s for the region as a whole (SEPD 1981). A 1981 Policy Statement (SEPD 1981) declared that, while the over-spill pupose had been achieved, new towns still had a role in promoting economic growth. This was best done by retaining the development corpora-tions which, 'with their integrated staff teams able to reach settlements quickly with industrialists and a sufficient housing capacity to meet the needs of any workers whom they require to bring in, provide the most effective means of managing towns until they approach completion' (SEPD 1981). When their role in promoting rapid economic growth had been fulfilled, the corporations could be wound up and their assets transferred to district councils and the SDA as appropriate. The housing role of the corporations, on the other hand, was to be further curtailed, both on grounds of demand and in order to further the policy of encouraging private development, in the new towns as elsewhere.

In November 1984, a further statement was issued, apparently confirming the corporations' life into the 1990s. In fact, this represents a significant weakening of this commitment. Under the previous arrangements, the corporations' life expectancy extended well beyond the 1990s as it was inconceivable that they would reach their targets before then. Now the Secretary of State proposed that, after 1990, the corporations will be wound up as and when they meet a 'population trigger' defined as a percentage of the target population. These population triggers are given in Table 2.2.

Table 2.2 Scottish new towns: trigger populations

Town	Trigger %	Population at trigger %	1984 population
East Kilbride	90	74,250	70,600
Glenrothes	79	43,000	36,750
Cumbernauld	77	54,000	49,500
Livingston	71	49,500	39,200
Irvine	66	63,000	56,400

The termination of support for the new towns can be examined from a number of perspectives. Firstly, the new towns are no longer 'new'. East Kilbride, for example, now demonstrates characteristics common to towns of a similar size and economic structure throughout Scotland – rising un-employment, skill imbalance, low levels of indigenous innovation and so forth. Furthermore, the dominance of foreign-owned companies in the town makes it markedly vulnerable to multinational disinvestment. Irvine, in contrast, has never realised its economic potential as a 'growth-centre', suffering unemployment rates consistently above the regional average. It is also becoming increasingly difficult for the Secretary of State to justify resource discrimination when the population growth rates of the new towns have fallen to a level similar to small town and suburban areas around the major cities.

There is also conflict between government expenditure on new towns and policies of urban renewal, particularly through the spatial investments of the Scottish Development Agency. It is becoming awkward to reconcile continued investment in the new towns when, in another part of St Andrew's House, the Secretary of State has approved a variety of policies aimed at rebuilding the inner cities to reduce, if not halt, the drift to greenfield sites.

In defence of the new towns, the development corporations will argue from two positions. In terms of population and housing, their case rests on indigenous demand for 'second generation' housing. They have always argued that they require '6(1)' consent to continue development for local need, originally in the form of public, now in the form of private, housing. In addition, they firmly believe that, in order to attract inward investment, they need an adequate supply of housing on offer. Secondly, they present their record on the attraction of industry, especially high technology firms, as evidence that they have played and will continue to play a crucial role in the economic development of Scotland. This argument may be valid in the case of Livingston and Glenrothes; one wonders if the same could be said about Cumbernauld, East Kilbride and Irvine!

From a political perspective, there may be a further contradiction. On the one hand, winding up the new town corporations has political currency in terms of reducing public expenditure and cutting out 'quangos'. On the other hand, there is the political cost to the Government of delivering the assets of the new towns into the welcoming arms of Labour-controlled regional councils and the younger, more committed members in some of the districts.

It is ironical that because of the introduction of the 'trigger' concept, the Labour councils in Strathclyde and elsewhere may now become the strongest supporters of further expansion of the new towns, hastening the time when the magic percentage is reached and the winding up process begins.

Planning in the 1980s

In recent years, there has been a great deal of disillusion about the planning system, which is widely seen as having failed to live up to the expectations placed in it or to carry on the work of the pre-reorganisation regional plans. As strategic planning was seen by Wheatley and the Scottish Office as the very *raison d'être* of the regional system, this is a serious question. Many of the criticisms have focussed on structure plans and their continued relevance in terms of their scope, their scale and the means of their implementation.

As far as the first is concerned, structure plans have tended to concern themselves rather narrowly with land use questions in a manner more reminiscent of traditional town and country planning than of the regional planning visions of the 1960s. The flexibility given to regional councils not to produce plans for the whole of their regions but to use a variety of planning instruments, notably regional reports, has not been exploited, nor has central government encouraged this. Instead, central and local government have persisted with a system designed originally for a system of unitary local government and with the problems of growth and development of the 1960s in mind. Indeed, it could be argued that, just as the 1948 Act rested upon assumptions derived from the 1940s which were to prove unfounded in the 1950s and 1960s, so the new system is facing the problems of the 1980s with tools designed for those of the 1960s. Structure plans may have been a good device for mastering and directing the pressure of growth in the 1960s. They are less suited to the problems of urban transformation and economic regeneration in the 1980s, when spontaneous pressures for growth are largely absent and more positive intervention is required. This is not to deny the need for strategic planning in the Scottish regions; rather, we are questioning the suitability of indicative planning documents of this level of abstraction as a means of achieving this.

Positive planning for the 1980s is, however, hampered by central government's continued virtual monopoly of the instruments of economic intervention. This results in a continued divorce of national-regional economic policy, pursued by the Department of Trade and Industry and the Scottish Office, from planning policies at the level of the regional councils. A number of joint economic development initiatives have taken place (discussed in the following chapters) linking the Scottish Office and the Scottish Development Agency with local authorities – GEAR, Area Projects, Enterprise Zones, Task Forces – but these have largely by-passed the structure planning machinery. Regional councils, eager to secure resources for economic development, have had to adapt their planning policies to the exigencies of other agencies as well as the private sector, rather than using structure planning as a basis for economic development. The result is that structure plans have become largely marginal to one of the main strands of contemporary urban policy. The difficulty is compounded by the lack of any clear spatial plan or policy at the Scottish level into which the various *ad hoc* initiatives, which in many cases may have some merit in themselves, can fit.

Problems of scale stem both from the division of the system between regions and districts and from the changing scale and incidence of urban problems. While in principle, regions are responsible for 'strategic' matters, it has proved notoriously difficult to define just what a 'strategic' matter is. This has caused problems for region-district co-operation and some fierce arguments over the call-in of planning applications by regions. So, although Strathclyde Region has called in only about 1 in 1,000 of Glasgow District's planning applications, these included some issues in which there was a fundamental disagreement over who should be responsible. The region sought for some time to restrict large retail developments in Glasgow on the grounds that this could prejudice the viability of shopping centres in other towns in the conurbation. Glasgow District, on the other hand, regarded this as a purely local matter, falling within its general responsibility for planning in the city. Even more contentiously, Glasgow District has refused planning permission for some of Strathclyde's own highway proposals on the grounds that these conflict with the city's planning priorities.

These problems stem partly from an unwillingness by city districts to accept the principle of two-tier planning – or indeed two-tier local government at all, and partly from what Wannop (1981) has identified as a gap in planning at the level of the cities. Structure plans cover whole regions, or large parts of them. Local plans cover small areas within cities. Consequently, a city like Glasgow has no overall plan, from either the region or the district. Structure plans, in Wannop's (1981) view tend to stop short at city boundaries, with proposals for the urban fringe but very little on the processes of physical change and development within city centres. They may have been more suited to an age when the priority was to bring in major developments like the motor plant at Linwood or the steelworks at Ravenscraig to Scotland than to the present age when attention is increasingly focussed on intra-regional disparities and the detailed problems of urban areas. The city gap is beginning to be filled, with work on city-wide plans in Glasgow and Aberdeen, but these in themselves may cause further jurisdictional arguments between local and structure planning authorities.

Many of the problems of implementation of structure plans stem from the two-tier local government system. Regional intervention in development control through call-in of planning applications is unpopular and is clearly intended to be exceptional. Yet, to avoid constant recourse to call-in, regions may feel it necessary to go into undue detail in their structure plans, so trespassing on the territory of local plans. As an alternative, regions may seek to protect their planning priorities through the provision or denial of infrastructure to new developments, but this will itself be an admission that the planning system itself is unable to cope with the issue (Keating 1982).

A practical problem arises from the lack of consistent time-scale for structure and local plans. In Aberdeen, for example, the first structure plan was due to run only until 1986, while local plans were still being produced in 1984, to run for five years. By the time the revised structure plan appears, the local plans will be in operation. So local plans are likely to continue to be produced without a structure plan framework.

Other implementation problems stem from the lack of co-ordination of structure planning with major public investment decisions, including the capital budgets of the regional councils themselves, or with corporate planning procedures. Structure plans are usually vague about the time scale for their implementation and planners have little influence over the priorities of major investment and service departments. Thomson (1984) similarly also found little evidence that, where local plans existed, they made much of an impact on the priorities of local authority departments.

Planning has been caught unawares by some recent developments such as the collapse of local industries or national economic decline. Wannop (1981) cites the case of the Clydebank where the council was still, in 1981, producing its local plan, started in 1975, though in the meantime there had occurred the run-down of the John Brown yard, the closure of the Singer works and the Goodyear Tyre factory, and the establishment of the Clydebank Task Force and Enterprise Zone. This points to the need for a more flexible type of planning, more adaptable to circumstances.

Planning failures and the recession have helped to generate an anti-planning mood sustained by the recent dominance of free-market and 'new right' ideology in government. Planning may be more difficult to sustain in a recession, when decisions about the location of development become a 'zero-sum game'. It is precisely at such times, however, that planning and the determination of priorities according to political choices is most vital in order to use resources efficiently.

Changing Direction

As we noted in chapter 1, the emphasis in urban policy began to shift in the mid-1970s to focus on the urban economic problem, particularly in the inner city. The most striking example of this reorientation in Scotland was the announcement of the Glasgow Eastern Area Renewal (GEAR) project.

Negotiations on a major programme of urban renewal in Glasgow began early in 1976, initially only between the Scottish Office and the SDA, then widened to include Glasgow District Council and Strathclyde Regional Council. The Scottish Special Housing Association, a government agency originally established in the 1930s to accelerate the pace of house building in the public sector, was also invited to these early talks. As was to become clear, GEAR was to continue the long tradition of using urban renewal in Glasgow to help solve the city's intractable housing problem. The chairman of the SDA, Sir William Gray, a recent Lord Provost of Glasgow, was, not surprisingly, an enthusiastic supporter of Agency involvement in urban areas – his Chief Executive and other senior officials were, in contrast, less than eager to divert the attention of the new agency away from what they saw as its primary purpose of sectoral intervention in the Scottish economy. In May 1976, with the support of the local authorities concerned, the Scottish Office formally announced potential expenditure of £120 million on a major programme of urban renewal in the east end of Glasgow. The Glasgow Eastern Area Renewal (GEAR) project was to be co-ordinated by the SDA, with the other participants retaining their existing powers and responsibilities.

Other areas in the city had been considered for this experiment in co-ordinated, 'comprehensive renewal': Govan, Maryhill and Springburn were

41

all similarly deprived and in need of massive public expenditure. It has never been made clear why GEAR was selected other than that the area had the 'best' combination of problems, planning background and political support.

A selection of statistics from the GEAR project serves to underscore its significance for contemporary urban renewal in Glasgow and the impact it had on urban policy and planning throughout Scotland. GEAR covers an area of 1,600 ha., some 8 per cent of the city of Glasgow; the population at the outset of the project numbered 45,000, having fallen from a high of 145,000 in 1952. In 1976, the area contained 42,000 jobs, a significant proportion of manufacturing industry in the city. Poverty and the attendant social problems could be found throughout GEAR, with a household survey finding a high incidence of long-term male unemployment, low household incomes, a high dependency ratio (based on the numbers of children, elderly, handicapped and permanently sick) coupled to dissatisfaction with inadequate social and health services. Physical decay was similarly obvious: 20 per cent of the land lay vacant, 12 per cent of all buildings were empty and the inner-core contained significant numbers of dwellings lacking basic amenities or structurally defective.

With this background, the product of economic decline, private disinvestment and institutional neglect, the SDA announced to a sceptical public a programme of action that would undertake 'in a co-ordinated way the comprehensive social, economic and environmental regeneration of the east-end . . . creating the conditions for the development of a balanced and thriving community.' An Urban Renewal Directorate was established in the Agency, staffed largely from the redundant Stonehouse design team. A complex management system was devised, including a Governing Committee chaired by a Scottish Office minister and attended by senior politicians from the local authorities and a Management Committee of senior civil servants and local government officials. At one time, 37 staff in the SDA's Urban Renewal Directorate were working on GEAR, servicing some ten officer working groups which brought together officials from all participating organisations under specific subject headings.

By March 1984, expenditure by the public sector in GEAR (largely capital expenditure) exceeded £212 million (table 2.3), distributed between housing (60 per cent), industry (13 per cent), community services (10 per cent), infrastructure (10 per cent) and the environment (7 per cent). A further public investment of £106 million is anticipated between 1984 and the completion of the project in 1987, bringing total public investment in GEAR over its 10-year life to £308 million. In addition, Leclerc and Draffan (1984) estimate that this public expenditure will lever some £117 million from the private sector, largely in the form of private housing and industrial building.

What is less clear is the extent to which GEAR attracted additional resources to Glasgow or merely redirected existing funds to the east end. Both Nairn (1983) and Joliffe (n.d.) contend that there was no additional housing

Table 2.3. Summary of project costs 1977-84 (£'000s).

Authority	Total costs of projects established 1977-84
Strathclyde Regional Council	
Infrastructure, transport	10,495
Education, social services, community	6,060
Protection services	4,262
Total	20,817
Glasgow District Council	
New housing	14,104
Modernisation, rehabilitation	23,038
Other	8,295
Total	45,437
Scottish Development Agency	
Land assembly – site preparation	9,365
Factory building	16,982
Environment, recreation, other expenditure	23,846
Total	31,433
Housing Corporation	
Local HA new housing	1,860
Local HA rehabilitation	58,820
Other	75
Total	60,755
Greater Glasgow Health Board	3,740
Manpower Services Commission	N/A
Other	
Voluntary organisations under urban programme	215
Total	£212,590

Source: *GEAR Project Report 1984*, SDA, Glasgow.

investment, particularly in the early years of the project. Expenditure by the SSHA and the Housing Corporation in GEAR enabled Glasgow District Council to redirect their housing investment to other parts of the city. Yet, despite the formal priority accorded GEAR by all the organisations involved, looking across the spectrum of public expenditure, there is no unequivocal evidence that significant additional resources were attracted to the city as a whole.

This investment has been translated into a variety of physical, economic and social changes in the east end of Glasgow – 83,000 sq. m. of factory floor space, 194 ha. of industrial land, major infrastructure improvements, 218 completed houses in the public sector and 5,800 modernised properties, 2,930 houses rehabilitated, a series of training initiatives sponsored by the MSC and a variety of educational, social and community projects focussed on pre-school education and on improving community facilities. Yet, while it is relatively simple to conduct an audit of physical development in the area, it is much more difficult to catalogue change, perhaps improvement, in the social and economic condition of the East End.

The question of measuring the impact of GEAR now fills an extensive library, recording and analysing the part the project played in changing the east end of the city (SDA 1980; Booth et al. 1982; Wannop 1983; Nairn 1983; Leclerc and Draffan 1984). Rather than reassemble this information and analysis, it is perhaps more valuable to examine ways in which the GEAR project, by far the largest innovation in recent Scottish urban policy, changed direction and emphasis over time and effectively redirected urban policy and urban planning throughout the rest of Scotland.

Although ultimately becoming remarkably similar to the comprehensive physical renewal schemes of the 1960s, GEAR was largely implemented in the absence of an agreed set of policies or any definable plan. Instead, parts of the project were based on existing priorities and commitments of the individual participants. Some, like Glasgow District, were able to work to established Local Plan guidelines (although in practice such policy frameworks were often ignored) while others, as in the case of the SDA's programme for environmental improvement, progressed on the basis of very short-term objectives, often responding to problems and opportunties as they arose. This reactive, some would say pragmatic, management style was also used to accommodate the often conflicting objectives of the participants and certainly was more acceptable to the sectoral, as distinct from the spatial, concerns of the SDA leadership. The GEAR 'Strategy and Programme', eventually published in 1980, some four years after the announcement of the project, was barely recognisable as a plan, containing no firm policy guidelines, no spatial strategy and no indication of programme targets, rendering policy evaluation almost impossible. It did, however, outline broad policy objectives and sought to reaffirm the commitment of the different organisations involved. In essence, therefore, it became a multi-agency agreement on the project's objectives, a model for co-ordinating area improvement that was to reappear throughout Scotland in the form of the SDA's Area Project agreements.

Whatever the benefits of this approach to comprehensive urban renewal, it became clear that the lack of fixed policy guidelines and a formal planning framework gave the GEAR team the flexibility to adapt the project in the light of rapidly changing economic and political circumstances. Thus GEAR encapsulates the shifting focus of urban policy after 1976. GEAR began with a commitment to social improvement, to addressing multiple deprivation, to improving welfare services, to 'overcoming social disadvantage' and to 'fostering residents' commitment and confidence'. It then inherited the economic and later the 'business' imperative of the SDA, paralleling a similar shift in UK urban policy. Programmes were designed to improve the economic competitiveness of the East End – infrastructure, factories, training programmes, marketing, image enhancement. By 1983, the SDA was actively promoting GEAR as a 'place to do business', with the publicity on the area changing from a focus on community development to the selling of floorspace. In a 1984 progress report, the Director of Area Development (the successor of the Urban Renewal Directorate) began a list of achievements in GEAR with mention of the conversion of the Templeton carpet factory into a Business Centre, the establishment of a Business Investment Park at Cambuslang, the development of two Business Development Areas, a listing of the number of new factory units opened in the East End, comment on a range of training initiatives sponsored by a private organisation and the opening of an Information Technology Centre. There were no headlines for social improvement now!

The implications of this reorientation was that a sizeable component of expenditure on GEAR was committed to infrastructure that no longer had a direct connection with the residents of the East End. By 1983, the project had begun to take on all the characteristics of comprehensive physical urban renewal to encourage commercial development where benefits would not necessarily be retained within the East End. Moreover, the business focus of GEAR also began to influence the substance of the programme, searching for symbolic rather than actual change, marketing the East End to the highest bidder. The symbol of environmental improvement effectively obscured the continuing deep-seated social and economic problems of the area, notably the persistence of high unemployment.

Perhaps the most significant characteristic of the GEAR project was the direct involvement of the Scottish Office in urban renewal and their use of a development agency to control implementation and direct public expenditure. Although the elected councils in Glasgow and Strathclyde retained control over their respective functions and remained equal partners in the renewal process, they nevertheless conceded overall control of urban change to central government and, crucially, were required to work within political, economic and administrative constraints that circumscribed local action. Once again, this experience in GEAR was to be replicated in other areas, addressing other types of problem. As in Leith and Clydebank, the respective local authorities involved in GEAR did not have much choice. To reject the 'partnership' in the project would have resulted in the loss of influence over urban change; to reject the offer of additional public expenditure would have been foolhardy. But the implications of the GEAR model of central involvement in urban renewal remain. As with the two Urban Development Corporations in England, when the 'signs come down', local government will be held accountable not only for any benefits of urban change but also for the problems that remain, and will be responsible for managing and maintaining the product of urban renewal in the absence of further additional resources.

3

CENTRAL INITIATIVES FOR
LOCAL ECONOMIC DEVELOPMENT

As the focus of this book is on local, urban economic iniatives in Scotland, we do not devote extensive space to policy that has a wider spatial focus, including national/sectoral and national/regional policies. However, the relationship between urban economic initiatives and national/regional policy raises a series of issues which are relevant to our theme of government's capacity to deliver coherent spatial policies and assist local economic change.

For the past three decades, UK regional assistance has been the main component of government's attempt to improve the performance of the peripheral regions and achieve a degree of spatial balance in the national economy. In the 1970s, regional policy was increasingly seen as at variance with other policies directed at urban economic improvement, and even with successive administrative changes government found it particularly difficult to target its industrial incentives, which were essentially demand-led, towards areas of severe economic distress. Despite the degree of administrative decentralisation in Scotland, regional aid throughout the 1970s continued to support industry, particularly in petrochemicals, located beyond the major cities.

Enterprise zone policy started life as a non-spatial initiative but was soon transformed into an instrument of urban and regional economic development; its relationship with other spatial policy instruments, however, remains problematic. Another actor in the spatial policy arena is the European Community, which has attempted to construct its own coherent regional policy in partnership with national government, and also with local authorities. The most ambitious initiative in this regard is the proposed Integrated Development Operation (IDO) in Glasgow. In this chapter, we review these national and European initiatives and assess their relationship to the urban redevelopment initiatives which are the main concern of the book.

Regional Policy

Regional economic policy can trace its origins back to the 1930s when the Commissioners for Special Areas were appointed in an effort to tackle the impact of the recession on the older industrial areas. In its modern form, however, it is a product of the 1960s growth philosophy and of a belief that, in times of overall full employment, both economic progress and social and political justice would be served by diverting industrial expansion from the congested to the depressed regions. The economic justification was based on the belief that encouraging expansion in those regions where there was unemployment would add to national output by bringing into use idle capacity as well as relieving the inflationary pressures which would arise from allowing industry to compete for scarce resources in the booming areas of the English Midlands and South East. It was thus a 'non zero sum' game, in which everyone was a winner. The social and political justification was that people in the depressed regions should have work made available to them in their home areas, rather than being forced to migrate.

The main policy instruments have been grants for investment, initially concentrated on manufacturing industry but now available to some service industries. There are now three types of grant, Regional Development Grants, payable automatically on capital investments satisfying certain requirements in eligible areas; Selective Financial Assistance, a discretionary grant for industry in eligible areas; and Office and Service Industries Scheme grants, also discretionary. Since 1975, Selective Financial Assistance has been administered by the Secretary of State for Scotland, who in 1984 took over responsibility for the automatic grants from the Department of Trade and Industry. From 1967 to 1976, a labour subsidy in the form of the Regional Employment Premium was available in eligible areas. For some years, the 'carrot' of incentives was accompanied by the 'stick' of Industrial Development Certificates (IDCs), required for industrial development in certain regions but, in the course of the 1970s, refusal of IDCs became an ever rarer occurrence and they have since been abolished.

The spatial focus of regional policy underwent a progressive widening in the 1960s and 1970s and has progressively narrowed since. The early regional aids were available for 'blackspots' of unemployment. In the Local Employment Act 1960, the idea of 'development areas' was introduced and by the late 1970s there were three classes of assisted area, Special Development Areas, Development Areas and Intermediate Areas, with varying ranges of incentives available in each. By 1974, with the designation of Edinburgh and Leith following an election promise by the incoming Labour Government, the whole of Scotland was an assisted area, with Special Development Areas in Dundee and over a large part of Strathclyde Region, as shown on map 3.1. The 1960s also saw the growth of regional planning (discussed in chapter 2) and the 'growth pole' philosophy in which the development of regions was to be led by their dynamic areas, but assisted areas policy was never integrated with this. Regional development grants remained largely automatic, despite the introduction of Selective Financial Assistance in 1972, so could not reflect the needs of planning strategies.

Most studies agree that regional policy measures have benefited the

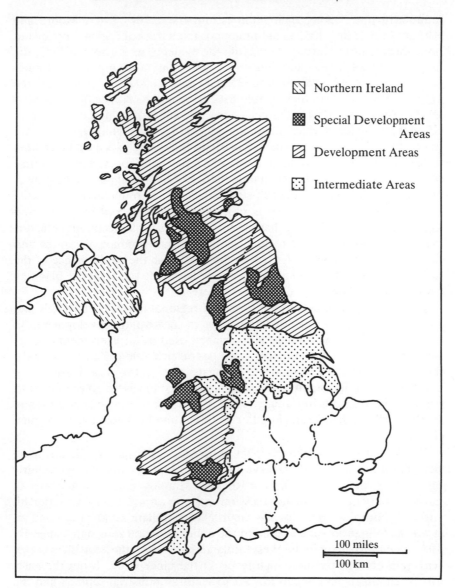

Map 3.1. Assisted areas, March 1972.

growth of manufacturing industry in Scotland (Lythe and Majmudar 1982).
Moore and Rhodes (1973) found that, during the period of active regional
policy (1961–71) Scottish manufacturing employment did better than in the
period of passive policy (1952–61) and were able to credit much of this to the
policy. They calculated that, for 1961–71, Scotland benefited by some
12–15,000 jobs in indigenous industry and some 34–38,000 jobs in incoming

manufacturing. Taking their findings into the 1970s (Tyler, Moore and Rhodes 1980), they find a continuing positive effect of regional policy but one which is not so strong. Surveying the evidence as a whole in 1983, the Department of Trade and Industry found that, allowing for multiplier effects, there were anything from 350,000 to 630,000 more jobs in assisted areas by 1979–81 than there would have been in the absence of policy (DTI 1983). They also draw attention to the 'plateau effect' noted by Moore, Rhodes and Tyler in which maintaining the policy at a given level may cease to create additional employment as, after a time, new jobs must be created to replace earlier policy-created jobs which have disappeared in the course of plant closures and other economic changes. Given that part of the growth pole strategy was to produce self-sustaining growth around major industrial developments, further doubt is cast on its effectiveness by Lythe and Majmudar's (1982) finding that the improved performance in manufacturing industry in periods of regional policy did not produce a spin-off into other sectors or services. Critics might see this as the consequence of the failure to integrate regional incentive policy with the regional planning exercises described in the previous chapter.

The same applied to another aspect of regional policy in the 1960s and 1970s, the 'arm-twisting' of large firms to locate new developments in declining regions, with financial assistance used as an instrument of persuasion. Scotland's most notable examples of such 'one-off' measures were the vehicle plants at Linwood and Bathgate, the steelworks at Ravenscraig and the aluminium smelter at Invergordon. By and large, these failed to produce the spin-offs into related industries which had been hoped for and by the 1980s all had been closed or were fighting last-ditch battles against closure.

By the late 1970s, the political consensus underpinning diversionary regional policy was breaking down. At a time of retrenchment, it was a fairly easy target for cutbacks and the Regional Employment Premium was an early casualty in 1976. As the recession and long-term deindustrialisation hit formerly booming areas like the English West Midlands and inner London, it was no longer possible to present the policy as a 'non zero sum' game. By 1983, unemployment in the West Midlands had passed the Scottish average, with pockets of extremely high levels in the inner cities. From the early 1970s, emphasis had begun to shift to sectoral industrial support and the rescue of large firms like British Leyland. At the same time, the spatial focus of policy came to rest upon the intra-regional shift from the inner urban areas, with the rise of inner city initiatives. The regional perspective in policy had never been strongly articulated, as a result of the failure to integrate inter-regional diversionary policy and the intra-regional planning initiatives of the 1960s and 1970s. With the increased emphasis on the one hand on the national/sectoral needs and, on the other, on the small urban scale, it now began to disappear altogether.

The effectiveness of regional aid was also called into question. Critics pointed out that subsidies to capital investment were often a poor way to increase employment and that many of the subsidies had gone to invest- ments, in many cases related to North Sea oil, which would have taken place anyway. In 1982, for example, of £238.6m paid out in Regional Develop- ment Grants in Scotland, £91.7m went to B P for the Sullom Voe oil terminal, £22.5m to Shell and Esso for the Moss Morran chemicals project and £10.2m to B P at Grangemouth (*The Scotsman* 28-11-83). Service industries con- tinued to be largely neglected, despite their potential for job creation, with available incentives aimed mainly at mobile office developments. Not only were regional policies not integrated with other spatial policy instruments but, in some regions, such as the West Midlands of England and inner London, regional policies appeared to be pulling in the opposite direction to the newer inner-city strategies.

Regional policy spending reached its peak in 1975–76, falling sharply with the abolition of R E P and again with the review by the incoming Conservative Government of 1979 (table 3.1).

The 1979 review, a cost cutting exercise, involved a 38 per cent reduction in regional aid and a reduction of its geographical coverage from 40 to 25 per cent of the working population over a three-year period (map 3.2). The Borders, Grampian and large parts of Tayside and Fife lost assisted status altogether and Central Region was demoted from development area to intermediate area. A further review was heralded by a White Paper in December 1983, in reality more of a 'Green Paper' making suggestions and inviting comments. It was made clear that the old argument about the economic rationale for regional diversionary policies no longer held sway and that the main justification for the policy must henceforth be social and political. A protracted period of inter-departmental haggling followed, with the Scottish Office seeking to maintain a strong commitment to the policy and to a generous demarcation of assisted areas. The result, announced in November 1984, represented a considerable setback. Scotland was to con- tribute some £90m of the total £270m cutback. Overall, the reductions represented about half the total budget for regional assistance and a third of the amount spent in Scotland. It is true that the Scottish share of aid is to increase from 41 to 51 per cent and the Scottish Secretary maintained that the money would henceforth not go to large developments which would have proceeded any way but to job creation. The Scottish T U C and C B I were nevertheless united in their view of the changes as disastrous. The three-tier classification of assisted areas is replaced by a two-tier scheme of inner development areas and outer intermediate areas. Only Arbroath, Dundee, Bathgate, Lanarkshire, Cumnock and Sanquhar, Kilmarnock, Glasgow, Irvine, Greenock and Dumbarton, were designated as inner development areas, with parts of the Highlands, Fife and Dumfries and Galloway as intermediate areas. Automatic grants in development areas were reduced

Table 3.1. Expenditure on regional preferential assistance in Great Britain, 1974/75 to 1982/83 (at 1982/83 prices).

Year	Total RPA expenditure (£m)	96 Total RPA accounted for by:				
		RDGS	SFA	REP	SDA & WDA	Other
1974/75	1,348	45.0	7.7	32.8	—	14.5
1975/76	1,530	48.6	9.8	32.2	0.9	8.5
1976/77	1,427	56.8	6.0	30.2	2.4	4.6
1977/78	883	77.6	8.8	0.6	6.3	6.7
1978/79	1,010	66.4	16.5	—	9.2	7.9
1979/80	780	58.8	13.3	—	14.4	13.5
1980/81	872	67.1	9.7	—	14.7	8.5
1981/82	939	70.3	8.6	—	14.2	6.9
1982/83	912	75.6	9.5	—	10.2	4.7

RDGS: Regional Development Grants.
SFA: Selective Financial Assistance under Section 7 of the Industry Act (including Office and Service Industry Scheme).
REP: Regional Employment Premium.
SDA & WDA: Expenditure by Scottish and Welsh Development Agencies on land and factories in Assisted Areas (excludes expenditure by SDA in descheduled areas of Scotland in 1982/83).
Other: Includes expenditure by English Industrial Estates Corporation, Highlands and Islands Development Board and the Development Board for Rural Wales; preferential payments under the Small Firms Employment Subsidy 1977-80 and a number of other small items.
All expenditure figures are gross and include payments to nationalised industries.
Source: RSA (1983) (original data from Department of Industry).

from 22 to 15 per cent, limited to investments which create jobs and subjected to a limit of £10,000 per job, except in the case of small firms. Grants were extended to a range of service industries. In the intermediate areas, only selective financial assistance will be available. As a gesture to the Scottish lobby, responsibility for the administration of automatic assistance in the development areas was transferred from the Department of Trade and Industry to the Scottish Office but, given the automatic nature of the grants, this has no policy significance. With the progressive reduction of the coverage of assisted areas, policy has reverted from the broad 'regional' perspective to a narrower 'blackspot' focus. It remains the case, however, that Scotland's major urban blackspots continue to be eligible for regional industrial aid, reinforcing the already tight focus of policy measures. The new towns, except for Glenrothes, and the major SDA urban regeneration initiatives continue to lie within development areas. It appears that this was not

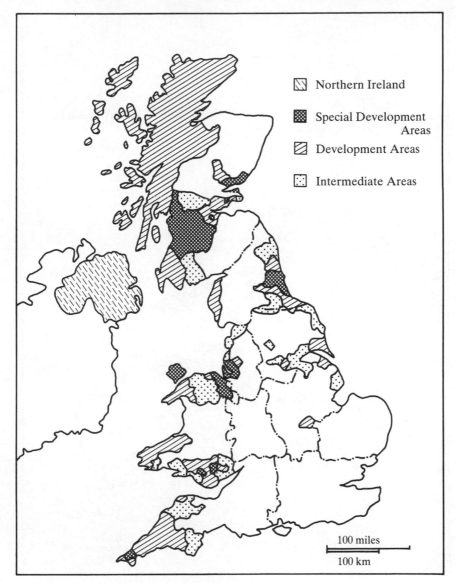

Key:
- Northern Ireland
- Special Development Areas
- Development Areas
- Intermediate Areas

100 miles

100 km

Map 3.2. Assisted areas, August 1982.

entirely accidental. Although the new assisted area boundaries were largely based on U K-wide criteria these were not applied entirely mechanically and it seems that the inclusion of Dundee in the list of development areas owed something to the fact that it was being promoted as a priority area through the project and the Enterprise Zone (map 3.3).

In justification for its measures, the Government pointed out that Scot-

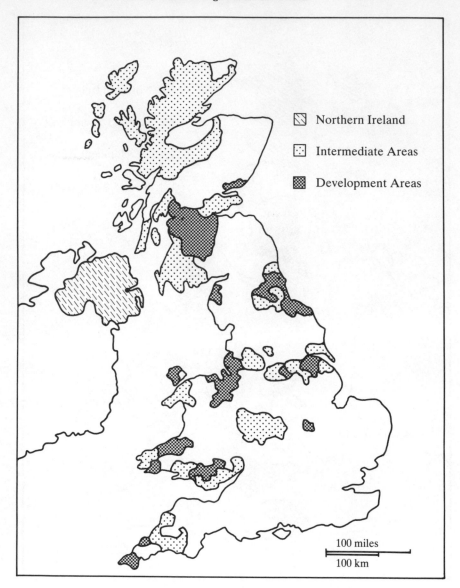

Northern Ireland

Intermediate Areas

Development Areas

100 miles

100 km

Map 3.3. Assisted areas, November 1984. Source: *Town and Country Planning*, January 1985.

land was 'now one of the most prosperous regions, with the third highest level of gross domestic product per head in Great Britain, compared with the eighth in 1971. Average full-time earnings of male manual workers were second only to the south-east of England; and, while Scotland had the worst unemployment rate in Great Britain in 1965, by 1984 there were four regions worse off – the North and North-West of England, the West Midlands and Wales. Scotland's industrial structure, according to the Government, was 'no longer a major disadvantage' (Scottish Office press notice 1362/84). Though putting a brave face on the outcome of the Cabinet battles, there is some evidence that the Scottish Office had found itself hoist on its own petard. Having boasted about the recovery of the Scottish economy and the glories of 'Silicon Glen', it was difficult to convince Cabinet of its continuing need for help or that its good fortune was only relative and not absolute, a product of the crisis of the English manufacturing areas.

Enterprise Zones

Enterprise zones were first suggested by Professor Peter Hall who, in 1977, proposed the creation of non-planning zones free of taxes, social services and government intervention of all kinds, to revive the depressed inner cities. In a modified form, the idea was taken over by Sir Geoffrey Howe, the Opposition spokesman on economic affairs, who was impressed by the analysis that urban economic decline was a consequence of state intervention, taxation and planning restrictions, which had stifled entrepreneurial initiative. Howe proposed zones, to be managed by a new type of agency, in which there would be:

An abandonment of planning controls, Industrial Development Certificates and Office Development Permits;

A reversal of the Community Land Act, with public authorities required to auction off their land holdings;

Exemption from Development Land Tax and, possibly, rates;

Guarantees against tax changes and nationalisation;

No government grants or subsidies;

No price or pay controls and a suspension of some or all of the provisions of the Employment Protection Act.

The free market basis of the scheme was still clearly evident but Howe's proposal recognised the impossibility of withdrawing services such as police, fire, roads, sewers and education, particularly if the objective was to encourage industrial development. In doing so, though, it raised doubts about the whole basis of the scheme. If industrialists were to continue to receive the benefits of public services, then to exempt them from the requirement to pay for them would simply amount to a public subsidy – quite the reverse of the original market idea. More fundamentally, to confine the benefits to industrialists in specified zones interfered with one of the principal features of a free market approach – the freedom to locate in the best sites, without costs being distorted by government policies. The argument about planning restrictions seems to have derived exclusively from experience in inner London, where conflicts over approprate land uses and industrial dispersal policies had led to refusals of permission for industrial developments. In Scotland, planning restrictions had been operated in order to protect areas of high amenity and encourage industry to locate precisely in the sorts of areas Howe had in mind.

When the Conservatives came into office in 1979 Howe's enthusiasm was translated into a Treasury initiative, considerably modified in turn by inter-departmental bargaining (Taylor 1981). The Department of Employment, under pressure from the trade unions, refused to agree to the suspension of the Employment Protection Act. The proposal to withdraw regional policy aids and other grants and subsidies was dropped after pressure from both industry and unions. The proposal to force public authorities to auction off land was dropped as unworkable and possibly very costly, though the intention was declared to select zones without substantial public land hold-ings. On the other hand, to maximise the attractiveness of the zones, the proposal for rates relief was definitely incorporated. Rates are not abolished in the zones but are paid by the Treasury, effectively constituting a public subsidy to zone occupants. This has led the Treasury to insist on tight demarcation of the zones and some rather eccentric boundaries, in order to exclude 'beneficial users', existing industries already paying rates who stood to make a windfall gain.

The implications of the proposal to abolish planning restrictions also caused some headaches, with local authorities which, such was the Govern-ment's urgency, had been approached before the legislation was enacted, pointing to further difficulties. It was accepted at an early stage that some restrictions to curb the nuisance value of certain activities would be neces-sary. Later, it was accepted that controls would be necessary on access to infrastructure such as water, sewerage and roads and on activities which could adversely affect neghbouring areas. For example, if unrestricted retail development were allowed, hypermarkets could come to take advantage of the (effective) subsidies and present unfair competition to retailers outside the zone. In some cases, shopping centres in which local authorities had a substantial investment could be threatened. This possibility was particularly obvious in the first Scottish zone at Clydebank and the restrictions negoti-ated there have since become virtually standard. There is a zoning scheme laying down that certain types of development are permitted automatically in certain parts of the zone, while others require planning permission in the normal way.

By the time the final Enterprise Zone proposals emerged, then, the idea had come a long way from the original free market concept and was begin-ning to look like an instrument of traditional spatial policy, a means of subsidising industry to locate in one area rather than another. There was, however, a continuing reluctance on the part of government to admit this and an insistence that the zones were not part of urban policy or regional policy. In England, implementation of the policy was given to the Depart-ment of the Environment and, despite the above disclaimer, to its Inner Cities Directorate. In Scotland, it was given first to the Scottish Office's

Urban Renewal Unit in the SDD and then transferred to the then Scottish Economic Planning Department; given the wide responsibilities of the Scottish Office, it was perhaps less important whether the zones were part of urban policy, regional policy or something else.

For local authorities, enterprise zones were a mixed blessing. Few were convinced of the analysis underlying the policy and many feared that, by cutting across their planning and development policies, reducing their planning powers and encouraging relocation of industry, they could cause problems. On the other hand, regarded purely as a package of financial incentives to industry – and the evidence is that this is how industrialists see them (Rodriguez and Bruinvels 1982) – they were a gift few authorities felt able to refuse. Instead, they have sought to tie in the zones to their own planning and development policies, turning the original idea on its head in the process.

For the first round of zones, sites were chosen by the regional offices of the Department of the Environment and the Scottish, Welsh and Northern Ireland Offices. The choice of Clydebank for the Scottish zone emerged from the working party under Gavin McCrone, Secretary of SEPD, which also produced the idea of the Task Force, to undertake responsibility for rebuilding the local economy (see chapter 5). It was because of this that responsibility came to be transferred from SDD to SEPD. The Clydebank zone is not quite continuous with the Task Force area but its 570 acres are included within it and its promotion is undertaken by the Task Force. The former Singer site, purchased by the SDA and renamed the Clydebank Business Park, accounts for 86 acres of the zone and is a central feature of the Task Force's efforts. In fact, although there is technically only one zone, 98 acres of it are within Glasgow and the zone consists of seven distinct, though contiguous, sites. Planning restrictions are generally lifted, except on developments over 4,250 square feet and for food and clothing retailing, but part of the zone is restricted to light industrial use and one area is subject to full planning controls. There was some argument over warehousing which might find the zone concessions attractive but has little employment potential, but in the event only whisky bonding was made subject to controls (Jordan and Reilly 1981).

Most of the land was in public ownership or, like the Singer site, was taken into public ownership, the main owners being the SDA, Clydebank District Council and the South of Scotland Electricity Board. Extensive site preparation and environmental improvement has been undertaken by the Agency. Infrastructure is the responsibility of Strathclyde Regional Council, though the region was unwilling to alter its capital spending plans to accommodate the zone in the absence of an extension of its total capital spending allocations. Attraction of industry and matching incomers with sites and premises is the responsibility of the Task Force. To this must be added the whole range of government incentives available outwith the provisions of the enterprise zone scheme. As the Task Force points out in its promotional literature, firms in Clydebank are also eligible for maximum assisted area incentives including regional development grants, selective financial assistance, aid under the Office and Service Industries Scheme and European Coal and Steel Community loans, as well as SDA assistance by way of fully serviced sites and premises, some at concessionary rates, loan and equity funding, business advice and loans from the Clydebank Enterprise Fund, administered by the Agency and the Bank of Scotland.

The result is an undoubted success in attracting industry. By April 1984, 229 companies had moved into premises in the zone, with a projection of 2,577 jobs. Of these, however, 58 companies, accounting for 602 of the jobs, were relocations, firms moving to take advantage of the zone concessions. Perhaps the best known of these was Radio Clyde who moved from the Anderston Cross Centre, a Glasgow city centre development already suffering from severe difficulties in attracting tenants and rapidly falling into decay. On the other hand, 1,551 jobs were in new companies, the balance being in branch plants. Most of the jobs, 2,098, were provided in SDA premises. Most of the jobs provided in privately developed premises were relocations or branch plants. It is clear, then, that the dynamic for new firm creation was coming from the provision of SDA premises and the offer of incentives. Overall, by Spring 1984, £19.5 million of public money had been invested in the zone, against £16.25 million of private money. The importance of the public sector effort was emphasised by Roger Tym and Partners in their review of the zones for the Government when they commented 'not only has the rate of development and employment been greater (at Clydebank) than in many other zones, but so has the degree of public sector involvement' (Clydebank EZ Bulletin, Spring 1984). By this time, the original enterprise zone theme, of liberating private initiative by removing public involvement had all but disappeared but it was still necessary to demonstrate some private leadership. Faced with the imbalance of public and private spending, the Enterprise Zone Bulletin (Spring 1984) ingeniously described the £19.5 million public investment as 'fast being over-hauled' by the £16.25 million private contribution.

The transformation of the enterprise zone policy into an instrument of public intervention only enhanced its attractiveness to local authorities while the Government's need to demonstrate success for its initiative implied that no effort would be spared to get industry into the zones. Above all, the designation of an enterprise zone became a propaganda bonus, giving the fortunate authorities a focal point for their advertising. So there was keen interest in the second round of zone allocations, in which two were to be given to Scotland. Although in principle there was to be open bidding in this round, the second zone was designated by the Secretary of State in 1982 in response to the closure of the aluminium smelter at Invergordon. The closure had led to a Scottish Office-led working party and then to the

Cromarty Firth Team on the task force model, led by the Highlands and Islands Development Board. At the time of the working party's report in March 1982, there was no suggestion of an enterprise zone, which the Scottish Office appeared to regard as a specifically urban policy and it seems that the announcement in July 1982 took most people by surprise. Highland Regional Council greeted the zone with a distinct lack of enthusiasm as their policy priorities were shifting to the needs of traditional industries in the rural and western parts of the region. Having invested so much in the industrialisation of the Cromarty Firth, they were reluctant to put more resources into coping with its deindustrialisation; and the Scottish Office was indicating that they could not expect resources for the zone. In fact, once the zone boundaries had been agreed between the Scottish Office and the region – after councillors had narrowly voted to accept the zone at all – its management was given over to the HIDB. This included the provision of infrastructure, including roads and bridges, which would normally have been the responsibility of the regional council, the cost to be met from the allocation of £10m which the Board had been given to deal with the closure issue and a small amount extra given later on. Most of the land was then taken into the ownership of the Board and the regional council and a scheme for its use devised by the Board. The zone consists of two parts, in Alness and Invergordon, drawn up, as usual, to avoid beneficial users. Areas were reserved for high amenity use and sites of various sizes parcelled up and serviced. Effective land-use planning is ensured through land ownership. Progress in developing the zone has been slow because of the need to prepare the sites and provide infrastructure and it would probably be fair to say that neither the Board nor the Region regard the attraction of industry to the zone, as opposed to other sites in the Cromarty Firth or other parts of the Highlands, as a major priority. In many respects, indeed, the zone is ill sited to attract incomers, being away from the shore where oil related developments could be encouraged.

Thereafter, bids were invited for the third zone. Four basic criteria were laid down by SEPD:

(i) the new zone should not be in competition with the existing zone at Clydebank or that to be set up at Invergordon;

(ii) a demonstrable need for action to redress the physical and/or economic problems of particular localities within the area concerned;

(iii) the site should be capable of early development;

(iv) the local authority or other eligible body is willing to accept fully the enterprise zone concept by relaxing its powers of planning control, speeding its decision making and co-operating closely with private sector to ensure the continuous release of land for development and the promotion and marketing of the zone.

This made it clear that only specific types of site would be likely to be eligible. Sites which were already developed were obviously ruled out; but equally, it would appear, were sites where there was no existing infra-structure or where there was a need for a great deal of site preparation. So by this stage the policy appeared as a means of bringing into early use sites prepared and serviced for industrial development. There were some twenty-five applications, some of which clearly did not meet the criteria. In selecting among those which did, the Scottish Office appears to have been swayed by a number of considerations, including political and geographical balance, the attitudes of the councils and devlopment corporations applying and the relationship of the enterprise zone to other initiatives. With one zone having gone to the west coast and one to the Highlands, it was almost inevitable that the third would go to the east coast, though it seems that this was not settled without some argument in the Scottish Office. Two applications were re-ceived from Tayside districts, Dundee and Angus. The Dundee application fitted the criteria quite well and was supported by Tayside Region which overcame its own political leaning to back it. On the other hand, there was some opposition to giving the zone to a Labour-controlled district which in the previous year had clashed with central government over spending. Angus' application was for a site in Arbroath, in the constituency of the Solicitor-General for Scotland. So a political balance was struck and the zone split between two districts, despite the fact that this breached SEPD's own criteria laid down in the invitations to bid, which stipulated that where a zone was split the parts should be separated by no more than quarter of a mile. The possibility of calling the result two zones instead of one was ruled out because of the insistence by the Department of the Environment and other territorial departments that Scotland was entitled to no more than three zones.

Dundee District, despite its Labour majority, which might have been expected to have ideological objections to the policy, was enthusiastic in its bid for a zone because of the financial advantages but mainly because of its usefulness in promoting the city as a site for investment. Their application presented the zone as an integral part of the Dundee Project, an SDA-led programme of urban economic regeneration (see chapter 5), with five separate sites – part of the port; the railway station and adjacent land; the airport; the proposed Technology Park; and the industrial estate at Wester Gourdie. Both district and regional councils believed that the zone would be wasted if it were not tied in closely to their existing economic development plans, with public authorities playing a leading role. As the district com-mented in its application:

> It is the coincidence between the diversity of development sites in the Waterfront area and the opportunities to release publicly-held land for private development by way of a planned initiative which can guarantee strong and effective promotion that makes the Waterfront area potenti-ally of national significance as an experiment EZ.

Planning controls would be relaxed but with the usual exceptions for danger-ous activities and safeguards retained for the airport approaches. In addition, controls were to be retained to safeguard the proposed Technology Park from the wrong sort of industry and restrictions placed on retail and residential development in the zone. What was not stressed was that, as most of the land was in public ownership, landlord control could be used to shape development, nor that, given the possibilities for speculators acquiring land in the zone, compulsory purchase powers might have to be used to bring about development and prevent the financial advantages of the zone ending up in the pockets of speculators. Designation of the major Project areas as the enterprise zone had a further advantage. In line with the remnants of the original philosophy, the Government had laid down that EZs should not involve increased public spending. In Dundee, the district was able to point out that the increased spending had already been committed under the Project and so could not be attributed simply to the zone.

Negotiations with the Scottish Office centred on the size and boundaries of the zone and the planning regime within it, the Government trying to rescue something at least of the original *laisser-faire* concept. Eventually, agreement was reached on 210.54 acres for Dundee and 87.5 acres for Arbroath, though officially there is only one zone, the Tayside Enterprise Zone. Dundee's part is in six separate locations, each of which is earmarked for particular types of development as follows:

1. Wester Gourdie   30 acres General Industrial Use
2. Technology Park   60 acres Technology Developments
3. Airport   30 acres Airport related
4. City Centre/Landfall 30 acres Commercial and high amenity
5. Port   30 acres Oil related
6. West Pitkerro   31 acres Greenfield site.

These sites are being promoted and marketed through the Dundee Project for appropriate types of development, with the initial emphasis on getting the Technology Park going and attracting a major hotel to the Landfall site. Public ownership of land is the main instrument to ensure that development conforms to Project Priorities and that prime sites are not 'wasted' on unsuitable development, though the absence of spontaneous development pressures means that the main emphasis is on attracting investment rather than control. In the Technology Park, an SDA-owned site in the Green Belt for which the Structure Plan had to be changed, tight controls are retained through land ownership and a Section 50 agreement putting obligations on future land owners (in the event of the Agency selling the land) to maintain it for high technology use. In the Wester Gourdie section, there is more of a free planning regime, but this section consists of a strip of land winding through an industrial estate to exclude existing users. This land was already available for industrial development without planning difficulties and the main effect of the zone designation, if industrialists do locate on the zone bits, will be to create two classes of users of the estate. In practice, enterprise zone provisions offer little incentive to build industrial property and any beneficiaries are likely to be tenants moving into SDA developments. This reinforces the lesson of Clydebank, that it is public investment in infra-structure and property, together with promotional work, rather than the marginal fiscal incentives of the enterprise zone which have the greatest potential for stimulating industrial development.

Angus District's application was for an enterprise zone split between a declining industrial area of Arbroath town centre and industrial estate, the two sites being just close enough to meet the Government's stated criteria. The estate was fully serviced and in council ownership, and one factory had already been set up. As in Dundee, the District's policy was to use the zone in pursuit of its own development plans rather than just designating a zone and waiting to see what would happen. The SDA had already agreed to a consultants' study of the central area, which duly bore fruit in the Arbroath Venture, one of the Agency's integrated area projects (see chapter 5). The council for its part wanted the whole of its planned industrial estate included, precipitating an argument with the Scottish Office over one existing bene-ficial user already there. There was a possibility that the firm in question would expand and, in any case, the council saw the preservation of existing jobs as being as important as the creation of new ones. There was another argument over restrictions on retail development which the District wanted to keep in order to preserve an existing town centre shopping development. In the event, the fragmented zone only allocated enough land to Arbroath to accommodate the industrial estate, with the town centre being dealt with through the proposed area project.

The Tayside enterprise zone represents an extreme case of the reversal of the original idea. Instead of zones of non-intervention where market forces could have free play, we see a planned, interventionist effort, led and financed by the public sector. Even the areal integrity of the idea has been shattered, with the Tayside zone emerging as a means of promoting specific industrial sites. The policy drift from the original concept must be attributed both to the unworkability of the original idea and to the deflection of the policy to the needs of the implementing agencies. Enterprise zones now look like a rather traditional spatial policy measure consisting of two principal elements, a package of fiscal incentives, notably the rates relief and the capital allowances, and a heavy promotional effort, the latter undoubtedly aided by the considerable political stake which central government has in being able to show results from the policy.

Whether enterprise zones as they have developed represent an appropri-ate response to the problem of urban economic decline is another matter. They are certainly costly, though establishing the precise totals of public expenditure in the zones is notoriously difficult. After the initial consultants' reports, the Government ended regular monitoring and produced only limited statistcs for 1983–84. In the first two years, when monitoring was in operation, it was calculated that £132.9 million of public money had been invested in all the zones (Roger Tyms 1984). Of this, £54.8 million was accounted for by rates relief and Initial Building Allowance (the tax concessions). For its report, after the ending of the regular monitoring, the government could only make estimates for the amount of investment in the English and Welsh zones and not for the Scottish ones. So it was unable to provide data on the amounts of investment allowances and grants paid in the zones after 1982–83 (DOE 1985). For the English and Welsh zones, the estimates suggest that, between April 1983 and October 1984, the zones attracted some £45 million of investment with the Government paying out £14 million in capital allowances and just over £19 million in rates (DOE 1985). These are simply the costs which were incurred under the EZ regime and exclude spending on infrastructure and allowances for which firms would have been eligible in the absence of the zones. The largest public investments have been at the Isle of Dogs, Clydebank, Corby and Swansea, where there are development agencies at work preparing land and buildings. Most of the fiscal incentives of the zones are related to property development and there has been a marked increase in building activity (Roger Tyms 1984). Much of the credit for this, however, must go to public programmes of land assembly and servicing; public ownership of land has been a crucial factor in our Scottish examples. In some cases, however, the lack of buildings is not the main constraint on development. Industrialists in Dundee have pointed out that the main constraint on development of the waterfront is the need for deepening of the river and modernisation of the harbour, neither helped by the enterprise zone measures. At Invergordon, the HIDB had had to undertake the servicing of the zone at considerable public expense despite the wide agreement that it is not the ideal site for industrial expansion and that the money could almost certainly have been applied to more effect elsewhere, including other sites in the immediate vicinity. So the uniform fiscal package may not be tailored to the needs of specific localities. The available information on the Scottish zones which, as we have noted, excludes the vital data on investment allowances, is given in table 3.2.

Table 3.2. Scottish enterprise zones.

Zone	Employment at designation	Employment Sept. 1984	Public sector infrastructure (£'000s)	Rates cost 1984-85[1] (£'000s)
Clydebank	2,825	5,500	6,000	1,700
Invergordon	103	100	1,000	17.1
Tayside	546	1,200	1,111	171.4

[1] Rates cost estimated for whole year on basis of figures for 1-4-84 to 31-10-84. Source: DOE (1985).

The simplified planning regime is said to be welcomed by developers (Roger Tyms 1984). This is not, however, the non-planning regime advocated by the original exponents of the enterprise zone idea. Development control procedures have been simplified but the negative planning of the past has been replaced by a very positive form of planning to match sites with suitable users. Land ownership is a major instrument of this. In 1982–83, only 8 per cent of the floorspace completed in the zones was undertaken under the simplified planning schemes and not either developed by a public agency or developed on land controlled by a public agency (Roger Tyms 1984). In Dundee, after the zone sites had been selected with such care, there was a determination on the part of region, district and SDA that the benefits of zone status should not be 'wasted' on random development but should contribute to the realisation of the priorities of the Dundee Project. Similarly, in Clydebank and Invergordon, public land ownership has been used as an instrument of very positive planning.

Another problem anticipated with enterprise zones was that firms might relocate, perhaps even with a net loss of jobs following modernisation, to take advantage of the zone privileges. There has been some evidence of this happening but of more concern is the finding of Roger Tyms (1984) that 85 per cent of firms would be operating in the same region in the absence of a zone and that only 4–12 per cent of new firms might not have been started without a zone. Of the relocating firms, some 90 per cent came from the same region, the remainder mainly going to the Corby zone. So enterprise zones appear to influence site location for firms but only to a limited extent firm formation or the decision to move into a new region. This implies that the gains of the zones are the losses of the neighbouring areas. This is only to be avoided by tying the zones into policies for the use of specific pieces of land and mounting an inward investment effort to attract in new developments, including those of foreign firms, as is the strategy in Dundee.

So, far from enterprise zones vindicating the policy of 'non-planning', their experience has confirmed the crucial role of public intervention in urban regeneration and the need for positive development policies to replace the negative planning controls of the past. In particular, the importance of land assembly and infrastructure and the provision of premises appear as key elements, combined with the availability of investment finance and promotional efforts to ensure that the policy is not merely relocating firms within the same region. In isolation from other measures, however, the policy may simply be a rather expensive means of shifting employment from one location to another. The experiment has brought useful lessons, though hardly those anticipated by its progenitors; we consider some of the implications of this in the conclusion.

European Initiatives

In recent years, much publicity has been given to the use of the various European Community funds for economic development in Scotland. Though the amounts of money involved are in fact quite small and subject, as we shall see, to 'non-additionality' rules, they do represent some addition to what would otherwise be available and the Commission has encouraged approaches from local authorities in order to consolidate support for the Community, traditionally very low in Scotland (Keating and Waters 1985).

The principal funds involved are the European Regional Development Fund (ERDF), the European Social Fund (ESF), funds of the European Coal and Steel Community (ECSC) and loans from the European Investment Bank (EIB). The ERDF was established in 1975, following British accession, in order to direct funds to needy areas of the Community and help counteract the tendency of the common market to concentrate development in the more favoured areas of the European 'golden triangle'. As a result of national jealousies, however, it emerged as little more than a means of reimbursing national governments for regional policy expenditures which they were undertaking in any case. National quotas were imposed, with a fixed share for each member state, disbursed in response to applications for investment and infrastructure projects in those regions eligible for national regional aid. The United Kingdom, like the other member states, then operates a 'non-additionality' rule, to the effect that expenditures on ERDF funded projects should not represent additional public expenditure. This means that where an ERDF grant is made to a private firm, this replaces an equivalent part of the national aid which the firm would be receiving. In practice, firms do not receive any money from Brussels at all. Central government merely has a proportion of the regional grants which it is paying approved by the Fund Management Committee as ERDF grants and keeps the ERDF money itself. In the case of infrastructure grants to local authorities, the money is passed on the authority which, having part of the money as a grant, saves on loan charges which it would have had to pay out if it had, as normal, borrowed the whole amount. EDRF funding does not, however, allow any authority to undertake capital spending which it would not otherwise have undertaken, as the project must still be accommodated within its overall capital spending limits. Even the advantage of the saving on loan charges is reduced by the fact that it is no longer allowed for in the Rate Support Grant. So the practical advantage to the local authority is the saving on the rate borne element of the loan charges. Where a grant is awarded to the Scottish Office for its own infrastructure projects, for example on trunk roads, the money remains in the Treasury and the only practical effect is the erection of signs on the project in question claiming ERDF funding for it. In practice, a fixed proportion of the UK's ERDF quota has been allocated to Scotland and a balance maintained between investment and infrastructure projects, within Community rules. From 1979, a non-quota element was introduced, amounting initially to 5 per cent of the Fund total, to be available for major programmes of development in any needy region of the Community.

All nine regional and all three islands councils in Scotland have received ERDF grants for their infrastructure programmes, though the involvement by districts has been less, reflecting their more restricted functions infrastructure provision. The non-quota section has funded local authority and other projects in steel and shipbuilding areas of Strathclyde, following a Community decision to use the section to cope with the problems of decline in these industries and is being extended to textile areas of Tayside. Several regions have forged direct links with the Commission in Brussels to find out what is going on there and to test to the full the eligibility criteria of the various funds.

The European Social Fund was established early in the life of the Community to provide funds to cope with the adverse effects of industrial change in the Community. Its main emphasis has been on retraining of workers displaced by the decline of older industries. There are no national quotas and, in the UK, there is some relaxation of the non-additionality rule. A substantial part of the UK's receipts go to the programmes of the Manpower Services Commission and to agencies such as the SDA and HIDB, where they are treated as non-additional, but where local authorities have been successful in gaining revenue support for schemes they have usually been allowed to retain the money. In recent years, there has been a substantial use of the ESF by authorities like Strathclyde and Tayside for employment subsidy schemes, with the regional council sharing the cost of maintaining or creating jobs which would not otherwise have existed. From 1984, new rules for the Fund have placed the major emphasis on employment and training for young people, with priority for the worst-off parts of the Community.

The European Investment Bank provides loans for capital projects in development areas and, although commercial interest is charged, the Bank is able, by borrowing on European markets, to obtain favourable rates. Scotland has made a great deal of use of this facility, accounting for some 25 per cent of all UK borrowing since 1973 (Keating and Waters 1985), mostly for water and sewerage, roads and industrial development projects.

For some years, the Commission has been trying to reform its 'structural' funds, to make them more of an instrument for genuine Community policies and forge closer links between recipients and itself. In 1981, it came up with a series of radical proposals for the ERDF, concentrating quota aid on specific regions chosen according to Community-wide criteria, greatly expanding the non-quota section and developing the idea of 'integrated operations'. Instead of individual projects, the quota section would be used to finance development programmes in the form of contracts between the Commission and national governments, with the involvement of local and regional governments in their negotiation. The non-quota section would be increased from 5 to 20 per cent of the total and be administered by the Commission itself. Integrated operations would be eligible for priority treatment. A further report in 1983 on the structural funds as a whole reiterated these proposals and gave further support to the idea of integrated operations.

A protracted period of negotiation followed until the final regulation was adopted in 1984 (Mawson, Martins and Gibney 1985). In the event, national quotas were retained in the form of upper and lower limits to funding for individual member states, though exactly how the share of member states within these limits is to be determined is not clear (the UK is eligible for between 21.4 and 28.56 per cent). It seems that the Commission intends the gap to be filled by development programmes, which are to account for some 20 per cent of all ERDF expenditure, though the level of Community funding of these – initially set high by the Commission to give maximum leverage over them – has been reduced. There are two levels of programme, Community and national, with the latter attracting grant of 55 per cent of the public spending on the programme and the latter 50 per cent with provision for 55 per cent in exceptional circumstances (Mawson, Martins and Gibney 1985). In practice even the Community programmes will be produced by national governments, with little Commission involvement. Additionality rules, which are the province of member states, will remain.

Effectively, therefore, there has been little move towards a genuine Community regional policy and the ERDF remains largely a means for transferring resources between member states. One proposal which has been retained, albeit in much reduced form, and which has gained a great deal of attention in Scotland, is the idea of Integrated Development Operations. These were pioneered in Naples and Belfast as a means of co-ordinating the various Community funds behind policies for urban renewal. It had initially been hoped that greater flexibility could be introduced in IDOs, with Community funds made available in non-Community policy areas such as housing but opposition from other member states largely prevented this: nor were non-additionality rules relaxed. So it was not easy to see just what the advantage of having an IDO would be, other than in promotional terms. With the revised ERDF regulation, the prospect opened of a higher rate of grant (through being counted as 'Community programmes') and of priority to applications for projects in IDOs, though it is by no means certain whether this will have any practical effect.

The first proposal for an Integrated Development Operation in Scotland has been for Glasgow. Following approaches from Strathclyde Region, with the support of Glasgow District, a consultants' report (Roger Tyms 1984) was produced, financed partly by the Commission. This was to set out the content of an IDO for Glasgow and the place of European funding in it. The report admits that there is 'no new EC budget specifically for an IDO: benefits lie in increasing the effectiveness of existing funds, in increased priority accorded to applications to existing funds and higher rates of grant, and in the unquantifiable gains following from a closer relationship to the Community.' The practical content of the proposal is in fact little more than a rehearsal of existing uses of Community funds in Glasgow – but without reference until the final section to the non-additionality rule – and a projection of them into the future. Local authority projects are also included but, given the inability of councils to commit themselves to major capital expenditures for a five-year advance period, only the EC contribution to them is specified, though this contribution will, of course, only be forthcoming if the local authorities proceed with the projects. Although the IDO is presented as an integrated package, its content is more of a shopping list of projects eligible for funding from EC sources. It is recognised, indeed, that the contribution of the IDO to inter-agency co-operation will be limited but hopes for better co-ordination between local agencies and the EC through the 'forward programme' for expenditure of £500m over five years. The whole problem with this is that, as we have noted, local authorities are simply not in a position to make such a forward commitment of their own resources and central government has given no indication whatever that it is prepared either to relax the non-additionality rule or to countenance higher levels of local government capital or revenue spending in IDO areas.

We must conclude, therefore, that there is a great deal less to the Glasgow IDO than meets the eye. It may have a certain promotional significance both for the local authorities and for the Community, which is anxious to publicise the disbursement of its funds. The existence of the IDO may give the authorities some leverage in pursuing applications for funding for projects from the ESF and the quota and non-quota sections of the ERDF, though this must be speculative. It does not, however amount to a development plan nor, indeed, to the sort of strategic intervention in selected projects which would have allowed the Community to target its resources on items central to its own policy objectives and to gain the maximum leverage over these. Instead, the funds will continue to be spread over a wide range of items as before, with local government seeking the maximum EC support for whatever projects it is pursuing and central government seeking to maximise the UK take from the various funds, without increasing overall public spending.

4

LOCAL GOVERNMENT AND
ECONOMIC DEVELOPMENT

Local authorities are by their very nature an important influence on their local economies. They are major employers and important customers for private industry. They provide essential infrastructure such as roads and water services; and their planning policies can encourage and discourage industrial expansion. In this chapter, we consider, first, the likely impact of local government expenditure on local economies, then the range of more explicitly 'economic' policies which councils have devised.

Local Government Expenditure

Local government expenditure is divided into two categories, capital and current (or revenue), which are treated differently for the purposes of management and control. Capital expenditure, on the creation of fixed assets, is subject to control by central government in the form of 'capital allocations' for each major service. These constitute permission to spend on capital account up to the amount allocated, the money being found mainly from borrowing. Interest payments and the repayment of capital borrowed are met from annual revenue expenditure. In addition, local authorities are permitted to spend on capital projects a proportion of their 'capital receipts' from asset sales, notably the sale of council houses. Revenue expenditure is spending on consumables such as salaries of staff and purchase of materials. This is financed from three sources: rates; Rate Support Grant and other specific grants from central government; and charges for the use of services. Housing finance is rather different. The cost of maintaining council housing is met from rents, a contribution from the rates and Housing Support Grant paid by central government to a limited number of councils. In this case, there is a link between capital and revenue spending as central government has in recent years set a limit on the contribution from the rates to the housing account and councils exceeding this have had their capital allocations for council housing reduced pound for pound (Midwinter, Keating and Taylor 1984).

The impact of local government spending on local economies is a controversial question. For some years, ministers and business interest groups have been complaining that rates pose a heavy burden on local business, reducing the level of business activity as a consequence. The impact of rates

69

on industry is lessened by the 40 per cent derating (formerly 50 per cent) which they enjoy. As a result of the 1985 revaluation, the burden on industry has been lightened further, though commercial ratepayers do not benefit substantially and have continued to complain loudly about their share. The Layfield Committee of 1976 tended to discount the importance of rates, pointing out that they constituted on average only about 4 per cent of business costs. More recently a study commissioned by the Department of the Environment (Crawford et al. 1985) examined the issue in detail. The authors confirmed that rates remained a 'relatively modest' cost incurred by business, citing evidence that rates were only equivalent to 2.7 per cent of industry's total wage and salary bill. For commercial activities, the impact may be slightly higher though available data here is presented differently. Birdseye and Webb (1984) quote evidence that rates amount to 11–12 per cent of non-labour costs in shops and offices. This is not to say that in marginal cases rates may not be the straw that breaks the camel's back but their political salience seems to be less a result of their absolute cost than of the fact that they are unrelated to profit levels and businesses are unable to reduce them as they can the cost of stocks, wages, investment and, indeed, Corporation Tax in a recession. Nor can businesses always see a tangible return from rates payments. Of course, businesses do gain from rate expenditure, directly through the provision of services such as refuse collection, policing and highways and indirectly from education but the relationship between the two is not always immediately apparent.

As far as the influence of rates on the location of business is concerned, the authors of the DOE study found no discernible impact in the case of manufacturing, retailing or warehousing and only a weak one, confined to London, in the case of offices. Their conclusion is that 'local authorities that have above average levels of rates or that levy above average rate increases, are probably not damaging their local economies' (Crawford et al. 1985).

The impact of local spending on the economy is equally controversial. Revenue spending on salaries of local government employees does, of course, add to effective demand in the local economy with favourable multiplier effects. However, in so far as it is financed through rates, the disposable income and hence the ability to spend on privately-provided goods and services of ratepayers is reduced by an equivalent amount. If increased local spending is financed by increased central government grants, on the other hand, there may be an increase in aggregate demand in the local economy though, local economies being inherently open, the multiplier may be small, much of the increased spending by council employees seeping out in purchases from elsewhere in the UK or abroad. Given that local councils are not able to borrow to cover their revenue expenditure and that central government grant and capital spending are tightly controlled, it is not in fact possible for councils of their own volition to pursue 'local Keynesianism', reflating their local economies by increased expenditure. Cuts in central government grants, on the other hand, will have a deflationary effect, forcing local authorities to reduce their employment or to increase rates, reducing the purchasing power of local households. This may be offset by whatever compensating increases in national government spending or reductions in national taxation filter down to the locality but, for any given locality, this effect will be small; and, in recent years, reductions in central grants to local government have been aimed at reducing the Public Sector Borrowing Requirement, with a net deflationary effect at national level.

Capital spending has different implications for local economies. Most of it goes directly to the private sector in the form of contract work, so creating private sector jobs. As it is financed largely by borrowing, there is no necessary offsetting reduction in private disposable income in the locality, though there is a long-term revenue cost in the form of loan charges for interest and debt repayment. Of course, it is not necessarily the case that capital spending projects will result in contracts for local businesses but in many cases, particularly for housing, they will do so and, as we shall see, it is possible for local councils to increase this effect through local purchasing policies. The effect of cuts in capital expenditure, on the other hand, will be to reduce demand for the services of local businesses.

Local government reorganisation was conceived in a time of expansion and growth. It was immediately followed by a period of retrenchment in public spending as, since 1976, successive governments have sought to limit and then reduce local government spending. Their reasons for doing so are contentious and sometimes rather confused but have all been related to central government's responsibility for the national economy and the supposed deleterious effects of local government spending on it. Under the Labour Government, from 1976, the emphasis was on the priority for the industrial strategy and the release of resources for investment. It was never clear just how resources would be transferred from local government spending to industrial investment and in fact the main impetus to spending cuts seems to have come from the International Monetary Fund as part of its conditions for the loan of 1976. Since 1979, the Conservative Government has placed the accent on reducing total public spending, of which local government spending is a part, in order to control the Public Sector Borrowing Requirement. The problem with this argument is that, apart from capital spending which is already tightly controlled by central government and has, as we shall see, fallen substantially, local government spending does not contribute to the PSBR as local authorities are not allowed to borrow to cover revenue spending. Ministers have also argued that rates pose an intolerable burden on households and commercial businesses, though from time to time they have been forced to admit that the burden of central taxation has actually increased more than that of rates. It has also been suggested from time to time that local expenditure is 'crowding out' private investment by pre-empting limited resources. This is a complex issue. Two 'crowding out' mechanisms are recognised in the literature (Heald 1983). One is physical where public expenditure pre-empts too large a share of physical resources, depriving the market sector. This is really plausible only in conditions of full employment and where public and private resources of material and man-power are mutually substitutable. The other mechanism is financial, where excessive public spending financed by borrowing or increasing the money supply drives up interest rates or inflationary expectations, depriving industry and commerce of investment finance. This mechanism cannot apply to local government revenue spending, in so far as it is financed from rates and charges. It can apply to that part of local government spending which contributes to the Public Sector Borrowing Requirement, that is spending financed by central grant and capital spending financed by borrowing, both of which are already controlled by central government, not by local authorities.

Finding a coherent strategy behind all this is consequently difficult but what does seem to impel the Scottish Office in its search for cuts are three considerations. First, there is the pressure of the Treasury, which regards local government expenditure for planning and control purposes as part of the Secretary of State's budget. So any overspend in relation to the planning totals in the annual public expenditure White Paper will count as a black

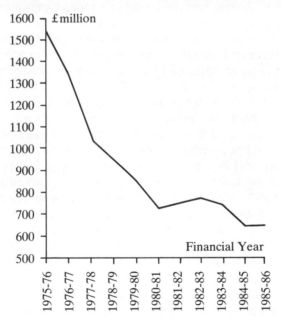

Figure 4.1. Estimated capital expenditure of Scottish local authorities at 1982-83 prices. (1975-76 to 1977-78 figures are estimates of capital spending from CIPFA *Rating Review*. The present system of capital allocations was introduced in 1978, and 1978-79 to 1984-85 figures are based on these, as supplied by Scottish Office Finance Division.)

mark for the Scottish Office. Secondly, there was, at least in the late 1970s and early 1980s, considerable pressure from ratepayers' groups and Conservative interests, particularly in Edinburgh, for the Government to intervene to curb rates increases. Thirdly, there is the belief that rates increases are damaging the health of industry and commerce.

Figure 4.1, based on CIPFA estimates and on capital allocations, indicates how total capital expenditure has been reduced since 1975, the largest cuts coming between 1975 and 1979 (in practice, spending may have been even lower, as a result of the tendency to underspend on capital programmes). The slight recovery between 1981 and 1983 was due almost entirely to the programme of grants for improvement of private housing. If our earlier argument is correct, this drastic reduction in capital spending will have had adverse impacts on local economies. This applies particularly to the large reductions in capital spending on council housing, illustrated in figure 4.2. This probably underestimates considerably the reduction in capital spending, since the capital allocations on which the recent figures are based include ambitious targets for council house sales. The largest cuts in regional

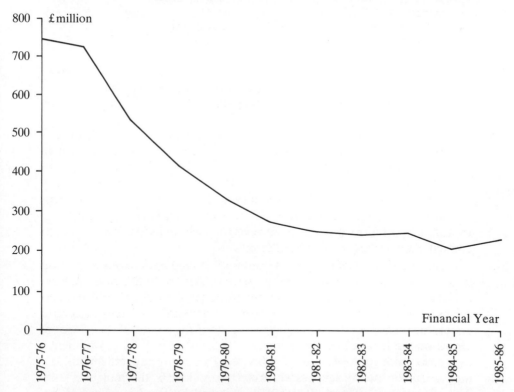

Figure 4.2. Capital allocations for housing review account at 1982-83 prices (GDP deflator). Sources: CIPFA *Rating Review*; Scottish Office.

council capital spending have come in education, with the end of the school building programme, while spending on roads has largely been maintained. This is evidence of an awareness on the part of central government of the importance of highways for economic development.

Figure 4.3 shows the pattern of revenue spending since 1978–79 at constant prices. As can be seen, there has been relative stability here, with total spending increasing by 2.6 per cent over the period.

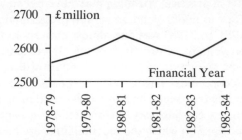

Figure 4.3. Current expenditure out-turns of Scottish local authorities at November 1982 prices. Source: Hansard, 27 July 1984, cols.857-8. Adjusted by local authorities' pay and prices index.

In 1979, the Conservative Government inherited a number of means of inducing councils to reduce their expenditure. These allowed it:

to reduce the amount of spending allowed for in the Rate Support Grant settlement;

to reduce the proportion of spending financed by grant, which under successive Secretaries of State has gone down from 75 per cent in 1976–77 to 56.4 per cent for 1985–86;

to use the abatement procedure popularly known as 'clawback' whereby – until 1984–85 – the RSG was reduced across the board where expenditure out-turns for Scotland as a whole were considered excessive.

In addition, advisory guidelines on revenue spending were issued to each council, though these had no legal force.

Figure 4.4 shows Rate Support Grant for Scotland back to reorganisation at constant prices, showing the progressive reduction. In this case, we have used two deflators, the GDP deflator and the index of local authority pay and prices. The former, a measure in terms of national resources of central government's support for local spending, reflects the impact of Rate Support Grant on the local economy. The latter, a measure of local government's own costs, taking into account, notably, local authority pay settlements, is a measure of the level of services which can be provided by the grant available. The discrepancy around 1979–80 is explained by the last stages of the Labour Government's incomes policy. By restraining local government pay increases up to 1979–80, this ensured that a larger level of service could be

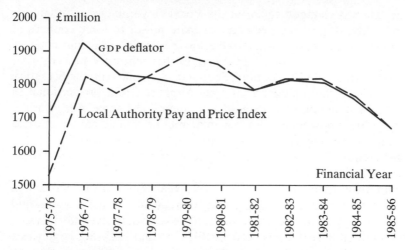

Figure 4.4. Rate support grant, Scotland, at 1982-83 prices.
Source : COSLA.

provided for a given level of grant. In the following years, this effect was removed by the Clegg 'catching up' pay awards and, since 1981–82, the two indices have not diverged substantially, both showing a marked reduction since 1982–83.

At the same time, Housing Support Grant has fallen in five years from £200m to £52m in cash terms and now only 26 of the 56 housing authorities receive it.

It was, of course, the Government's intention that councils should respond to cuts in central support by reducing their own expenditure. In fact, with revenue spending more or less stable, cuts in central support have led to increases in rates. So, by pursuing the objective of cutting its own support for local spending, central government was undermining another objective, to keep down rate increases. To some degree, there was a deliberate policy to transfer the burden of local spending on to local ratepayers, hence the cut in the proportion of relevant expenditure (accepted as the proper level by central government) financed by grant. To this effect, though, was added local government's unwillingness to reduce expenditure to the levels provided for in the Government's guidelines. So, over the years, the Secretary of State has added a series of selective powers to the general ones which he inherited.

The first stage was the Local Government (Miscellaneous Provisions) (Scotland) Act of 1981, allowing the Secretary of State to withdraw Rate Support Grant selectively from councils planning 'excessive and unreasonable' expenditure. The criteria for action were so widely defined as to give him virtually unfettered discretion. These powers were first used against seven councils in 1981 (Midwinter, Keating and Taylor 1983c). The next year, the law was changed again, in the Local Government and Planning (Scotland) Act, to give the Secretary of State power to force councils to make refunds to ratepayers and strike a lower rate. In 1983, four councils were forced to cut their rates. In 1984, further statutory powers were taken, in the Rating and Valuation (Scotland) Act, allowing the Secretary of State to make the abatement of Rate Support Grant proportional to each council's spending over its guideline figure. The same Act gave the Secretary of State powers to set a legal maximum rate fund contribution to each council's housing revenue account, adding a legal sanction to the financial sanction already existing in the form of the corresponding reduction in capital allocations.

To summarise, then, there have in recent years been substantial cuts in local government capital spending, a small increase in revenue spending and cuts in central support for local spending. At the same time, average domestic rate bills doubled in real terms between 1979–80 and 1985–86, largely as a result of the withdrawal of central government support. The net effect on local economies cannot but be adverse, with increases in local taxation not even being reflected in improved local services or contracts for local business.

Local Economic Development Policies

The importance of local government plans and policies to industry was recognised by the Wheatley Commission but, as we have seen, the 1975 reform did not redefine the economic role of the local authority. Rather, the traditional view prevailed, that economic and industrial policies are a matter for central government, with local government's role being to ensure that its environmental and social policies create a favourable climate for industry. In recent years, economic development has become a major priority for some local authorities. There are several reasons for this. The recession and mounting unemployment of the 1970s and 1980s have posed severe problems for the communities which councils represent; and, as we have seen, there has been an increasing recognition that many of the problems of urban decline and deprivation have an economic base. At the same time, the run-down of national regional policy has led some authorities to try and fill the gap through measures of their own to attract and maintain industry. In England, there has been an ideological dimension, with left-wing authorities, like the Greater London Council, the West Midlands Metropolitan County Council and Sheffield City Council developing their own 'alternative' economic strategies (Boddy and Fudge 1984). In Scotland, this theme is largely absent. The 'new urban left' here have shown little interest in economic and industrial policies, concentrating their attention on resisting spending cuts and on housing and social services.

The range of 'economic' activity available to a local authority is considerable, from facilitating policies to create a favourable climate to measures of direct intervention. We have categorised them under six headings.

Administrative Reorganisation. Economic development is not a statutory function of local government and does not feature in the traditional list of council departments but some local authorities have reorganised their decision-making and management systems to ensure that greater emphasis is placed on the needs of economic development. All regional and islands councils have industrial development officers, though only a minority of districts do. More elaborate arrangements exist in some large authorities, particularly those which have adopted corporate management systems. Responsibility tends to be vested in planning departments or Chief Executive's departments but policy has to be implemented through operating departments such as Roads or Estates, so that a strong corporate management system is necessary to bend departmental decisions to the corporate priorities of economic development. In Strathclyde Region, the Chief Executive's Department houses the Economic Policy Group, responsible for general economic policy matters including research, lobbying and area projects and the Industrial Development Unit with operational responsibility for implementing the industrial aspects of the strategy, including the promotion of inward investment. On the members' side there is an Economic Strategy sub-committee of the Policy and Resources Committee which takes a strategic view of the implications of the Region's economic strategy for all its services. There is also an Economic and Industrial Development Committee corresponding to the Industrial Development Unit, with more specific tasks. So the distinction between 'traditional' industrial development activities and the more recent corporate, policy-oriented approach is apparent on both the members' and the officials' side. In Grampian, the North East of Scotland Development Association (NESDA) predates local government reform – and North Sea oil. Originally a joint body, it was taken over on reorganisation by the Regional Council and has begun to develop a strategic approach to industrial sectors, developing contacts with industry and concentrating on the needs of the rural areas which have missed out on the oil boom. In Tayside, economic development issues are handled by the Planning Department, with the Tayside Regional Industrial Office (TRIO) as its operational arm. At member level, matters are handled through the Planning, Policy and Resources and Finance committees. These are the most elaborate of the regional council arrangements. In Lothian, economic development was not given priority under the former Labour administration – in contrast to Labour councils elsewhere – but there is now an Industrial Development Officer. On the elected member side, there is an Industrial Development sub-committee of the Policy and Resources Committee. In the cities, too, the picture varies. In 1980, Glasgow reorganised and formalised its economic development activities. There is now an Economic Development Bureau grouping five departments, which produces a rolling five-year plan. On the members' side, there is an Employment sub-committee of the Policy and Resources Committee responsible for economic policies and initiatives. There remains, however, a divorce between the economic plan and local land-use plans. While local planning continues to provide the policy framework for physical renewal, it is almost oblivious to economic change or the wider policy framework. The Glasgow economic development programme also suffers from being the recipient of cuts, with economic initiatives often seen as expendable. In Aberdeen, there is an Industrial Development Committee which since 1983 has been developing a strategy for economic development to replace the previous *ad hoc* approach; this followed the loss of development area status and hence of national regional aid for the city. In Dundee, the convener of the Planning and Development Committe has a general responsibility for industry. In 1982, it was decided to create a Centre for Trade and Industry with its own director to handle industrial promotion and development. This came immediately into conflict with the 'one-door' approach being promoted at the same time through the Dundee Project, which we describe below and, after some wrangling, the post was down-graded. Edinburgh, like Lothian, has until recently had little by way of formal commitment to industrial development.

Bending of Existing Policies. One of the purposes of administrative re-organisation for economic development is to encourage the bending of councils' traditional mainline functions to the needs of industry and employment. Corporate objectives usually emphasise the needs of economic growth while structure plans have placed a major emphasis on action to stimulate industrial development, as have Transport Policies and Programmes. Strath-clyde's structure plan follows its 1976 Regional Report in identifying employment, together with action to combat deprivation, as its key objectives. In Grampian, the two structure plans emphasise the need to promote employment in the rural area, away from the major oil developments. Lothian's structure plan is less ambitious, concentrating on land use matters. Tayside's Regional Report declared the highest priority to be the creation of jobs and the reduction of unemployment and the Economic Policy statement adopted by the council proposes the infrastructure decisions should reflect this. The structure plan has a wider set of seven aims, one of which is related to the improvement of job opportunities. Central Region's three structure plans are addressed primarily to other agencies, with the council's own work being guided by a regularly updated regional report. This gives the 'highest priority' to the creation of jobs. As we have noted, however, structure plans are only as effective as the means for implementing them and, while plans can allocate sites for industrial development, they cannot in themselves bring that development into being. Local government capital spending is closely controlled by central government through a series of block allocations for the major services and it is not open to a council to increase its total capital spending as a means of providing jobs or stimulating the local economy. Even within the block limits set by the centre, much local authority infra-structure investment is determined by the existing pattern of development and the need to cater for movements in population, leaving an extremely limited margin of strategic choice. This is even more true of revenue expenditure on services such as education and social work which tends to be dictated by statutory requirements and numbers of clients. The function most directly relevant to economic development is the building and improvement of roads and all regions claim to give priority in their road programmes to the schemes with a potential for creating jobs. Some steps have been taken in further education to provide training geared to local employment needs but the main problem tends to be not lack of trained manpower but lack of job opportunities.

Another way in which traditional services can be made to help economic development is through local purchasing policies. Legally, councils can accept tenders for the supply of goods and services some 5 per cent above the lowest bid, but giving local firms preferential treatment. Glasgow has introduced such a policy, with local firms given a second chance to match outside tenders.

Provision of Land and Factories. A more direct form of help for industry is the provision of land and factories at commercial or below-market rates, though the latter are fairly strictly controlled by law. COSLA's 1980 survey found that all regions and island authorities as well as 96 per cent of responding districts were involved in the acquisition and servicing of sites, with 89 per cent of regions and islands and 87 per cent of districts involved in the erection of factories. Five of the regional and island authorities allowed 'stepped rentals' (deferred payments) on advance factories. Under the Inner Urban Areas of 1978, certain councils have enhanced powers, including that of declaring Industrial Improvement Areas (IIAS). Although the Act applied in Scotland, there were no special Urban Programme allocations as in the English partnership areas, the reason being that in Scotland and Wales comparable finance was available from the development agencies. So IIAS took some time to arrive here, there being little incentive for local authorities, and the Urban Programme in Scotland continued to focus largely on social objectives. By the early 1980s, however, a number of authorities had begun to approach the Scottish Office with IIA proposals and were directed to the SDA, the result being the small area projects which we examine below, with local authority powers combined with Agency resources for environmental improvement and investment. The clearest examples of this occurred in Monklands District, where the background work to establish an IIA in Coatbridge resulted in the designation of the Coatbridge Project. This became perhaps the closest Scottish equivalent of an English IIA, with the Project focussing almost exclusively on sites and environmental improvement to attract and assist industry.

A more interventionist variation is for the local authority to purchase the premises of a firm in difficulty and lease it back, so providing the firm with working capital and relieving pressure from creditors. It is recognised, however, that there are dangers in this approach. The firm is deprived of collateral for further credit and the authority risks being left with an expensive but useless asset if the business does eventually fold.

Joint Ventures. Given the limited resources which local authorities have available for economic ventures, it is often more profitable for them to try and lever money from other sources through joint initiatives. Area projects in conjunction with the SDA are analysed below. There have also been joint initiatives with the Steel Corporation subsidiary BSC Industries in Strathclyde, providing alternative employment for redundant steelworkers. Funding for this has also been available from the European Coal and Steel Community. Manpower Services Commission projects, notably the Community Programme, for people who have been unemployed for some time, exist across Scotland, with local authorities acting as sponsors. In Glasgow, there is a major Community Programme initiative under the title Project 80s, which places unemployed people in temporary work, mainly in the council's own Leisure and Recreation Department. Strathclyde and Tayside regions have made great use of the European Social Fund to provide employment subsidies to firms taking on or retaining workers who would otherwise have been unemployed (Keating and Waters 1985).

Recently, a number of councils have hosted MSC-sponsored Technical and Vocational Education Initiative Schemes to provide vocationally-relevant education in schools. While the extra resources provided by the MSC make this a tempting proposition, requiring little or no bending of councils' own budgets, it does risk creating distortions in the educational system, undermining the comprehensive principle and recreating the old distinction between 'academic' and 'technical' education, children and schools. The programme is spatially-specific, targetted at areas of deprivation and high unemployment but implicitly confirms spatially-organised class patterns by providing differing types of education, with very differing employment and life prospects for children of different areas. It thus marks a radical break from the Plowden philosophy of equipping children from deprived areas with the means to compete in the wider higher education and employment markets. There is a further danger that, by training children too early in existing technologies, the programme will deprive them of the adaptability which could come from a more liberal education and which will be at a premium in tomorrow's world. Nor can such training initiatives make much impact on the problem of youth unemployment which is caused essentially by the lack of job opportunities and not by a deficiency of skills.

Other activities are aimed less at joint action than at persuading other agencies to pursue favourable policies. Advocacy is explicitly recognised by Strathclyde and Tayside as an important function and councils have lobbied central government over regional aid and EEC additionality rules, threats to major employers such as the Ravenscraig steel works and other matters.

Promotion of Inward Investment. At one time, a great deal of effort was being devoted by local authorities to persuading firms to come into their areas from overseas as well as other parts of the United Kingdom. This was limited in the Local Government and Planning (Scotland) Act of 1982, which lays down that district councils cannot advertise for investment outside their own districts without the approval of the region and regions cannot promote themselves abroad without the approval of the Secretary of State, which effectively means that their efforts must be channelled through the Locate in Scotland unit. While districts often claim that the restriction is irksome and unnecessary, most were in fact running down their own efforts before 1982. Glasgow, notably, had mounted a big effort for a few years but to little effect and had decided that the district's resources could more fruitfully be employed in helping small and local businesses, with promotional efforts concentrated on improving the city's general image through the 'Glasgow's Miles Better' campaign. Inward investment promotion is still carried out by all regions and new towns in the form of press advertising, exhibitions and seminars, promotional literature and participation in Locate in Scotland activities though, given the small amount of mobile investment available, this can cause considerable friction.

Direct Aid to Firms. Direct aid by local authorities in Scotland to firms is widespread but small in scale. Several of the larger councils have business development officers to provide advice to small firms, particularly those just starting up. Grants and loans, are available, again on a small scale, in most regions. NESDA in Grampian claim a 90 per cent survival rate for firms assisted in this way. With a budget of £350,000, they have created or safeguarded employment at a cost of about £400 per job, a fraction of the cost of job-creation by regional development grants, though the council recognises that their scheme can only to a tiny extent offset the loss of development area status. In areas such as Strathclyde and Dundee, where regional development grants are still available, local authorities see their role more in terms of dealing with those firms which fall through the regional policy net, usually because they are too small. Generally, indeed, this sort of activity in Scotland is on a small scale, with no attempt at economic interventionism of the sort practised in London, the West Midlands or Sheffield and in particular no attempt to take equity stakes in firms.

One reason for local government's limited economic role is simply financial. The main source of revenue for economic development activities in section 83 of the Local Government (Scotland) Act, which allows local authorities to spend up to the product of a two penny rate on any activity which is in the interests of their population, free from the restrictions of the *ultra vires* rule. Although the use of this for industrial development was, after some confusion, specifically sanctioned in legislation in 1982, no authority has made full use of the power. Indeed, up until 1980, no Scottish authority had made any use of the power. Unlike the English metropolitan counties, Scottish regions have heavy service-provision responsibilities, with little spare capacity for ventures into new areas. It is difficult to justify spending extra on what may appear to be risky and speculative economic ventures with other services pressed for cash; and any extra spending risks pushing councils over government guidelines, exposing them to automatic and selective grant penalties. Nor have Scottish authorities followed the example of some English councils and earmarked a proportion of their pension funds for local industrial investment. Instead, they have sought access to the larger funds of the SDA through joint initiatives, a course not open to English authorities, though some of the large Scottish authorities are now starting cautiously to explore the possibilities of establishing investment funds.

Another reason for their caution is ideological. Conservative councils are naturally suspicious of state intervention and selective subsidisation of industry, preferring indirect forms of help. Grampian, for example, has declined to use the European Social Fund for employment subsidy schemes on the lines of those in Strathclyde and Tayside. Perhaps more surprisingly, the Labour left in Scotland has not taken up economic interventionism as a major issue even where it has been in power, as in Lothian before 1982, in Edinburgh after 1984 or in Stirling, Dundee or post-1984 Glasgow. All this has certainly made for a more harmonious relationship between central and local government on economic development than exists in the English conurbations where the interventionist economic policies of the metropolitan counties and the GLC is cited by central government as one reason for their abolition.

Local government's economic activities are on a very small scale compared to those of central government and its agencies. It is all the more important, then, that they should be clearly focussed on activities where they can make an impact. This has involved a long learning process, with councils discovering those areas where they have a role to play and moving from 'scatter-gun' approaches towards forward-looking strategic ones. Glasgow, from trying to operate across the board, has settled for a role in assisting very small firms with small loans and grants and business development advice, filling in the gaps left by other agencies. In Grampian, where there is no support from national regional policy and, until recently, little by way of an SDA presence, the local authorities have taken more of a leading role. Aberdeen has adopted a strategy for manufacturing industry based on support for existing firms, attracting new firms from outside and stimulating new home grown firms, with a concentration on small and medium sized enterprises. For Grampian as a whole, NESDA have adopted a strategy for key industrial sectors, with the involvement of local industrialists. The cohesiveness and sense of regional identity in Grampian facilitates such a strategy, with firms encouraged to help each other by bringing opportunities to the notice of prospective suppliers through a system of consultative committees and NESDA sponsoring regional brand names in agricultural and fisheries products. In a larger and more heterogeneous region like Strath-clyde, this is not possible and the council's main strategic planning is focussed on the twelve Economic Priority Areas – all old industrial areas – identified in 1981. These are to be the subject of wide-ranging economic and environ-mental improvement programmes, with the financial help and co-operation of district councils and the SDA. Though the region has sought, for example by its 'bombshell' in 1981 when it announced its EPAs before consulting the SDA or central government, to take the lead in the development of local economic strategy, the policy is crucially dependent on the co-operation of the Agency. In other regions and districts, there is much less of a strategic approach to economic policy, with councils tending to react to opportunities or problems as they occur. Indeed, even in Strathclyde and Grampian, policy must to a considerable extent be reactive. In the current climate, all job opportunities are to be welcomed, even when most effort is being put into specific sectors and areas.

Another problem facing local authorities is the attitude of central govern-ment to local economic policies. Broadly speaking, central government has welcomed and encouraged those activities which create a favourable climate for industry, for example the provision of industrial estates or road building, but frowned upon more direct involvement. This is partly a matter of ideology. A Conservative Government committed in principle to non-inter-vention in industrial policy is not likely to smile on such intervention on the part of local government. There are also fears about unfair competition between subsidised and unsubsidised firms, which might simply lead to new firms displacing existing ones with no gain in output or employment. Com-petition between areas, too, could get out of hand as regions and districts compete for mobile investments. There is some evidence of councils seeking to 'poach' firms from others with tempting offers of premises and grants, though at the existing level of local authority support and with attention focussed on indigenous industries, this has not become a major problem. Central government has also expressed concern that unrestrained local government activity could undermine its own spatial policy priorities; but, while this could have been a problem in the past, nowadays local authorities may be justified in asking how much of a national spatial economic strategy exists to be undermined. It was disquiet about the economic policies of some of the more radical councils in England which led the Government to attempt to remove the right to use the 2p rate product for this purpose, an attempt which was defeated following a campaign in the House of Lords. It is also an important reason cited by the Government for the abolition of the metropolitan counties and the Greater London Council. In Scotland, while the Government is not particularly happy about councils giving loans and grants to firms, the issue has not assumed major proportions, given the limited amounts involved and the absence of an ideological challenge by the councils involved.

Local government has long argued that its central role in economic development has been in the field of sites, services and environmental improvement, providing the physical and psychological conditions for industrial investment. Despite the protestations of the Conservative Government, local planning authorities have not obviously acted against the interests of industry. In fact, development control policy has, particularly since the mid-1970s, encouraged some forms of industrial expansion. Environmental improvement, especially along transport corridors, has long been a component of physical strategy for economic development. Considerable expertise has developed in terms of site selection, purchase and improvement; an expertise that has been harnessed by the SDA. Whether environmental improvement has any direct bearing on economic development is open to some doubt and is the subject of detailed research by the DOE but it nevertherless has been the dominant strand in the planners' response to urban decline.

5

SDA INITIATIVES

The Development of the Area Approach

We have seen that, on its establishment, the Scottish Development Agency was given a very general brief which it had itself to translate into concrete policies and programmes. One specific task which the Agency was given by central government in 1976 was the co-ordination of the ambitious GEAR project which we have described in chapter 2. In 1979, an SEPD working party set up to look at the problems of the Garnock Valley in Ayrshire following the closure of the Glengarnock steelworks recommended an SDA task force. Similarly, in 1980, an Agency-led task force emerged from an SEPD working party on Clydebank. These were emergency measures for areas hit by sudden and drastic industrial closures. Their spatial focus is narrow, their objectives to get as many jobs as possible in to replace those lost and their methods informal. In Clydebank, for example, the task force consists of four SDA officers with a very general brief and the focus is on developing the Business Park on the former Singer site. There are no specific job targets, no formal involvement by local authorities and no withdrawal date. The Task Force can draw on the expertise of the Agency across the board, to bring industrial promotion, investment, factory building, environmental improvement and small business advice powers to bear as well as preparing 'business packages' for incoming firms, with details of aid available from all sources; in 1980 Clydebank was also chosen as the site for Scotland's first Enterprise Zone. By Spring 1984, some 229 companies had moved in, with job projections of 2,577, 2,098 of them in SDA premises. This is certainly an impressive achievement, though replacing only a quarter of the 10,294 jobs lost in redundancies between 1975 and 1980 (we have discussed the Clydebank experience above under Enterprise Zones).

Despite their success in providing jobs, however, the task force model could not be extended indefinitely. It was possible to argue for Clydebank and Garnock Valley as special cases and in Clydebank the presence of the Enterprise Zone made it politically necessary to produce results. With only a limited amount of industrial investment available, it was not possible to make every declining industrial town a special case. The Agency further feared that the Scottish Office might be tempted to use it as a permanent 'fire brigade' for crisis areas. To pre-empt this, it would need to develop its own area-based strategy, focussed on areas with the greatest potential for contributing to the Agency's overall objectives. Formalising its area approaches would have other advantages. It would enable the Agency to put its relationships with local authorities on a clearer basis, after allegations that it was ignoring regional structure plans, and to ensure that infrastructure development was complementary to its own plans. It would also satisfy an internal need, by bringing together the Agency's own divisions in a planned and forward-looking rather than merely reactive approach. So, in 1981, an Area Programme Development Division was set up within Planning and Projects to develop co-ordinated policies for area development and a new Area Development Directorate established for their implementation. A decision was taken to spend 60 per cent of the Agency's 'targetable' resources in area projects.

While the initiative for the area project policy appears to have come from the Agency itself, it was quickly accepted by the Scottish Office. Some of the advantages from the point of view of central government are clear. An economic dimension can be given to urban policy without giving additional economic powers to local government itself. We have seen that the existence of the Agency is one reason why Scottish local authorities have not attempted elaborate interventionist strategies or to raise investment funds themselves. At the same time, the SDA enables the Scottish Office itself to avoid becoming directly involved as the Department of the Environment has in the English Inner Partnerships. Area development, as well as being a highly visible form of activity, is probably also regarded as politically more acceptable than the Agency's investment activities.

The approach is not, however, without its ambiguities. The 60 per cent target of resources for area projects represented an aspiration rather than a commitment. Some forms of spending, for example on environmental improvement, can be allocated quite easily to areas but investment proposals in area projects must satisfy the same criteria as elsewhere. This basic dilemma in spatial economic policy is further illustrated in the choice of locations for area projects. A policy of going to the areas with the most problems or the highest unemployment is alien to the philosophy of the Agency, which is to seek out potential and to create in Scotland internationally competitive industry. Formalisation of the area approach and breaking with the 'fire-brigade' model of Clydebank and Garnock Valley was intended to enable the Agency precisely to seek out the most promising areas. Yet it remains under some political pressure to provide a visible response to the needs of the worst hit areas and to balance its geographical coverage. So the formula is now that it will go to areas where there is the greatest gap between 'potential' and 'performance', allowing it to consider both opportunities and problems. In the first of the new-style projects, in Leith, there were few difficulties of this nature. The site was chosen partly from political prudence, lest the SDA be seen as too exclusively a west coast agency but also because, its decline not being far advanced, it could be 'pulled round' rapidly. The first area project in Strathclyde, for Motherwell, was less clear cut. Motherwell featured on the Regional Council's list of twelve Economic Priority Areas and work had been going on for some time on possible responses to steel closures. Concern was mounting about the threat to the Ravenscraig works, reprieved after a prolonged campaign in 1982 and there was clearly pressure on the Scottish Office to make a gesture to the area (Gilchrist 1985). The Agency, however, insists that what brought it to Motherwell, in pursuance of its general philosophy, was the potential for improved performance of the local economy, pointing to the natural advantages of the area, including its location, access to the rail and motorway networks and the availability of maximum regional development grants. There are two problems with this. Firstly, some of these advantages are far from natural but are the result of government policies aimed at overcoming natural disadvantages. Secondly, several other parts of Strathclyde Region could probably point to the same combination of favourable features. So the decision to come to Motherwell represented both economic and political opportunity.

The same is true of the extension of area projects to Tayside Region in 1981 following a visit by the SDA chairman and pressure from the local authorities for a greater agency presence, especially in Dundee. The first project was for the Blackness area of Dundee and took the form of a programme of industrial and environmental improvement to a small area. It was followed by a much more ambitious scheme, the Dundee Project. This started life as a Waterfront Project suggested by the local authorities following early approaches by the SDA which was still keen on putting more resources into the city. The consultants, possibly with some prompting from the Agency, then broadened out the idea to include the whole city, on the grounds that the waterfront developments could not be seen in isolation from those elsewhere. From the point of view of the area development staff of the Agency, this would have the further advantage of bringing together all the SDAs activities in Dundee. The expansion of the Project – and the consultants' report itself – raised some political difficulties, however. In the first place, the consultants had advocated sectoral initiatives in electronics and health care. This was treading on the toes of the Agency's sectoral staff who, at that time, saw their work in aspatial terms. There was further resentment at the approach of the consultants who were seen as having taken too broad an approach to sectoral studies, rather than the detailed firm-by-firm approach which the Agency had been developing in its own sectoral work. Nor was the report received uncritically by the local authorities, who thought that the consultants had failed to use their own knowledge and experience.

A whole-city project was, however, appealing to the Agency, allowing it to channel its own resources to Dundee, promote its own proposals there and provide a single forum for discussions and negotiations with the local authorities. A crucial point in the consultants' report was that Dundee suffered from a poor 'image', which deterred investors. This was a delicate matter to handle, for the negative image encompassed both the former old-fashioned and sometimes corrupt Labour Party and union machine and the more recent left-wing city administration, with its controversial links with Palestinian and other Arab interests. A hidden agenda item in the genesis of the project was consequently a wish to remove or at least tie down Dundee District's independent industrial promotional efforts. There were some officers in the District who sympathised with the need to improve the City's image and who saw the Project as an opportunity to effect change in their own authority and increase the priority for industrial development. Some councillors who had been little involved with the early negotiations on the project, however, soon became suspicious about the lack of control which would follow, as did some of the officers. So Dundee's attitude was that the project would not encompass all industrial development activities in Dundee but only specified measures on specific sites, with collaboration on promotion. On the other hand, the District naturally welcomed the extra resources which the Agency was proposing to bring to Dundee and saw possibilities for developing projects which they had had under consideration for some time. These uncertainties over what the project would include, and the SDA's insistence on getting from the local authorities more specific and binding commitments than had been the case in either Leith or Blackness, prolonged negotiations but in November 1982 an agreement was signed, with resource commitments from each of the participants and the project Steering Committee, under the Agency's Deputy Chairman and a Project Team, under the Deputy Director of Area Development, established.

Following these precedents, projects have since been established for Coatbridge, Arbroath, Kilmarnock, Wigtown, and Denny and Bonny-bridge (map 5.1). While all are based on 'project agreements', each initiative is different, reflecting the peculiar circumstances of each area and the different agencies involved; and, as can be seen from a comparison of Leith and Dundee, initiatives also vary greatly in terms of scale, financial commitment and economic objectives. The Agency itself draws a distinction between the task forces for Clydebank and Garnock Valley, the integration area projects and the 'self-help' initiatives such as those in Port Dundas (Glasgow) and Kilmarnock, where other agencies – in these cases the district councils – are expected to take the lead role (Gulliver 1984). Projects being negotiated at the time of writing will assign the lead role to the private sector, a development which we discuss below.

It is tempting to see area projects merely as an assisted areas policy. Locations are discussed with the Scottish Office, all the projects have been sited in areas hit by industrial closures and there is little doubt that eyebrows

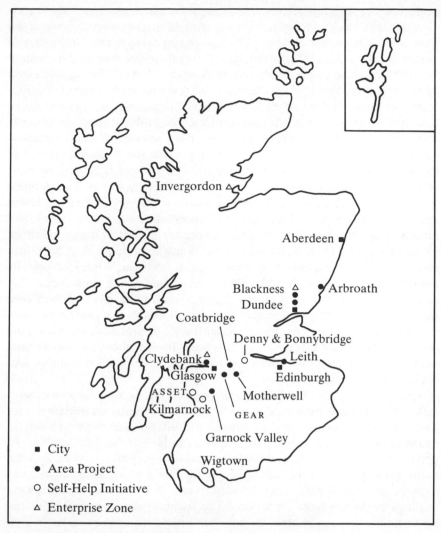

Map 5.1. Area projects in Scotland (adapted from Gulliver 1984, p.324).

would be raised in the Scottish Office if a major area project were sited outside the assisted areas for regional policy. Yet the Agency insists that it is not an assisted areas policy and can point to Linwood where, following the closure of the Talbot plant, there was no large-scale intervention, to justify its claim that it is seeking potential, not problems. Part of our difficulty in interpreting all this is penetrating the language which must, at any given time, be used to legitimise intervention. As a regional development agency dedicated to creating competitive industry, the SDA must use the rhetoric of opportunities; this has become increasingly the case under the Conservative Government pledged to increasing the sway of market forces, in which the Scottish Office cannot be seen to be harbouring lame ducks. In the case of enterprise zones, as we have seen, this goes as far as dressing up intervention and subsidy in the language of non-intervention. So both the Agency's own instincts and the thrust of government policy are to go for areas of development potential. On the other hand, political pressures and the immediate concerns of ministers point to a concentration on problem areas, particularly those hit by major closures. As far as the location of area projects is concerned, the best we can say in summary is that the Agency must pursue its policy of putting its resources into the areas where there will be most return with an awareness of the political environment in which it operates. There must be a balance between east and west, the cities, the small towns and the country and, indeed, between Conservative and Labour areas; and neither it nor the Scottish Office can ignore the impact of major industrial closures and the need to be seen to be doing something. Scottish Office ministers themselves, indeed, encapsulate this dilemma. While ideologically committed to the survival of the fittest and against saving lame ducks, they do, as territorial ministers, feel obliged to make the most of their own interventionist initiatives for Scotland. So, although the general message coming from government is about concentrating on profitable industries, the short-term pressure is often to go into areas like Motherwell or Greenock when major closures threaten and to do fairly conventional things like building advance factories.

The procedure for establishing area projects has become fairly standard. After an approach by a local authority or on the Agency's initiative after discussion with the local authorities, consultants are commissioned to examine the area, its assets, potential and needs. This has been a source of considerable annoyance to some local authorities, who complain that the consultants have merely taken their own data and rehashed it at great expense for the Agency; on the other side, it is claimed that the local authorities do not have the expertise to identify economic and industrial opportunities. What is clear is that the consultants' report serves a vital political function in providing a source of information independent both of the Agency and the local authority and in justifying Agency intervention in commercial terms.

The report has usually been followed by the negotiation of a project agreement, specifying the contributions to be made by the SDA and the relevant regional and district councils. Since 1982, there has been an insistence on the part of the Scottish Office for a specified private sector contribution as well, a requirement which considerably delayed the completion of some agreements. The project agreement is a formal but legally non-binding statement setting out the project's objectives, targets for job creation, time scale and administrative structure. Early agreements, such as that for Leith, were couched in fairly general terms, with little by way of specific commitments or targets but later ones have been considerably tighter. They are a mixture of generalised objectives and specific proposals well captured in this description of the Dundee Project's strategy: 'to increase investment, development and employment opportunities in Dundee by focussing upon the development of technology industries in the city and upon specific sites adjacent to the river Tay and the City Centre to accommodate a Technology Park and commercial, hotel and tourist facilities. These emphases will be complemented by the development of a number of city-wide opportunities – the further development of the conference and tourist markets; in subcontract, joint venture and licensing opportunities with individual companies; in the North Sea oil sector; in research and development within the University and intraining initiatives. Further, the project will co-ordinate and integrate these and all other Agency initiatives in Dundee.' The generalised policy objectives are usually accompanied by a target for job creation. The reason for this is presumably presentational. SDA rhetoric usually stresses the needs of competitive industry and not job creation which, in today's conditions, is a very different matter; nor is it possible with any accuracy to predict the impact on employment of the various measures laid down in the agreement. Yet employment is what the local authorities are looking for from area projects and job creation, as something which can, albeit with difficulty, be measured, is a major element in the evaluation of projects.

Resources

The inputs of each of the parties are specified with more or less precision. Agency spending is on environmental improvement, industrial buildings and investment. The environmental expenditure can be specified with some precision and firmly committed. Industrial building is more difficult, depending on demand and the take up of premises as they are provided. Investment is the most difficult of all to target. Not only do the opportunities need to be present but investment proposals in area projects must satisfy the same criteria as proposals elsewhere. At one time, there was some resulting tension between the Agency's sectoral and area teams, with the former insisting on an essentially aspatial approach to investment and the latter seeking to harness investment to project aims. This is now much less apparent, with the dominant philosophy being that of backing opportunities. So projects are not to be seen as a mechanism for diverting investment resources into needy areas; at most they provide the means for bringing out opportunities in specific areas. Data is not available on the extent to which the project policy has shifted investment resources as, in the absence of the agreements, investment may have gone into those areas in any case. Dundee, for example, was already receiving a substantial amount of SDA support before the project (*Scotsman*, Dundee Project advertising feature,

20-11-84). Figures released in December 1984 in reply to a Parliamentary question indicate that little of the Agency's investment budget is in practice going to project areas (table 5.1). Bearing this in mind, together with the small proportion of the total Agency budget which is devoted to investment in any case, we must regard the SDA's principal contribution to areas projects as lying in the fields of environmental improvement, factory building, promotion and advice.

The regional council's input is usually in the form of infrastructure, notably roads and water provision. It is notoriously difficult to determine how much of this is 'new money' and how much would have been spent in any case. Local authorities' total capital spending is rigidly controlled by central government in a series of blocks so that, if a region were to spend more on a road in an area project, this would have to come out of savings elsewhere in its roads and transport capital budget. The Scottish Office does not officially take cognisance of project agreements in determining local government capital spending limits, though there is a suggestion that Tayside may have been more favourably treated because of the Dundee Project. In any case, the major road schemes specified in project agreements have been items to which regional councils were already committed in their Transport Policies and Programmes so perhaps the most that can be said is that their inclusion in the agreement may have saved them from postponement and cutback in a time of retrenchment. For district councils, the commitments are even less specific. In Dundee, for example, the District is committed to capital spending in such general terms that almost any item in its capital budget could count towards the specified £500,000. Table 5.2 summarises the financial commitments for the major projects.

Other local authority commitments are to administrative support for the project and the secondment of staff to the project team. In addition, regional councils may be required to amend their structure plans, for instance to accommodate high technology industry on high amenity sites in the green belt, a factor which caused some delay in the finalisation of the Dundee Project.

The resources brought into area projects must, of course, be seen in the context of overall public expenditure and investment trends, the general effect of which has been to take resources out of Scotland's cities. Figure 5.1 plots Rate Support Grant (RSG) for the four cities and Motherwell since 1976–77 at constant prices. Motherwell stands out as having lost heavily, as has Glasgow since 1980. Dundee's RSG, on the other hand, has more or less kept pace with inflation. Even more striking is the picture with regard to Housing Support Grant (HSG) (figure 5.2). All the districts have lost heavily, with Motherwell, Dundee and Edinburgh ceasing to receive HSG altogether. Until 1980, Glasgow's loss of HSG was to some extent offset by increases in RSG but since then it has been losing both. On the capital account, there is a similar pattern. Table 5.3 shows capital allocations for the

Table 5.1. SDA current investments by constituency as at November 1984.

Constituency	No.	Value £	Constituency	No.	Value £
Aberdeen North	6	302,174	Glasgow Govan	15	355,236
Aberdeen South	24	1,418,876	Glasgow Hillhead	7	53,923
Angus East	20	1,609,018	Glasgow Maryhill	4	426,532
Argyll & Bute	6	80,538	Glasgow Pollok	8	66,073
Ayr	14	402,461	Glasgow Provan	3	16,585
Banff & Buchan	19	253,510	Glasgow Rutherglen	20	2,804,264
Caithness & Sutherland	1	4,941	Glasgow Shettleston	27	266,526
Carrick, Cumnock &			Glasgow Springburn	3	14,405
Doon Valley	24	3,525,086	Gordon	15	501,837
Clackmannan	8	58,319	Greenock & Port		
Clydebank & Milngavie	24	499,254	Glasgow	14	726,754
Clydesdale	18	173,646	Hamilton	15	1,343,091
Cumbernauld & Kilsyth	21	1,193,118	Inverness, Nairn &		
Cunninghame North	42	1,557,213	Lochaber	13	1,771,638
Cunninghame South	10	344,711	Kilmarnock & Loudoun	28	1,104,797
Dumbarton	21	784,163	Kincardine & Deeside	7	143,633
Dumfries	30	504,925	Kirkcaldy	17	624,050
Dundee East	3	69,905	Linlithgow	4	78,307
Dundee West	24	383,953	Livingston	34	1,799,170
Dunfermline East	13	117,580	Midlothian	15	190,028
Dunfermline West	14	477,683	Monklands East	15	163,906
East Kilbride	23	513,473	Monklands West	2	24,387
East Lothian	25	361,672	Moray	20	912,870
Eastwood	2	60,294	Motherwell North	16	145,053
Edinburgh Central	17	581,924	Motherwell South	7	44,905
Edinburgh East	3	54,850	Orkney & Shetland	8	193,062
Edinburgh Leith	16	1,201,552	Paisley North	12	488,267
Edinburgh South	5	455,192	Paisley South	2	104,684
Edinburgh West	6	385,149	Perth & Kinross	34	789,156
Falkirk East	8	167,973	Renfrew West &		
Falkirk West	19	674,313	Inverclyde	29	1,822,723
Fife Central	13	370,188	Roxburgh &		
Fife North East	10	67,757	Berwickshire	42	734,757
Galloway & Upper			Stirling	22	1,174,912
Nithsdale	21	541,879	Strathkelvin &		
Glasgow Cathcart	7	24,332	Bearsden	3	179,733
Glasgow Central	50	9,012,335	Tayside North	6	378,892
Glasgow Garscadden	3	14,618	Tweeddale, Ettrick &		
			Lauderdale	27	960,682
			Total	1,064	48,653,413

(i) Investments include: Mortgages, Site Loans, Rural Loans, Shares, Loans to Large/Small Businesses and Leg-Up Loans.

(ii) The figures provided show net current investment and exclude receiverships.

Source: *Hansard*, 6 December 1984.

Table 5.2. Area projects.

Project	SDA budget	RC budget	DC budget	Private sector
ARBROATH	*£759,650*	*£750,000*	*£380,000*	*£401,650*
	£70,650 – running costs	£15,000 – running costs	£15,000 – running costs	£16,650 – running costs
	£75,000 – premises provision (new build)	£555,000 – road and traffic schemes	£120,000 – improvement to premises	£25,000 – premises provision (new build)
	£464,000 – environmental improvements	£57,000 – improvements to harbour	£5,000 – tourism	£360,000 premises provision (conversion)
	£150,000 flood prevention of Brothock Burn	£75,000 relocation of lorry park	£240,000 – premises provision (conversion)	
		£48,000 flood prevention of Brothock Burn		
BLACKNESS	*£6 millions*	*£2,035,000*	*£150,000*	*£1 million*
	£3.8m – new factory floorspace, conversion of existing factory floorspace, yards development, acquisition of land and premises	£1,085,000 – acquisition, site assembly and implementation of highway improvements, improvements to footpaths, street lighting improvements	£125,000 – financial assistance to firms	£600,000 – industrial building
	£1.8m – landscaping of vacant land, clearing derelict buildings, preparing derelict land for industrial use, improving existing building stock, studies	£600,000 provision of water and sewerage services	£25,000 – project development/management through project officers	£400,000 – commercial building
	£200,000 – financial assistance to firms	£200,000 – other works and additional sewerage works		
	£200,000 promotional programmes, sponsorship of MSC special training initiatives, business/community support, provision and maintenance of project office	£125,000 – financial assistance to firms		
		£25,000 – project development/management through project officers		

94

Project	SDA budget	RC budget	DC budget	Private sector
CLYDEBANK (no project agreement)	*£21 millions* Agency expenditure to 31.3.84 was £19m £14.1m – factory construction £2.1m – environmental improvements £1.2m – acquisitions It is assumed that the remaining £800,000 was spent on running costs	It is estimated that the Regional and District Councils will contribute a combined total of £2m		*£18.2 millions* £6.3m – industrial building £11.9m – commercial building (to 31.3.84)
COATBRIDGE	*£10.715 millions* £4.125m – provision of premises £3.335m – site assembly and site preparation £1m – financial assistance to firms £1.820m – environmental improvement £435,000 – upgrading watercourses	*£3.65 millions* £2.1m – sewer replacement £1.55m – road improvements	*£600,000* £400,000 – financial assistance to firms £200,000 – provision of premises or workshops	*£2.4 millions* £1.3m – commercial building £1.1m – industrial building (to 31.3.84)
DUNDEE	*£18 millions* Agency expenditure to 31.3.84 was £4m £1.1m – factory construction £1.2m – environmental improvements £1.6m acquisitions It is assumed that the remaining £100,000 was given over to running costs	It is estimated that the Regional and District Councils will contribute a combined total of £6m		*£1.2 millions* £1.2m – industrial building

95

Project	SDA budget	RC budget	DC budget	Private sector
GARNOCK VALLEY (no project agreement)	*£19 millions* Agency expenditure to 31.3.84 was £18m £9.6m – factory construction £5.1m – environmental improvements £300,000 – acquisitions It is assumed that the remaining £3m was given over to running costs	It is estimated that the Regional and District Councils will contribute a combined total of £3.5m		*£200,000* £200,000 – industrial building
KILMARNOCK VENTURE	*£525,000* £75,000 – running costs of the Business Development Unit £450,000 – provision of small units by the Business Development Unit	*£36,000* £36,000 – running costs of the Business Development Unit	*£453,000* £153,000 – running costs of the Business Development Unit £300,000 – provision of small units by the Business Development Unit	*£36,000* £36,000 – running costs of the Business Development Unit
LEITH	*£7 millions* £5m – provision of premises (new build and rehabilitated or converted) site assembly and site preparation £1m – financial assistance to firms £1m – environmental treatment	No formal financial commitment	No formal financial commitment	*£4.8 millions* £4.2m – industrial building £600,000 – commercial building
MOTHERWELL	*£37 millions* £37m – provision of premises, workshop development, financial assistance to firms, environmental improvement	*£14 millions* £14m – infrastructure	*£6 millions* £3m – provision of premises, workshop development and environmental improvement £3m – environmental improvement in housing areas	*£59.3 millions* £41.9m – industrial building £17.4m – commercial building

Project	SDA budget	RC budget	DC budget	Private sector
WIGTOWN	£639,000 £456,000 – set up, and running costs of the Wigtown Rural Development Company £183,000 – environmental works	£60,000 £60,000 – set up, and running costs of the Wigtown Rural Development Company	£20,000 £20,000 – set up, and running costs of the Wigtown Rural Development Company	£214,000 £200,000 – from the Scottish Tourist Board for tourism £14,000 – set up, and running costs of the Wigtown Rural Development Company
DENNY BONNYBRIDGE	£2,790,000 £1,500,000 – environmental programme £250,000 – financial assistance to firms £410,000 – acquisition and servicing of industrial site in Denny Remainder for consultancy services, community business, MSC 'top up', promotion of new starts and enterprise development	£552,000 £75,000 – financial assistance to firms £66,000 – community business support £66,000 – training and education staff £290,000 – factory units in Bonnybridge £25,000 – improved directional signposting £30,000 – MSC 'top up'	£215,000 £15,000 – private sector-led marketing initiative £60,000 – industrial site in Bonnybridge £110,000 – small units £30,000 – MSC 'top up'	

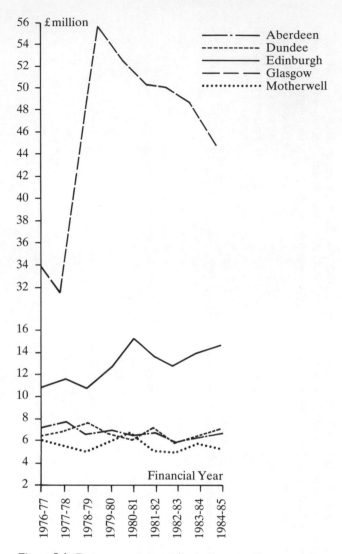

Figure 5.1. Rate support grant (including specific grants) for
four cities and Motherwell at constant 1982-83 prices (local
authority pay and price index).

five districts since 1978–79. Once again, Motherwell stands out as a heavy
loser, with a capital allocation running at only half its 1978–79 level. With 80
per cent of households in council tenancies, Motherwell was unable to take
advantage of the increase in allocations for private sector house improvement to the same degree as, for example, Edinburgh, which received a large
input of resources from this programme. Overall, between the arrival of the

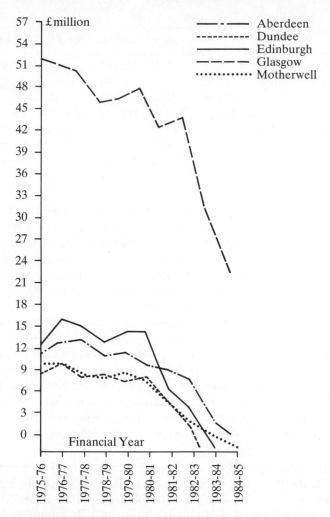

Figure 5.2. Exchequer subsidies/housing support grant for the
four cities and Motherwell at constant 1982-83 prices. Source:
CIPFA *Rating Review*.

Conservative Government in 1979 and 1984–85, Motherwell lost £34.87
million in capital spending on district services alone, at 1982–83 prices. This
is almost equivalent to the whole of the SDA input to the Motherwell Project
(£37 million). In the same period, it lost a cumulative £32.5 million at
1982–83 prices in Housing Support Grant and Rate Support Grant (including specific grants). Edinburgh, on the other hand, has seen its levels of
capital spending maintained and its RSG (including specific grants) increased, though it, too, has lost all its Housing Support Grant. In the same
period, Glasgow lost some £76 million in HSG, RSG and specific grants.

(£m)

City/Town	1978-79	1979-80	1980-81	1981-82	1982-83	1983-84	1984-85
Aberdeen	26.28	24.20	18.36	17.89	15.93	15.22	12.86
Dundee	16.99	16.47	13.75	12.55	16.08	14.93	13.93
Edinburgh	39.65	30.46	28.41	34.11	37.87	34.41	29.94
Glasgow	129.10	123.15	104.11	101.18	104.38	108.93	120.43
Motherwell	16.63	17.83	13.78	12.35	10.90	9.13	8.12

Table 5.3. Local authority capital allocations for the four cities and Motherwell at constant 1982-83 prices. Source: Scottish Office Finance Division.

Dundee, while losing its Housing Grant, has seen its RSG maintained and improved slightly, though the figure for 1984–85 will be reduced by the abatement at the end of the financial year. Its capital allocations are also down since 1979–80, representing a cumulative loss of £11.1 million at 1982–83 prices. This is a large figure in comparison with the planned project expenditures of £18 million for the SDA and £6 million between the region and the district.

Nor is it always possible to argue that cuts in support for district councils have been matched by increases for the corresponding regions. Figure 5.3 shows that, while Strathclyde did indeed gain Rate Support Grant up until 1981–82, it has since been losing it. It is of course impossible to attribute a precise proportion of the gain and loss to any one town or city within the region but at least it is clear that, in the period of the Motherwell Project and the Glasgow initiatives, the region as a whole has been losing RSG. The figure shows the same picture for Tayside, of which the city of Dundee forms half the population.

For capital spending, figure 5.4 shows that Strathclyde has experienced continued reductions in capital allocations, leaving little scope for extra spending in area projects. Tayside is a little different. After a period of reduction, capital allocations were increased from 1982. It is thought that the Dundee Project may have had a part to play here, though no official cognisance was taken of it.

There is no allowance made for area projects in current expenditure guidelines for regions and districts, either. These are now calculated according to the 'client group' method and, while there have been considerable fluctuations in our case-study areas, they bear no discernable relationship to urban regeneration programmes.

In the light of these figures, it is clear that, whether or not money coming into these areas through the projects is 'new' or not, they are losing out on external funding overall. Given the overall cutbacks in capital spending, it is further clear that any resources which local authorities are putting into area projects must be at the expense of other parts of their areas.

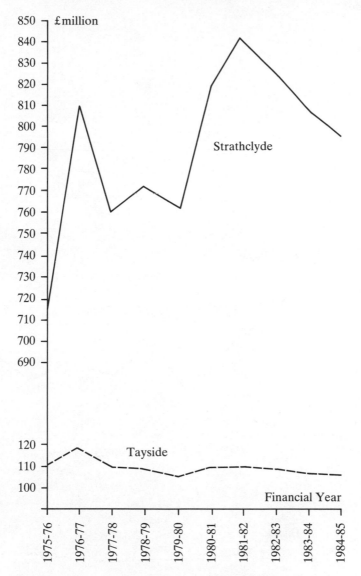

Figure 5.3. Rate support grant, Strathclyde and Tayside regions, at 1982-83 prices (G D P deflator). Sources: C I P F A *Rating Review*; Scottish Office.

Working Relationships

The formal project agreement as a quasi-contractual relationship is a new development in the public sector in Britain, though common enough as an instrument of intergovernmental relations in France and elsewhere. Its

101

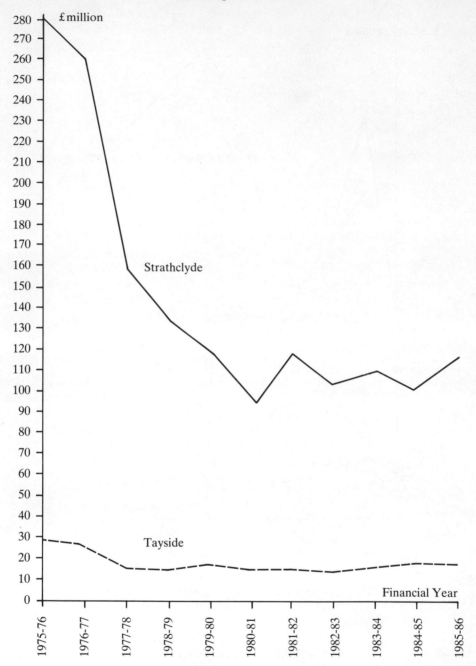

Figure 5.4. Estimated capital expenditure, Strathclyde and Tayside regions, at 1982-83 prices. Sources: CIPFA *Rating Review*; Scottish Office.

practical significance is less clear. The Agency's view is that it is the mechanism through which it has secured complementary local authority action for its area interventions but, as we have seen, the practical effect on local government activity has been small. More important, perhaps, has been their symbolic role in providing a focus for publicity and promotion of areas to investors – and the framework they provide for continuing co-operation through the various project teams and steering committees. The commitment to a particular scheme in an inter-agency agreement, even though the scheme may have been scheduled already, might help to secure its future in a time of general cutback. There is evidence, indeed, that local authorities have been very reluctant to postpone or cut back on infrastructure developments featuring in project agreements, despite the overall capital reductions which we have observed. It must be said, too, that the period 1981–84 was a learning one in which the principle of project agreements was being developed and refined. However, instead of being developed into sophisticated intergovernmental planning systems, providing a measure of certainty to each party but retaining enough flexibility to cope with the unforseseen, they are now being abandoned. This appears to reflect the move on the part of central government away from planning and towards market solutions. This entails the disaggregation of urban problems into their component parts and a restriction of public agencies to a servicing and reactive role, with the pattern of development determined by the private sector. We consider the emerging pattern of area development more fully below.

The style and character of area projects varies considerably, as do the mechanisms by which the generalities of the project agreement are translated into operational terms. The small projects, such as Blackness in Dundee or Port Dundas in Glasgow, are relatively straighforward, being effectively Industrial Improvement Areas with Agency involvement in environmental work and access to Agency investment and business advice services. The project teams of seconded officers, which may be led by the Agency or by the District Council, can have a close knowledge of the area and the firms in it and the clear remit of promoting the maximum industrial development. Some of the recent small projects have been designated as 'self-help' efforts, with the Agency agreeing to support and aid projects led by district councils, as in Port Dundas, or by enterprise trusts, as in ASSET or Kilmarnock, an approach further discussed in chapter 7.

Large projects are more difficult to pin down in terms of their operational objectives or even, sometimes, their geographical extent. In Motherwell, the project covers an extensive area but only a part of the District. In Dundee, following the consultants' report, the proposed project was extended from the Waterfront to cover the entire District, the argument being that the economy of the city needs to be seen as a whole and opportunities exploited wherever they might be. Another less explicit motive in this case appears to have been a desire to take the promotion of Dundee's image out of the hands of the City council.

Given the wide-ranging brief of these large projects, it was necessary to focus attention on key objectives and projects in the course of implementation. These range from the very general and intangible to the most precise and specific. At a general level is the promotion of a favourable image for the area to attract inward investment; this goes along with an intensive 'marketing' exercise in the UK and, through Locate in Scotland, abroad. Then there are specific spatial and sectoral initiatives identified in the project agreement or subsequently. Finally, there is general business development work aimed at existing or new local businesses.

We have referred to Dundee's poor 'image' which was said to deter potential investors. A key part of the Project involved the promotion of a more favourable image of the city as a whole to potential investors and this applies also to other projects.

'Flagship' developments are also important in relation to the image problem. In Motherwell, a great deal of emphasis was placed on the Food Park, a site for the development of food-processing industries in which the consultants' report had identified potential. By developing the Food Park – and indeed by the choice of name for this industrial estate — it was intended not only to provide jobs in the food-processing industries but to change the image of Motherwell generally, associating it with new and expanding industries rather than old and declining industries like steel. In Dundee, a similar purpose was served by the Technology Park, a high amenity site for high technology industries, in the green belt and owned and promoted by the SDA, with the help of its enterprise zone status. Indeed, in the two years following the signing of the project agreement for Dundee, the Technolgy Park emerged as the key element by which the project would succeed or fail, with intensive effort being made to secure the first company. Others, it was assumed, would then follow more easily.

Environmental improvements are, of course, an important element in the promotion of a better image for an area and we have seen that a large part of Agency spending has been on this. The resulting high profile, though, caused some cynicism in Dundee as the more concrete items such as the development of the Technology Park were delayed.

Promotional activity takes the form of advertisements and a copious supply of literature extolling the virtues of the areas in question as well as more focussed efforts to attract firms through the Agency's contacts and Locate in Scotland (LIS). Given the shortage of mobile investment, it is perhaps not surprising that local authorities tend to complain about the performance of LIS. LIS has the task of bringing industry to Scotland as a whole and will tend, therefore, to show potential investors its best sites, whether these be in project areas or not. Many of the new high technology investments which are so sought after have gone to the new towns whose life has, indeed, been prolonged because of their value in bringing industry into

Scotland. By late 1984, Locate in Scotland had assisted with the introduction of only five companies to the area projects. To compete effectively for LIS attention, the project areas must be able to show that they have the potential to compete in specific sectors hence the search for sectoral opportunities.

The larger projects have increasingly emphasised these sectoral initiatives. In Motherwell, the potential in food industries was identified in the consultants' report and accepted by the Agency and local government. In Dundee, matters were less simple. High technology, health care industries and North Sea oil related industries were identified as sectors of potential growth by the consultants. These were, of course, among the SDA's own priorities for industrial growth in Scotland though the Agency Planning and Projects staff on the sectoral side appear to have been sceptical of Dundee's claims. North Sea oil development was believed by many to be committed irrevocably to Aberdeen, with Dundee too late to get in on the act. Nonetheless, some work has been undertaken in this field, with a new consultants' report in 1984 on opportunities in rig inspection and repair concluding that, at £250,000 per rig visit the business would not be viable. A knowledgeable member of the project steering committee was able to correct this figure to £500,000 and the consultants' blushes spared by a hasty alteration in the report to £500,000 per year (rig visit every two years); but it was considered too late for Dundee to get into the business. Work on the attraction of health care industries and the high technology effort, concentrated on the Technology Park has, as we have noted, become a prominent feature of the whole project strategy.

Spatial initiatives, including site acquisition, property development and infrastructure improvement, the very essence of the smaller projects such as Blackness and Port Dundas, also take up a large part of the time and resources of the larger projects. In Motherwell, the agreement stipulates that, out of a total public sector budget of £57 million, £27 million is to be spent on the development of premises and £14 million on infrastructure. In Dundee, there is a similar emphasis. This is concentrated on a number of sites identified in the Project, in the Technology Park and the Waterfront area, the former a high amenity site in the green belt, the latter a series of largely derelict industrial sites. Nearly half of the Agency's capital spending is to be for the Technology Park, emphasising its role as the 'flagship' for the project.

Business development is encouraged through the provision of advice as well as premises. The idea is that projects should provide a 'one-door' approach for businesses starting up or seeking to expand, pooling the services of the SDA and regional and district councils and advising on assistance available from central government sources. In Dundee the establishment of the project office has led to a marked increase in enquiries, with some 25–30 counselling sessions being held per week one year into the project. In addition, short courses have been held on business start-ups. In

Motherwell, since the formation of the Enterprise Trust, much of the business counselling work has been passed over to them, in a pattern which is likely to become more general.

Area projects are intended to provide a co-ordinated approach to urban economic renewal, so that a great deal depends on the quality of the working relationships established for their implementation. There is typically a Project Steering Committee at senior level, with representatives from the SDA, the region, the district and the private sector, with the task of setting the general strategy and receiving monitoring reports. The Project Team is in charge of day-to-day management and consists of officers seconded on a full or part-time basis from the participating agencies. In the larger projects, the SDA input is co-ordinated through the Area Development Directorate but in the smaller projects the team deals directly with the Agency's operational divisions. In fact, it tends to be at the level of the project team that operational strategies are forged and priorities decided, the steering committee meeting too infrequently to have a major impact (figure 5.5).

In general, relationships appear to be quite good, especially in comparison to relationships in some of the English urban initiatives, such as the Inner City partnerships (Stewart 1982; Cox 1980). One reason for this is no doubt the limited functional scope of the projects, which, unlike the English partnerships and indeed GEAR, are fairly tightly confined to economic and industrial objectives. Local authorities do not, in general, feel that they have been displaced in their legitimate functions which are largely unaffected by the project agreements. This marks a step back from the ambitious attempts at global solutions to the problem of urban decline based on the 'multiple deprivation' or 'cycle of deprivation' theories but it is clear that the Agency was never happy about its involvement in social policy issues in GEAR, seeing this as a diversion from its true economic role. From the point of view of local authorities, area projects are thus a means of gaining extra resources for economic development and a way back into the inward investment promotion role lost in 1982, at very little cost either financially or in loss of autonomy. One exception to this occurred in Dundee where the project, covering the whole city, was intended by the region and the SDA to subsume the whole of their economic development role in the city. They were also anxious that it should take in the whole of the district's role too; but, as this would have left the district without an independent role in the field, it did not agree and established its own Centre for Trade and Industry at the same time as the project. The difficulties this presented for the 'one door' approach were not resolved until, following an internal row, the role of the Centre was downgraded. The absence of a direct role for central government helps relationships, too. While the SDA is, of course, a central government agency, it is not a central department and is not regarded with the same political suspicion and resentment as, for example, the Department of the Environment in the English partnerships.

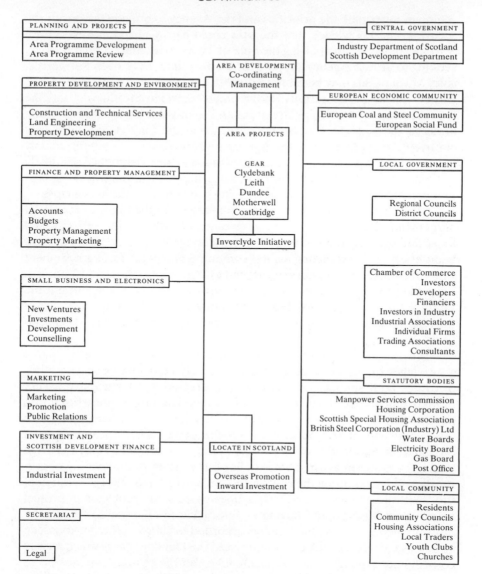

Figure 5.5. Co-ordination and management of area projects.
Source: SDA Annual Report 1985.

We have seen, of course, that the Agency does view area projects as a means of committing local authorities into complementary actions for its own initiatives and uses its freedom to locate in order to persuade councils to co-operate as the price of getting Agency support. Local authorities have responded to this in different ways. Strathclyde, when it launched its twelve Economic Priority Areas initiative in 1981, took the view that it was for the

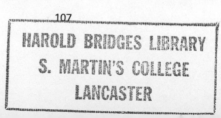

region to determine the priorities and the Agency to provide the resources, secure in the knowledge that the SDA could hardly abandon west-central Scotland or even avoid putting the bulk of its resources there. Other regions, seeking to attract Agency support for the first time, have been less aggressive. Much of this may be more to do with style than with substance. There turned out to be no serious disagreement between Strathclyde and the Agency over economic priority areas and joint work is proceeding on the areas in the region's list. In any case, given the limited local authority contribution to projects and the Agency's insistence that it is interested only in the economic potential of areas, the attitude of the local council is unlikely to be the major determining factor in a decision to locate a project – except in the improbable event of a council being competely hostile in principle.

Conflict has, however, not been totally absent in the implementation of agreements. Delays have occurred because of cutbacks in both SDA and local authority funding, though the project agreements do seem to have been effective in protecting capital commitments on the local government side. In Dundee, the region even agreed to increase its roads contribution to keep the project on target. Generally, however, budgetary delays put the Dundee Project back considerably in its first year to the embarrassment of the team, who had already mounted their publicity effort and raised expectations.

More serious problems have at their root a basic dilemma of spatial approaches to economic development, namely their relationship to other priorities both spatial and sectoral. The SDA project teams have a very limited control over finance and, though spending targets are written into project agreements, each item must be justified to SDA headquarters in Glasgow where it will be assessed on the same basis as proposals from elsewhere in Scotland. This is entirely in line with the philosophy that area projects are not an assisted areas policy but a means of discovering opportunities and maximising the contribution of each area to the regeneration of the Scottish economy. However, it does cause some problems in project teams, with Agency staff having to refer back to Glasgow so frequently. Staff, in their turn, envy the freedom accorded to the SDA office in Aberdeen to dispose of its own budget, in contrast to the Dundee office, which merely co-ordinates Agency activities in Dundee. So the tension may not be so much between agencies as within agencies, with project staff agreed on priorities but having to convince their own sceptical colleagues. This is a recurrent problem with LIS, suspected by people on the east coast of favouring the west and by people in the cities of favouring the new towns. As we have noted, its brief to act for the whole of Scotland leads it to promote the best locations, rather than favouring the most needy, so that area teams need first to promote their areas to LIS for the latter to promote them abroad. This is beginning to happen, for example with the Dundee Technology Park and the Motherwell Food Park, but it is a long and difficult process.

Other frictions have arisen within local government as members of project teams have insisted on priority for their schemes at a time of general retrenchment. There have also been the usual personality clashes. Generally, however, the finding is of good working relationships.

Evaluation in Area Projects

Given the generalised nature of the objectives of area projects, evaluation is notoriously difficult. Indeed, scientific evaluation of the impact of projects is impossible given the lack of comparable control areas which could be used to assess likely outcomes in the absence of the intervention. Other problems are psychological and political. Area projects are intended, among other things, to increase morale and improve the image of the area; this requires a constant stream of good news and success stories to create a bandwagon effect. So there is a strong temptation to produce favourable reports, particularly on 'flagship' schemes like the Dundee Technology Park and the Motherwell Food Park, to sustain the momentum. Much of the reporting coming from the projects themselves is of this nature, consisting of glossy brochures extolling the success of the venture and claiming credit for all job creation in the project area.

SDA headquarters, however, needs more rigorous monitoring systems and these are being put into effect. Monitoring is of two types, management performance monitoring and impact monotoring. Management performance monitoring is done by the Area Development Directorate and includes data on meeting targets specified in the agreement and numbers of contacts made with firms. Given the generalised nature of the objectives of the projects, impact monitoring has perhaps inevitably concentrated on employment creation. This operates at two levels. There is monitoring of the local economy generally, to chart its performance, using Department of Employment and MSC data, and there is monitoring of the performance of individual firms aided by the project. Net job creation in firms aided by the Agency is credited to the project. In addition, a register of firms is built up from contacts which firms may have with the project, even though this does not lead to Agency assistance. The coverage thus built up varies considerably. In small areas such as Clydebank, Garnock Valley or Port Dundas, it may be possible to have a 90 per cent or more coverage of local firms and so a very precise idea of local industrial change. In larger areas like Dundee and Motherwell the coverage will be smaller and more random, including only directly aided firms.

This method of evaluation is still rather imprecise. The assumption that jobs created in aided firms would not have come in the absence of the project may not always be justified, especially if one counts total net job creation, but it is probably the only basis of calculation available. The more generalised effects of the project, in improving an area's image or even the effects of investment in infrastructural and environmental improvements, however, do not feature in the calculation, so that the impact may actually be under-estimated. Again, there is a major difference between small-scale projects and the larger ones. In an area like those of the Clydebank or Garnock Valley task forces it may be reasonable to assume that, in the absence of the intervention, industrial expension would have been negligible. In a larger economy such as that of Motherwell, let alone Dundee, the project is only one of many influences at work. Evaluation by job creation raises another problem. Increasingly, the SDA sees its aims in terms of the creation of internationally competitive industry rather than employment, and industrial modernisation can often serve to destroy rather than create jobs. So provision of jobs does not necessarily tell us about the success of area projects in contributing to this wider aim.

With these caveats, figures on the impact of area projects do show some positive results. Up to late 1984, some 1,719 companies had been assisted in Agency-led projects (GEAR, Garnock Valley, Clydebank, Leith, Blackness, Motherwell, Dundee and Coatbridge). 16,432 jobs have been safeguarded, according to the SDA, against 4,377 lost in assisted companies. Job creation patterns vary from one project to another. In Clydebank, where virtually the entire economy had to be rebuilt, job creation has been high (1,968 jobs), though significant proportions of these are short-term construction jobs or relocations. In Garnock Valley, Blackness and Motherwell, new jobs were more significant than transfers, but in Leith and Coatbridge, the balance is reversed. The impact on the local economies as a whole is very difficult to measure. Unemployment in all the project areas except Coatbridge had increased over the project period and, in Clydebank, Leith, Motherwell, had increased faster than the Scottish average. On the other hand, the Agency are no doubt right to point out that the increase would have been even greater in the absence of the projects. Table 5.4 gives a summary of progress on the major projects up until March 1984.

The Future of the Area Approach

Area projects are established for fixed periods of three to five years on the clear understanding that, at the end of this time, the Agency will terminate its formal involvement so as not to become locked into a few areas and to retain its freedom of action. This is a very short time scale in which to effect major changes in the urban economic and physical environment and hopes have been expressed that some of the projects might be extended. In any event, arrangements for termination must be made at some stage and work has already begun on this. In Garnock Valley, the ending of the Task Force led to a successor organisation, the Garnock Valley Development Executive, supported by BSC Industry, the Clydesdale Bank, General Accident Assurance, Cunninghame District Council, Strathclyde Regional Council and the SDA. A similar pattern is likely to develop for other projects with the business advice and development role taken over by enterprise trusts, and local authorities looking after physical development. What is less clear is what will happen to the marketing and promotional work, including the relationship with LIS, for which enterprise trusts are largely unfitted in terms of resources, contacts and skills. Agency investment finance might be more difficult to secure in the absence of the project team, though it would still be available as elsewhere.

More generally for the future, the Agency is beginning to move away altogether from formal projects with written agreements; the last of these is likely to be the Arbroath Project, started in 1984. There is a feeling that Agency leadership has imposed too great a strain on manpower and that, in any case, the formalised project arrangement may have encouraged over-rigid attitudes on the role of the participants. So there has been a growth of the local authority-led and the 'self-help' style of project, such as those for Port Dundas and Kilmarnock. In Port Dundas, the lead is taken by Glasgow District Council, in the context of a formal agreement. In the case of Kilmarnock, arrangements are less formal, with no written project agreement. Two longer-term trends are likely further to de-emphasise the area project idea. One is the political pressure towards privatisation, with the Agency being pushed by central government into leaving business advice to enterprise trusts. This has happened already in Motherwell, with the Mother-well Enterprise Trust taking over most of the business advice work. The other is the growing convergence of the Agency's area and sectoral approaches, with more emphasis being put within area projects on the need to explore and realise sectoral opportunities. Of course, we have seen that, following the early 'fire brigade' operations, area projects have had to justify themselves in economic terms, as a contribution to the creation of competitive industry. The difficulty for the analyst is in distinguishing changes in the rhetoric by which intervention must be legitimised from changes in the rationale for the intervention itself. The very language used becomes a barrier to understanding, employed, as it is, to justify what is proposed in ideologically acceptable terms and to create the 'image' which is so important a part of the policy itself. Allowing for this, there is now less emphasis on physical redevelopment and property as a feature of area projects and more on firms and sectors. The absence of project agreements, the reduced concentration on physical development and the increased role for private initiatives such as enterprise trusts amount to a major downgrading of the physical planning and spatial dimension of Agency work which could have considerable implications for the future. The integration of spatial planning and economic development policies in the context of area projects was a form of 'positive planning' with potential for development, meeting some of the criticisms which we have noted of the traditional planning system. Certainly, policy was never entirely integrated. We have noted the relatively small input from LIS and the Agency's investment division into area projects; but, without the project machinery, these are likely to continue to be

Table 5.4. Scottish Development Agency area projects: summary description to 31.3.85.

Project	GEAR	Clydebank	Leith
Project type	Comprehensive urban renewal	Task force	Integrated
Period of project	1976-87	1980-	1981-86
Total estimated investment private/public	£470.5m	£69.9m	£54.7m
Total Agency investment	£78m	£25m	£12m
Agency expenditure to 31.3.85	£58m	£22m	£11m*
Agency factories completed	242	182	49
Area	949,967 sq. ft.	683,999 sq. ft.	41,300 sq. ft.
Cost	£21.1m	£14.1m	£1.6m*
Agency environmental improvement schemes completed	277	24	71
Cost	£16.4m	£3.1m	£5.5m
Land acquisitions	£9.6m	£1.2m	£0.8m
No. of property and business enquiries	4,000	2,800	5,200
No. of new companies	275	285	124
Jobs created and provided for	4,000	3,000	1,450
Private investment			
Industrial building	£48m	£7.4m	£5.3m
Commercial building	£33m	£14m	£0.8m
Private housing			
Homes completed/under construction	1,900	100	1,288
Cost	£47.5m	£2.5m	£24.8m
Homes programmed	1,200	1,200	574
Cost	£30m	£24m	£11.8m

* Includes pre-project expenditure. Source: SDA *Annual Report* 1985.

divorced from spatial priorities.

An early example of the new approach is the proposal for a Glasgow City Centre project focussed on the needs of business development, with an emphasis on the service sector. Although this is being supported by both regional and district councils, their input is likely to be modest. Although some of the early proposals involved physical renewal and design, these were seen as flowing from the needs of business development and were not discussed with the responsible local authorities. They were in any case later reduced in scope as it was made clear that the project would not represent another attempt at comprehensive urban renewal. The same applies to the

Motherwell	Dundee	Coatbridge	Inverclyde	Total
Integrated	Integrated	Integrated	Private sector led integrated	
1982-87	1982-85	1983-86	March 1985-	
£179.6m	£86m	£28.2m		£888.9m
£37m	£18m	£10.7m		£180.7m
£15.8m*	£8m	£7m	£1.03m*	£122.8m
111	17	34	Nil	635
454,438 sq. ft.	134,156 sq. ft.	356,919 sq. ft.	Nil	2,620,779 sq. ft.
£5.5m	£1.4m	£2.2m	Nil	£45.9m
123	10	46	Nil	551
£5.8m	£1.5m	£2.4m	Nil	£34.7m
£0.3m	£2m	£0.2m	Nil	£14.1m
2,153	2,500	923	Nil	17,576
137	150	60	Nil	1,031
1,352	2,300	837	Nil	12,939
£38.2m	£15m	£2.4m	Nil	£116.3m
£23.8m	Nil	£2m	Nil	£73.6m
1,758	1,000	Nil	Nil	6,046
£40.4m	£25m	Nil	Nil	£140.2m
881	900	350	Nil	5,105
£20.2m	£22m	£8.75m	Nil	£116.8m

ideas being worked out for an Inverclyde Project, based on Greenock. When the closure of the Scott Lithgow yard appeared imminent, there was considerable Scottish Office pressure on the Agency to mount a major rescue operation for the local economy. With the yard secured for the immediate future, the emphasis has shifted towards a business development programme, with strong private sector leadership.

Similarly, in the proposals being developed for a rural initiative in North Perthshire, there is less emphasis on physical renewal and infrastructure and more on business development, the aim being to identify and exploit the natural resources and assets of the area.

The new approach may have considerable implications for local authorities. Although they continue to be involved in the development of projects, the reduced emphasis on planned development reduces their role in the realisation of the schemes. At the same time, the reiterated concern with the promotion of competitive industry implies a further downgrading of job-creation as a target. As it is jobs with which local authorities are basically concerned in their economic development role, this may lead to separate job-creation initiatives in local government. We have noted the separate policy in Strathclyde for community business, seen largely in terms of social policy. Employment creation as social policy is likely to continue to grow, marking a further disintegration of the economic and social policy spheres whose integration was such an important feature of the urban initiatives of the 1970s such as GEAR and the English partnerships. The implications of this policy disintegration are further explored in our conclusion.

community are involved in decision making process

benefits community as a whole socially + economically

As the communities gain not individual organisations

6

COMMUNITY-BASED LOCAL ECONOMIC DEVELOPMENT

The Origins of Community Business

While much of the recent interest in local economic development has concentrated either on the attraction of inward investment or on support for small firms, a complementary, community-based alternative has attracted attention from both government and the private sector. This different approach to the creation of local economic growth – in essence jobs – attempts to redefine and re-orientate economic development, replacing the profit-centred goals of commercial enterprise with essentially non-profit, welfare-based, objectives. Three characteristics differentiate community business from the mainstream activities of local developments:

(1) a different concept of ownership and control where decisions are taken by representatives from the community served by the enterprise, not solely by those participating in the business organisation;

(2) any surplus income (the term profit can be misleading) is directed towards developing the wider community interests and not always towards improving the performance of the business concerned nor for individual gain; and,

(3) the goal of community business is not commercial success per se but the pursuit of economic and social improvement that will benefit the community as a whole.

This review of community initiatives focusses attention on the practicalities of community business in Scotland but also examines its diverse conceptual framework. Such diversity stems from, for example, the traditional British co-operative movement, from European experiments with worker control of industry and from the expansion of community development in the USA, embracing ideas extending from radical community control through to conservative neighbourhood protectionism. Drawing on data collected by Hayton (1983), McArthur (1984) and the Planning Exchange LEDIS series, we examine the organisational framework of community business and make a preliminary review of its impact on local economic change. Brief case studies of three separate initiatives illustrating a range of different activities – property management, home production/marketing and the provision of neighbourhood services – form the basis of our tentative evaluation of

115

community business in Scotland.

As with recent developments in the private sector, it is important, however, to place the role of community business in perspective. A directory of community business covering the central Lowlands cites only 35 individual organisations (CBS 1984), probably involving less than 450 jobs. Furthermore, it is estimated that in 1984 community business in Scotland as a whole, employed no more than 1,000 people, including home producers and the growing army of community business development officers (McArthur 1984). And despite the rhetoric of undying support for small, community-based, industry, total government assistance in this sector was less than 1 million pounds in 1984–85. The significance, therefore, of community business is unlikely to be its net contribution to the Scottish economy, be that in terms of jobs, output or innovation. The potential benefit of this alternative approach to local economic development needs to be seen more in terms of the location of the modest benefits of community business and the wider improvements for the community as a whole, in particular, the value of local control over social and economic change. Further, this modest set of initiatives must be viewed in terms of their demonstration effect, as an illustration to government and to community groups of the potential for locally-guided development.

The 'alternative' sector in economic development covers a broad church of ideas, concepts, even philosophies ranging from enterprises almost indistinguishable from mainsteam profit-centred organisations through to neighbourhood-based community action initiatives that are wholly dependent on external subsidy. This diversity of purpose and the attendant organisational differences leads to a confusing terminology that is not assisted by the introduction of an American lexicon, itself awkward to translate across the Atlantic. What follows may offer a degree of clarification:

(1) The Non-profit Sector: an American term used to denote 'organisations that are private in structure (non-governmental) yet not profit seeking. What is more, they perform functions judged to be publicly relevant or socially desirable, on the basis of which they are then exempt from federal income tax' (Salamon 1984). Organisations in this sector cover activities that range from recreation through religion to education, health care and the arts. Community development agencies, including those active in local economic processes would fall into this category, but only where they did not support commercial, profit-seeking enterprises;

(2) Not-for-Profit Organisations: a term commonly found in American literature, defining enterprises that operate alongside the private sector, that have developed accounting systems that return any operating surpluses either back into the enterprise or redirected into other not-for-profit, often community-based, activities;

(3) Community Business: 'a trading organisation which is set up,

owned and controlled by the local community and which aims to create ultimately self-supporting jobs for local people and to be a focus for local development. Any profits made from its business activities go either to create more employment, or to provide local services or to assist other schemes of community benefit' (CBS, quoted in Pearce 1983); and

(4) Workers' Co-operative: simply defined as commercial business owned and controlled by the people working in them. Thornley (1981) suggests that workers' co-operatives should be based on six principles: (1) autonomy, (2) employee ownership of limited share capital, (3) one person, one vote, (4) formal direct employee participation, (5) profit-sharing, and (6) limited return on capital. From this definition, workers' co-operatives differ significantly from community businesses but are nevertheless included in this review because of their historical importance in determining the commercial objectives and organisational style of many community-based enterprises.

Even with these definitions, however, the range of different community businesses is still very confusing. For example, some enterprises aim to become self-sustaining (i.e. free from direct and indirect public subsidy) as quickly as possible while still ensuring that any operating surpluses are automatically re-cycled; others do not seek to lose their public support, some in fact consider it one of their key functions to continually search for additional public finance; some, but only a few, have the ambition to move out of the arena of community business into the mainstream of competitive industry. Pearce (1984) argues that all community business should attempt not to become profitable but, within the particular objectives chosen by the organisation, should seek 'maximum feasible viability'. If this requires permanent subsidy then so be it. The key characteristic of community business is to achieve improvements for the local community not for the enterprise itself.

The origins of community business in Scotland can be traced back to a variety of different influences, with individual organisations selecting the most appropriate 'mix' of objectives and management styles that fits their particular situation. Despite this diversity however, the desire to create employment and at the same time return local control over decisions that affect the performance and direction of the 'business' lies at the heart of the movement. Workers' co-operatives, numbering some 600 in the UK, employing over 6,000 people (1983), demonstrate these objectives. But unlike the co-operative movement in Europe, particularly in Italy, experiments with workers' co-operatives have not traditionally been regarded as viable alternatives to privately owned and profit motivated business. Trade unions, government and the voluntary sector have, with certain exceptions, shown little interest, ignoring the historical successes in Britain and remaining largely ignorant of contemporary developments in France, Italy and Spain. Only the Mondragon experiment in northern Spain caught the attention of the major trade unions but it is ironic that this well-publicised initiative may be the least relevant to the British scene.

Renewed interest in workers' co-operatives stems from the famous 'Benn' experiments in industrial democracy when, working through the National Enterprise Board, the 1974–79 Labour Government briefly supported co-operatives at Meriden, Kirby, and at the *Scottish Daily News* in Glasgow. The initial success – then the spectacular failure – of these experiments increased awareness in co-operatives, not least in the Industrial Common Ownership Movement, and led to the formation of a central loan fund administered under the 1976 Industrial Common Ownership Act. In 1978, the Co-operative Development Agency was given the task of promoting co-operatives throughout the UK. Initiatives in Scotland were organised through the Scottish Co-operative Development Committee (SCDC), repre-senting the STUC, the Co-operative Union, the WEA and the Scottish Council of Social Service. The membership of SCDC clearly demonstrates the poten-tially conflicting objectives inherent in workers' co-operatives: permanent, unionised labour against temporary, perhaps even voluntary, workers; community education against profitable business; profit-sharing within the enterprise against the distribution of surpluses throughout the community. Because of these and other conflicts, SCDC has found the promotion of workers' co-operatives a difficult task but, in contrast, has had considerable success in mobilising support, convincing local government, the trade unions, even the SDA, that co-operatives are a viable alternative, in certain circumstances, to traditional means of generating local economic develop-ment (Campbell 1983).

Incorporating workers' co-operatives in local economic strategy has, to date, figured prominently in only one part of Scotland. Based on rural initiatives in Europe, particularly in the remote parts of western Ireland, the Highlands and Islands Development Board (HIDB) launched a 'Community Co-operative Programme' in 1977, targeted initially in the Western Isles. Based on the concept of community involvement in the provision and improvement of basic services – retailing, local transport and community facilities, the co-operatives have branched-out into profit-seeking activities such as tourism, home production and fish farming. Some co-operatives, such as the Harris initiative have exploited indigeneous skills and resources, building a series of experiments – home production and marketing, tourism, a museum and a community centre – around the Harris Tweed industry. By 1983, the HIDB had established 20 co-operatives, stretching geographically from Ness at the Butt of Lewis to Appin in Argyllshire, involving activities as diverse as refuse collection, brewing and soft-energy generation. This model of government support for co-operatives has not, as yet, been replicated by the SDA in the industrial heartland of Scotland. Indeed, there is some evidence that despite the limited success of the HIDB in stimulating com-munity-based workers' co-operatives and the exhortation of SCDC, the SDA will only very reluctantly consider financial support for this alternative to mainstream business development.

If the influence in Britain of the European co-operative movement has been limited, the impact of experiments from the 'non-profit' sector in the USA has been considerable. The transfer of innovative policy in the field of urban affairs has a long, if not particularly distinguished, pedigree (Boyle and Rich 1984) and since the late 1960s, community experimentation has commonly featured in the exchange of ideas, most recently as part of a Tri-National study of urban policy funded by the German-Marshall Fund in 1979. Significantly, this review involved Colin Ball and John Pearce both of whom subsequently became active in the development of community business in Britain.

Pearce and others were introduced to a sector of the US economy that for a British audience is both enlightening and confusing. Enlightening, for it contains a vast array of neighbourhood and community agencies most adept at leveraging finance from both public and private sectors and able to demonstrate success with remarkably sophisticated community businesses in some of the most distressed neighbourhoods in urban America (Newnham 1980); confusing, because this sector also includes voluntary agencies involved in a wide range of public, social and educational services that would be included in the public sector in the UK. Salamon (1984) estimates that, in 1980, the non-profit sector employed some 4.6 million people, had expenditures of $114 billion accounting for 5 per cent of GNP and absorbed $40 billion of federal support. Neighbourhood business organisations form a very small proportion of this total but, significantly, constitute part of the US economy that is now long established and accepted by government and the private sector as a viable means of providing jobs, goods and services outwith the mainstream commercial sector.

The picture is further confused in that this tradition embraces ideologically opposed concepts. On the one hand, stemming from the initiatives of the Ford Foundation and the federal Office of Economic Opportunity in the 1960s, Community Development Corporations were created to stimulate local, neighbourhood, improvement, including economic development. Organisations such as the Local Initiatives Support Corporation (LISC) in the South Bronx, New York, were initially charged with the aim of stimulating neighbourhood action, improving political awareness and expanding local opportunity. 'Originally, many . . . saw Community Development Corporations as political institutions as much as economic ones, arguing that the condition of poor neighbourhoods was a question of powerlessness, not just poverty, and that economic and political development had to proceed apace' (Mier and Wiewel 1983, 317). Reviews of CDCs often found that neither objective was successfully achieved, not least because of inherent conflict between political goals and the commercial objectives of the business ventures. These, more radical initiatives, were highly dependent on public support, and with the federal budget reductions imposed by the Carter administration then more vigorously by Reagan they were forced to adopt a more commercial stance and at the same time seek support from other sources.

This brought CDCs into competition with local, voluntary organisations that reflect a very different political philosophy. The US has a long tradition of community support based on a much more conservative political agenda. This is what Berger and Neuhaus (1977) termed 'mediating structures' – 'initiatives standing between the private lives of individuals and the large institutions of public life. Mediating structures may be churches, ethnic groups, neighbourhood associations, families or voluntary organisations within the community' (Woodson 1982, 136). Building on work begun by the Commission on Private Philanthropy and Public Needs, the American Enterprise Institution (AEI) was instrumental in funding research into mediating structures across almost all sectors of US domestic policy. This research was based on a set of conservative principles that sought to '(1) remove the non-needy from income maintenance programs; (2) improve the work incentive of social programs; (3) tighten up claims review, returning programs to their original intention; (4) redesign programs with uncontrollable cost limits; (5) rely to a greater extent on the resources of the private sector to meet our social needs' (Meyer 1982, 30).

This combination of demands to reduce the role of government, increase involvement by the private sector and focus neighbourhood action on the creation of viable business was an attempt to bridge the liberal and conservative traditions. Hence, in the late 1970s, the Carter administration was supportive of a partnership between corporate giving, government assistance and local initiatives to encourage urban economic development while, at the same time, the Independent Sector and the Heritage Foundation, two conservative organisations, were just as active in promoting private sector involvement in the same fields.

The non-profit sector and corporate philanthropy became the talisman for the Reagan administration. Building on information collected by the AEI (see McKinnon et al. 1982) and by the prestigious Committee for Economic Development, Reagan established his Presidential Task Force on Private Sector Initiatives to promote private sector leadership and explore ways of encouraging essentially private sector strategies for local economic growth. Without any obvious framework or even structured rationale, the Task Force collected a series of largely unconnected case-studies (see Fosler and Berger (eds) 1982) documenting corporate involvement in a number of different locations, including the famous examples of Pittsburgh, Baltimore and Atlanta. Yet as Salamon (1984) argues, the administration failed to grasp the concepts involved in the mediating structures project, reducing the idea to exhortation of voluntarism while at the same time reducing the funding to local, neighbourhood groups working with training, small business development and community development. Hence, with one hand, the administration supported private sector involvement in community-based business development but on the other effectively weakened its support through budget cuts and changes to the tax system. 'The administration was content to rely mostly on rhetoric, while putting uncritical faith in the workings of its economic development program to revitalise the nonprofit sector' (Salamon 1984, 284).

Whatever the ideological differences, the past two decades of interest in community enterprise in the US demonstrates a number of characteristics that have been significant for community business in the UK. The positive side of the balance sheet records success in terms of:

(1) local business innovation;

(2) high risk ventures but at relatively low cost;

(3) corporate, government, community liaison; and

(4) focusses attention on the problems of specific neighbourhoods.

On the debit side of the balance sheet:

(1) underfunding (from both the public and private sectors) creates problems, especially the failure to build on an initial injection of capital;

(2) lack of clear objectives and conflicting orientations;

(3) lack of organisational and managerial continuity; and

(4) a failure, by sponsors, to appreciate the frailty of many neighbourhood organisations and the difficulties they can face, particularly in terms of job security.

Recent programmes demonstrate that where government support is lacking or insufficient, its replacement by corporate and/or foundation money is never sufficient. Furthermore, private sector sponsorship can re-orientate community enterprise towards activities that are much closer to the mainstream commercial system. The original emphasis on job creation, small business assistance or improvement of local services can be replaced by programmes of physical development where there are tangible pay-offs for the private sector donor. Community development is replaced by a search for corporate profits.

The Organisation of Community Business in Scotland

Community businesses are characteristically small, geographically specific, financially insecure and managerially complex. To be successful, those involved in the 'business' need to understand the product or service 'inside out', must have correctly identified the market and be familiar with the competition; have skills in business management that range from an understanding of employment protection legislation through to property management; and at the same time have an understanding of public policy and knowledge of the complex system of public support for small businesses. And to cap it all, it helps if they have experience of working with the voluntary sector. In other words, community business requires more than entrepreneurial flair!

This section attempts to review the growing network of agencies – public and private – that now encourage and support community business and includes comment on the various grants and loans available to this 'alternative sector'.

At the national, UK, level, community business is perhaps too new, too small and too 'different' to figure prominently in industrial, regional or urban policies of government. As in the USA, it nevertheless has considerable appeal to both right and left; the right consider it as an alternative to state support for industry and the left champion its collectivist deals. Both the Department of Industry and, particularly, the Department of the Environment have indicated general support for the concept of community business but have not supported this rhetoric with substantial resources. Community business was reviewed by the 1983 Environment Committee and suggested by Lord Scarman as an alternative to inner-city unemployment, particularly in the black community. Once again, the influence of American experience was obvious in the Scarman recommendations. Potentially, the Manpower Services Commission (MSC) could play a significant role in the development of community business but experience to date suggests that the MSC concentration on temporary employment schemes mitigates against the goals of permanent employment through viable community business (Pearce 1982). Furthermore, the MSC has been reluctant to allow its Enterprise Allowance Scheme (that pays, at 1984 prices, £40 per week to the unemployed to start their own businesses) to be used by those working in community business. The rules state that the Allowance can only be paid to the self-employed.

As shown in table 6.1, central government, at least in Scotland, supports community business through Urban Aid, a 75 per cent grant for approved projects channelled through local authorities. Projects eligible for Urban Aid were revised in 1981 to include local economic development, allowing neighbourhood enterprise initiatives to apply for these valuable funds. It is impossible to obtain total Scottish Urban Aid expenditure on community business but McArthur (1984) estimates that in 1984–85 twelve organisations in Strathclyde Region received £440,000: £262,000 in recurring revenue (given over a 3- to 5-year period), £139,000 in capital grant and the remainder in non-recurring revenue. Such funds are vulnerable to change in government policy with community business finding the 33 per cent reduction in Urban Aid introduced in FY84/5 very difficult to replace from alternative sources.

Using the Urban Aid pool, local government has been the most accessible source of financial assistance for community business. The amounts involved are, however, very modest. In addition to the Urban Aid contribution, Regional and especially District Councils have offered help in the form

Table 6.1. External development funding for community businesses at mid-1984.

Source	Type of funding
Local Government (Regional and District Councils)	Urban Aid Programme (25% local government contribution and 75% Scottish Office) giving 3 or 5 year funding; Premises and land – often at a peppercorn rent; Small one-off payments – e.g. to buy stock or commission market research; Loans Mandatory and discretionary rate relief
Scottish Development Agency	Capital conversions of buildings to work-spaces, followed by an agreed yearly return on investment between s d a and the community business; Loans
Manpower Services Commission	Community Programme – 12 month sponsorship of temporary work schemes which can sometimes be turned into a business enterprise
European Economic Commission (Social Fund)	Funds are now available for vocational training for the unemployed, for helping develop local employment initiatives and for certain innovative schemes. All European Social Fund grants must be matched by an equal public sector contribution
Community Business Development and Advisory Agencies (Community Business Central, Community Business Scotland, Strathclyde Community Business Ltd)	Consultancy and start up grants Some capital grants and loans
Enterprise Trusts	Consultancy assistance, e.g. product development Occasional grants and loans
Charitable Trusts	Small grants and donations
Public and Private Sector Companies	Occasional one-off donations for particular purposes, e.g. market research Occasional secondment of staff Donation of goods and materials
Banks	Very conservative lenders to any new businesses, especially community businesses

Source: *Community Business in Scotland – Directory* (1984).

of property (often vacant school premises or empty council houses), management assistance and, in some cases, small cash payments to overcome short-run cash-flow difficulties. Local government can also offer the potential of rate relief and the possibility of including community businesses in local purchasing agreements. Limited funding – often in the form of 'gap' finance is also available from Community Business Scotland (CBS), a co-ordinating organisation operating as a central resource for local initiatives and acting as a lobby for increased finance and interest in the community business movement.

Table 6.1 illustrates other, very limited, sources of external funding. Together, Enterprise Trusts, charities and the private sector offer little tangible support although this may increase when community business can attain a higher profile and, crucially, demonstrate a degree of commercial success. Perhaps the greatest assistance that the private sector can offer will be the purchase of goods and services from individual community businesses. This commercial acceptance will then allow individual community businesses to seek financial assistance from the highstreet banks. At this early stage in the development of community business, any involvement by the banks has been in the form of donations. The National Westminster Bank, for example, gave £3,000 to help establish Govan Workspace in Glasgow.

The relationship between community business and the Scottish Development Agency (SDA) is complex. On the other hand, since 1979 the Agency has chosen to support businesses that 'demonstrate that they are, or have a reasonable prospect of, operating with commercial viability . . . there must be at least a reasonable prospect that the business will operate profitably after any grants and associated subsidies have been eliminated from its trading projections'. Furthermore, 'the Agency does not have a social remit and, since most community businesses have dual social and economic objectives, they have proved to be difficult areas of business development' (Fisher 1984). The SDA state that they will only assist community business where traditional business criteria are applied and where there is evidence of other support from the private sector.

On the other hand, the SDA has assisted various community enterprises, notably in terms of small-firm advice and with the provision of industrial premises. More conspicuously, they also assist community business in a number of the Project Agreements. Despite the philosophy of directing assistance only towards commercially viable businesses, the SDA is now participating in the development of Strathclyde Community Business (SCB) Ltd. SCB Ltd is committed to assisting a variety of different projects, some working with commercial criteria, others having definite social goals. This suggests that the SDA is keeping an open mind on community businesses, and will give support and financial assistance on the basis of particular, local, circumstances.

If sources of finance for community business are both limited and constrained, information, advice and encouragement is in plentiful supply. At the UK level, the Community Business Ventures Unit, a product of the Trinational Project in 1979, was set up to encourage the development of community business. It was particularly interested in assessing the availability of funds, exploring:

> funding partnerships between community-raised finance, private sector finance, local government finance and central government finance; through collective involvement of local people, community organisations, private companies, trade unions, local government departments, and through the legal, administrative and managerial frameworks of community companies limited by guarantee and registered as charities.

In 1982, with support from the Tavistock Institute, the Centre for Employment Initiatives continued this role and, through its publication *Initiatives* now acts as a central clearing house for information on community business throughout the UK.

In Scotland, LEAP (Local Enterprise Advisory Project) was established in 1978 as a three-year experiment to examine ways of creating employment in areas where the objectives and activities of the official economic development agencies were seen to be inadequate, even, inappropriate. The stated objectives of LEAP offer an insight to the particular social and economic direction of this organisation:

> (1) to work in the first instance with specific community groups in the East End of Greenock, Ferguslie Park (in Paisley) and Govan (Glasgow) to encourage and support the investigation, design and preparation of locally based job schemes;
> (2) to establish contact with various external agencies with relevant skills and resources and help community groups negotiate these resources;
> (3) to build up a resource bank of information, ideas and specialist expertise which will be available to local groups;
> (4) to arrange appropriate training, workshops and seminars and to carry out relevant data collection on behalf of local projects;
> (5) to evaluate the experience and assess the implications of that experience for both the policies and practice of external agencies and the validity of such an approach as this to the creation of employment; and
> (6) to extend, after a certain period, the work to additional groups who may approach the project for assistance.

Originally based in Paisley College, LEAP secured Urban Aid finance through Strathclyde Regional Council and operated with one full-time officer, John Pearce, and a part-time secretary. After its early success in Ferguslie and Govan, LEAP was given further Urban Aid support up to 1984 and was able to expand its staff and the services offered. LEAP, and in particular the enthusiasm of Pearce, has been a key factor in the development of community business in Scotland. It would not be an exaggeration to suggest that all community businesses in Scotland have, at some stage in their evolution, received assistance from the LEAP team. Moreover, Pearce was also instrumental in setting up Community Business Scotland (CBS) to extend the promotional activities of LEAP throughout the country.

LEAP has done more than assist with individual initiatives. Perhaps its most significant role has been in convincing government that community business should form at least part of local economic strategy. Furthermore, Pearce argues that community business can become pivotal in terms of overall community renewal by emphasising 'community development first, business development second'. Strathclyde, Central and more recently Lothian Regional Councils have developed economic policies that now recognise community business, while a series of District Councils, including West Lothian, Glasgow and Inverclyde commit funds for local community business schemes. Local authorities active in this area, however, attach considerable ideological baggage to their support: members conceive of community businesses as vehicles for tangible community assistance; officers can use community business as a means of gaining political support or, if in close contact with local activists, can develop strong links into the community, bypassing political networks; community workers and the individual community business activists perceive community business as a means of achieving direct action but operating at arms length from the bureaucracy of local government. In terms of neighbourhood politics, community business has something for everyone œ

The logical evolution of LEAP led, in 1984, to the creation of Strathclyde Community Business (SCB) Ltd, a unit funded partly by the Regional Council but acting independently of committee or departmental control. It is significant that support for SCB developed from the social and community strategies of the regional council and not from the economic policies discussed in chapter 4. Overall policy and financial authorisation is made by a Board of Management, made up of representatives from the Regional Council, the SDA, Glasgow District Council and Community Business Strathclyde, federation of local initiatives operating in the region. SCB Ltd retained many characteristics of LEAP while gaining a number of new functions. First, due to the increased level of funding and the commitment of the SDA, it now has the ability to authorise loans, occasionally grants, for new community businesses. Second, Pearce has attempted to implement the community policies of the Regional Council, as outlined in the 'Social Strategy for the 1980s' (SRC 1983), through developing community business as an agent for local development (see figure 6.1), particularly in areas, like the major public-housing estates, where other forms of economic and industrial development are ineffective. Pearce also argues that the development agency model is the only way in which private sector resources can be attracted into

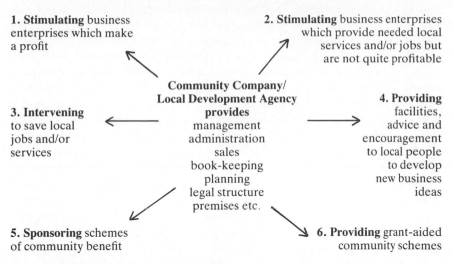

1. Stimulating business enterprises which make a profit

2. Stimulating business enterprises which provide needed local services and/or jobs but are not quite profitable

Community Company/ Local Development Agency provides

3. Intervening to save local jobs and/or services

management administration sales book-keeping planning legal structure premises etc.

4. Providing facilities, advice and encouragement to local people to develop new business ideas

5. Sponsoring schemes of community benefit

6. Providing grant-aided community schemes

Figure 6.1. The community business as an agent for local development.
Source: Pearce (1983).

such areas of social and economic deprivation (Pearce 1983).

McArthur's survey of community businesses in Scotland (1984), perhaps the first attempt to collect comparable data, identified 25 separate 'businesses' employing, in total, 430 people. He estimated that an additional 300 jobs had been created through home production, with another 170 people employed in ancillary enterprises, giving total employment in community business of less than 900. The average size of the workforce in each enterprise was 5 with the largest having 19 employees, Hayton (1983) found similar figures when he reviewed community businesses in 1983 but found larger numbers of part-time workers particularly in the home-produced knitwear industry. McArthur also found from a questionnaire survey of employees that community businesses in Scotland were addressing social as much as economic problems in specific communities. 93 per cent of those employed in community businesses included in his survey had previously been unemployed, students or housewives; 69 per cent were classified as being 'long-term' unemployed, being previously out of work for more than one year, many with a history of recurrent spells of unemployment. Nonetheless, over half those included in the survey had some form of school, trade or other qualification and one-third had previously been in professional, managerial or skilled occupations.

Attitudes to their involvement in a local economic (social) experiment varied significantly. Those employed in schemes funded by the MSC indicated a strong desire to secure permanent employment, often in a conventional workplace setting; employees in schemes with more permanent funding demonstrated a stronger commitment to community business, 59 per cent content to remain outside the traditional workforce. However, 75 per cent of those surveyed felt that their present job was temporary and there was a general perception that their employment and their employer was in some way exceptional. This suggests that community business is still considered experimental and, as has been the case with other innovations, generates strong feelings – some avid supporters of the experiment, others expressing concern about their future prospects. Pearce (1984) suggests that this fear is a reaction to the fact that the proportion of MSC temporary jobs that eventually become permanent is very low. This problem has led community business, and the various umbrella organisations, to focus attention away from increasing the number of separate initiatives to concentrating on improving the 'conversion rate'; the proportion of temporary subsidised jobs that eventually become financed through the operation of the 'business'. The survey reveals that community business is also concerned with offering better chances to the unemployed, particularly school leavers. Local community business can act as an introduction to the 'work-place', improving the basic skills of those facing long-term unemployment.

The irony is that to overcome these organsational weaknesses can lead community business away from its original objectives. 'Involvement in business activities requires community organsations to become increasingly sophisticated. Without conscious and continuous effort, they can become strikingly similar to other businesses' (Mier and Wiewel 1983). This is based on the US experience of not-for-profit organisations but the message is also appropriate in the Scottish situations. The commercial criteria applied by the sponsors (SDA, local government and the private sector) and the obvious economic benefits sought by policy-makers may be at variance with the goals of community development and a local response to economic distress.

For at the heart of the community business concept lies a different approach to local economic development. Merely to replicate mainstream private sector activity in areas previously abandoned by the market is to ignore the economic circumstances that exist in certain communities. Therefore, despite its modest scale and the questionable impact it can have on aggregate economic growth, community business does represent a dimension of local economic strategy that is designed to address the deep-seated socio-economic problems of particular areas. To quote John Pearce:

> There is some evidence now that community business can play and should play a part in any local economic development strategy. That is not to say it is an alternative to other policies, nor is it to make exaggerated claims about the number of jobs which can be created in this way. It is simply a recognition that community business is one way of making some progress in those areas where other forms of economic and industrial development are ineffective. It is a recognition that economic and social problems must be tackled together and that there is an important role for self-help and local collective action.

Turning to examine the types of products and services offered by community business in Scotland, figure 6.2 demonstrates much more variety than any discernible pattern. Based on the 1984 Community Business Scotland Directory (with information covering only enterprises operating within Strathclyde, Lothian and Central). Figure 6.2, for Strathclyde Region, shows that only business advice centres, craft-shops, the provision of community workspace or workshops and home-produced knitwear are common to four or more community businesses. Rather than attempt to describe all these diverse activities and review the different managerial systems that have developed, three case studies of reasonably well-developed community businesses will be used to illustrate the practical problems and potentials of this alternative approach to local economic development.

Govan Workspace Ltd: in 1978 an informal employment study group was established by the Govan Area Resource Centre to examine the problems of lack of employment in the Govan area of Glasgow. Two community-based initiatives emerged from this review. One was Govan Enterprises Ltd, a company formed to create jobs in the area. After a number of trading problems, and some difficulties with temporary funding, Govan Enterprises successfully developed GEEZ, a wholesale trading company distributing a product called 'Bombay Mix' (!) through central Scotland. The second project was Govan Workspace Ltd, formed to provide low-cost, small industrial premises in the area. This had been identified as a major impediment to attracting new companies to the area and, presumably, to the development of new, local small firms. Govan Workspace Ltd became a property management company, limited by guarantee, but does not have charitable status. Hence all profits must either be re-invested in the company or used for the benefit of the local community.

A long search for suitable premises eventually identified a bakery, once owned by Lyons, which was then bought by the SDA, on behalf of Govan Workspace Ltd in 1981. Subdivision of the factory began in 1983 and was scheduled for completion by the end of 1984. Conversion would result in the provision of 48 units, ranging from 500 sq. ft. upwards. Govan Workspace Ltd will be responsible for letting and management of the refurbished property. While this development work was proceeding, a vacant school building, in the heart of Govan, was renovated and made available for new, small businesses. At a cost of £92,000, funded through Urban Aid and Strathclyde Region, 25 small units were created, none bigger than 600 sq. ft. By 1983 there were 24 small businesses in the school, ranging from a computer maintenance company to a TV repair shop, glazier, model maker, printer, even a company preparing and distributing sandwiches. Together, they employed 80 people and it was estimated that 40 of these were new jobs. What made these premises different from others available in the Glasgow area was the policy of 'easy-in – easy-out': short-term (monthly) leases, payable in advance with rental charges as low as anything available

Community Business and Location	Art Work	Building	Business Advice	Business Services	Café	Caneware	Contract Cleaning	Clothing Alterations and Repair	Community Workshop	Copying	Craft Shop	Furniture Manufacture	Gardening	Graffiti Removal	Home Repairs
Ad Hoc Crafts, Ayr											■				
Arden Community Workshop, Thornliebank, Glasgow									■						
Bambee Products Ltd, Bellshill								■							
Erskine Enterprise Group, Erskine									■					■	
E.I.B. Developments Ltd, Erskine			■												
Fairfield Printers Ltd, Govan, Glasgow	■									■					
Flagstone Enterprises Ltd, Ferguslie Park, Paisley														■	
Forgewood Enterprises Ltd, Forgewood, Motherwell			■	■	■	■			■						
Garnock Workspace Ltd, Kilbirnie															
Goodwill Incorporated Ltd, Maryhill, Glasgow															
Govan Enterprises Ltd, Govan, Glasgow															
Govan Workspace Ltd, Govan, Glasgow			■	■											
Greater Springburn Ents Ltd, Springburn, Glasgow															
Group Kilmarnock											■				
Levern Enterprises, Priesthill/Nitshill, Glasgow															■
'Many Hands', Maryhill Community Business Ltd, Glasgow		■											■		
Poldrait Service & Industry Ltd, Bridgeton, Glasgow		■					■				■				
Port Glasgow Community Ents Ltd, Port Glasgow											■	■			
Possil Local Enterprise Group, Possil, Glasgow															
Provanhall Holdings Ltd, Easterhouse, Glasgow		■	■	■											
South West Greenock Community Workshop, Greenock									■						
Tass Community Enterprises Ltd, Saltcoats											■				
Valley Crafts, Kilbirnie															
'Via', Home Prod. Sales Org. Ltd, Govan, Glasgow															

Figure 6.2. Matrix of community businesses in Strathclyde Region and their products/services. Source: Community Business in Scotland, 1984 Directory.

House Board-Up Service

House Clearance

Joinery

Knitwear

MSC Managing Agency

Packaging 'Bombay Mix'

Printing

Quality Seconds

Recycled Electrical Goods

Recycled Furniture

Shop

Shops To Let

Site Clearance

Stone Cleaning and Restoration

Thrift Shop

Toy Manufacture

Transport

Typesetting

Upholstery

Voluntary Service Work

Workspace

on the market. Rental also includes a service charge covering heating, lighting, security, etc.

Govan Workspace Ltd has been very successful in adding to the range of industrial premises in the Govan area. It has also helped to create a number of new jobs. It has also successfully convinced both the SDA and Glasgow District Council that it is a viable local property development/management company. They have probably been less successful in satisfying other, local, objectives. The jobs created have not necessarily benefited local residents and it has been argued that the provision of managed work-space can be more effectively provided, and at about the same cost, by the private sector. That being said, Govan Workspace Ltd has become the model for community-based managed work-space throughout Scotland.

(Information source: LEDIS no.A5 1983)

Port Glasgow Community Enterprise Ltd: was conceived as a company to create locally owned and controlled businesses to provide a range of services and to create local employment, built around the idea of 'home production'. In April 1982, Port Glasgow Community Enterprises Ltd was registered as a company limited by guarantee, having charitable status, and controlled by a Board of Directors elected from a membership drawn from the local community. Finance for the Company, as opposed to individual projects, came through Urban Aid. In 1981 a major revenue grant application was approved providing the salary of a general manager and secretary who inherited the task of running a home producers' shop trading under the name of PEGLEG – Port Glasgow Local Enterprise Group.

The focus on home production of knitwear, clothing, leather goods and soft toys was the result of a consultancy exercise, funded by LEAP, that undertook a review of local potential and developed an initial production and marketing plan. The local District Council, Inverclyde, was persuaded to provide rent-free shop premises for the first two years of the project. PEGLEG opened for business in December 1980 with a full-time shop manageress, an assistant funded through YOP and a number of volunteers. Technical assistance was given by a part-time secondee from Coats Paton, organised through SARC. Goods were 'manufactured' by some 120 home producers, with a standard pricing system organised through the shop. Acting on another initiative from LEAP, a Home Production Sales Organisation (HPSO) was set up to be responsible for attracting orders and also to organise the distribution of work among the producers. HPSO's costs are covered by taking one-third of the wholesale price of all goods sold. A full-time sales consultant was employed to concentrate on marketing a limited range of products, attempt to improve quality, build-up production of knitwear and look for new markets. Initial problems included poor quality, late delivery and the competition with other local outlets. Hence the HPSO looked beyond the Scottish market for new outlets, eventually finding business in London.

The HPSO breaks new ground for community business in Scotland. Even with the difficulties of short-term (Urban Aid) finance and the problems of attracting skilled manpower, HPSO widens the horizons of community business and may offer a genuine chance of income distribution between different areas, not merely redistribution within one, economically distressed area. John Pearce and SCB sees this aspect of extending the product reach of community businesses as crucial for the development of the 'movement' in future years.

(Information Sources: LEDIS no.A14 1983, Hayton 1984)

Provanhall Holdings Ltd: a multi-functional company, limited by shares, created to provide jobs and local services in Easterhouse, a large post-war housing estate on the outskirts of Glasgow. Provenhall has developed three activities: retail management, a local building service and the construction and letting of managed workspace. Provenhall as a history that begins in 1977 when the Easterhouse Festival Society was set up to promote a summer arts festival. With the deterioration in the local economy and the incidence of very high unemployment (in pockets over 50 per cent of the male workforce) in the peripheral estates, the Society formed the Easterhouse Employment Initiative Group. Although subsequently replaced by a residents group, the Festival Society successfully obtained support from Strathclyde Regional Council, through Urban Aid, to develop an employment strategy. A community worker was hired to explore ways in which a community company could be established. In December 1980, Provenhall Holdings Ltd was incorporated as a company limited by shares, having a subscribed capital of £100. The reason for selecting this form of incorporation, as opposed to a company limited by guarantee, was to engender greater community involvement through the purchase of shares by local groups. In the event, this caused a number of problems leading to substantial underfunding of the company. To get round this problem, a separate charity, the Easterhouse Community trust was founded. This now acts as the Company's fund-raising organisation.

The company's first project was the conversion of six vacant ground-floor flats into shop units. The premises were given to the Trust, rent-free, on a 21-year lease by Glasgow District Council. The Council also met the costs of materials for extensive renovation. These units now house a variety of small businesses including a launderette, hairdresser, clothes shop and solicitor's office. In essence, this represents community business developing basic, local services in an area ignored by the private sector. The Company's second project was to obtain further work for the building team formed to renovate the shops. The Company successfully won a contract from Glasgow District Council to convert a disused school building into workspace (on the Govan model). This will eventually provide nine units – six small workshops and three offices. The Trust will act as the workshop management, funding the staff from Urban Aid support. Albeit on a small scale, the

activities of Provenhall are significant for community business demonstrating that 'community contracting' can be a viable alternative to either Direct Labour or private contracting. This role for community business has raised the political temperature in a number of areas. Central government supports the concept as a way of reducing the bureaucratic and monopolistic delivery of local services provided by local government and as yet another way of cutting direct public expenditure; the Trade Unions (both manual and non-manual) view community contracting as a potential threat to their industry, as a threat to organised labour and as an invitation to 'back-door' privatisation. This reaction has had unfortunate consequences for community business as the concept of community contracting could not only improve the delivery of local services, e.g. school meals, home helps, street maintenance, but could provide valuable employment opportunities for local residents and, crucially, give local communities control over the pace, direction and level of local services.
(Information Sources: LEDIS no.A17 1983, Pearce 1984)

The Potential of Community Business

Despite the well-intentioned rhetoric accompanying community business in Scotland, its achievements have fallen far short of its goals. The vision of a radical, alternative, orientation for local economic development, involving employee control, community re-investment of surpluses and widespread community involvement, has given way to what McArthur (1984) calls the 'practical and more immediate considerations' of raising finance, sustaining momentum and reaching modest job creation targets. Nevertheless, success can also be measured in terms of the movement's ability to challenge the conventional wisdom of local economic development, ensuring that the concept of community-based enterprise is at least on the agenda of regional and local development agencies. The evolution of LEAP into Strathclyde Community Business and its success in promoting community initiatives in some of the most deprived communities in Scotland suggests that local government and eventually the SDA are prepared to commit resources to schemes that fall outside the traditions of supporting privately-owned, profit-seeking, business.

Since the late 1970s, the expansion of community business in Scotland has, however, to be viewed as a component of social policy as much as a part of local economic strategy. Many initiatives have been of the 'make-work' variety, targetting MSC funds, Urban Aid, and s83 sources at short-term job creation projects. A number of community businesses, especially those located within large public-sector housing areas devoid of almost any form of legitimate employment, have not pursued the concept of recycling surpluses into the community nor have they sought to reduce their dependence on public subsidy. Instead, such initiatives should be examined as an extension of social policy, building on the foundations of traditional community development. Nonetheless, John Pearce and others argue that while commercial success should not be the sole criterion for evaluation, community business is more than a convenient 'band-aid' for areas experiencing severe economic distress. Community business can become the basis upon which long-term economic growth can develop. His model of community business as the agent or catalyst for local economic development attempts to extend short-term job creation into stimulating an indigeneous entrepreneurial environment in areas ignored or neglected by the market place. As with the exaggerated claims made by the enterprise trust movement, community business is not short on evangelistic fervour!

As seen in the development of community-based economic development agencies in the USA, the recent initiatives in Scotland demonstrate the difficulties of achieving the complex, often conflicting, objectives set for small-scale community businesses: (1) as an alternative to the private-sector, small firm focus of conventional economic policy; (2) yet, as a mechanism for releasing the commercial potential of deprived areas; (3) as an extension of social programmes enhancing neighbourhood control; yet, (4) focussing on the problems of job creation; (5) as a means of effecting community control over local services; while at the same time, (6) searching for a means of leveraging private investment. Perhaps the limited achievements of community business reflect these contradictory objectives that merely serve to dissipate impact across too many sectors, too many different organisations.

Because community business tends to be administered, funded and analysed from an economic perspective, the indicators of performance suffer from the same weaknesses affecting conventional local economic policy. As with many spatial policies, community business cannot control against the exporting from the local area of employment and other benefits induced through public subsidy. Jobs may be targeted at local residents but the multiplier effect may have little direct bearing on the local community. Furthermore, the higher skilled, better paid jobs, particularly in the management of local projects, may not be available to local residents. In addition, the provision of public subsidy for local goods or services delivered through community business may have a negative effect, reducing the competitiveness of existing local firms and individuals. The creation of subsidised employment in one community may be at the expense of non-subsidised jobs elsewhere. Some argue that support for community business can have an overall negative effect in that it may replace experienced with inexperienced business, introducing a higher chance of business failure. Supporters of the community business concept argue that to engender local commercial development in areas neglected by the private sector will have an economic cost that must be borne by areas that demonstrate locational, economic advantage.

Community business also suffers from organisational weaknesses that need to addressed if they are to make a significant contribution to local economic development. Evidence from the analysis of well-established neighbourhood enterprises in the USA (CURA 1984) and from commentary on recent initiatives in the UK highlights several organisational issues critical for long-term development. Even the very best support from agencies such as Community Business Scotland or SCB cannot compensate for weak or absent local leadership. The most effective community businesses demonstrate strong community leadership (often the catalyst for the origins of the enterprise) and effective leadership at the operational level. Secondly, the temporary, vulnerable, funding structure of so many community businesses is perhaps the weakest link in translating short term initiatives into more permanent enterprise. The scale of support is often less significant than certainty and consistency. The best that can be said of much of the funding for community business in Scotland is that it is consistently uncertain! Self-generated income, surpluses or profits are the key to longevity but the pursuit of surpluses raises the central dilemma of balancing the financial demands of the 'business' and the original objective of re-cycling profits into the community at large.

The Port Glasgow example highlighted the common problem of finding and retaining professional and/or managerial staff. Competent staff provide the bridge between community leadership and the workforce and are the key factors in the funding, management and development of the enterprise. This unusual combination of skills required by community business has not been easy to find and the comprise of hiring either traditional community development officers or managers direct from the mainstream private sector has often not produced the desired effect.

Studies of community business in the USA pinpoint the need for developing skills in 'political marketing'. In order to balance often conflicting interests and to extend fund-raising activities, community business needs to build a network of contacts throughout the local economic development community. Moreover, to attract significant support, particularly from the private sector, individual enterprises must demonstrate abilities recognised by outside interests: commercial acumen will be the measure applied by the private sector (and the SDA); skills in community mobilisation will be sought by the social work community; job creation will be the bench-mark set by the political system. Skills in political marketing are also required to sustain momentum at the community level, ensuring grass-roots support for targetted funding. The most obvious organisational weakness is perhaps the most difficult to overcome, namely, the development of technical/business competence. This can only fully be achieved through experience but evidence shows that learning from demonstrable success, avoiding the more obvious failures and using whatever assistance is available within and outside the local community, in exactly the same way as business 'buys' expertise, can help build this capacity.

7

PRIVATE STRATEGIES FOR LOCAL ECONOMIC DEVELOPMENT

The Role of Enterprise Trusts

Origins

The reorientation of urban policy in the late 1970s placed new public responsibilities on the private sector. In an attempt to reduce public expenditure yet maintain their urban programme, government looked to the business community as a new source of funds. Furthermore, the concentration on business development and on creating an environment for local economic recovery required the skills and expertise apparently available in the private sector. The positive response of the private sector was based on the concept of 'corporate responsibilities, where business, it is argued, cannot sensibly contract out of concern for and involvement in our economic and social problems' (BIC 1981). This admittedly flimsy concept is then translated into practice through a related, and considerably more robust concept of 'mutual aid or mutual self-help' where advice, encouragement and resources for local business growth are provided directly or indirectly by private companies trading profitably in the same local area.

Successfully combining corporate responsibility, mutual aid and the assistance of senior cabinet ministers, the national business lobby has mobilised support for an organisation entitled 'Business in the Community' (BIC) that has in turn stimulated the local enterprise trust or enterprise agency. In Scotland, the first trust was established in May 1981; at the end of 1984 there were 24 such trusts, operating in towns as far apart as Fraserburgh and Cumnock and in situations as diverse as inner Glasgow and rural Dumfries.

Private sector interest in local economic development is not the result of a single significant event but is instead the outcome of a complex inter-play of forces. There is firstly, the tradition of 'mutual aid' between individuals, firms and corporations in the private sector. Industry and commerce has had a long collective interest in local and national economic affairs. The first chamber of commerce, for example, was founded in Glasgow in 1783 and by 1860 thirty local organisations had formed the Association of British Chambers of Commerce. In 1983 there were 87 chambers of commerce affiliated to the Association, organised into 12 regional chambers. Collectively, chambers of commerce claim to represent over 50,000 businesses (Foster 1983), including the top '200' firms in the UK. While each chamber is organised to reflect local circumstances, they exist to represent local business interests on issues such as taxation, and especially local rates, commercial law, business regulations, industrial policy, transport and local planning. Their role in direct mutual aid has, however, not been well-developed and although some 50 per cent of the income of individual chambers comes from firms with less than 25 employees few activities of chambers of commerce are aimed at supporting or assisting small firms. It is also suggested that because office-bearers in chambers of commerce tend to be drawn from medium and large firms whose direct interests do not lie in the small firm sector, the concept of mutual assistance between companies has not been, until recently, a central activity of many chambers of commerce.

At the national level, the Confederation of British Industry (CBI), an organisation representing the interests of some 16,000 firms, has had a very limited role in encouraging mutual support between private companies. The CBI has, not surprisingly, traditionally encouraged its image as the spokesman for large firms, representing the interests of some 40 per cent of its members who have employees in excess of 200. It did, however, establish a Smaller Firms Council in the mid-1970s to develop the interests of this sector.

With the deepening economic recession in 1979–80 the CBI took a very active interest in local economic issues and in creating its Special Programmes Unit focussed attention on employment strategies within a framework of Community Action Plans (SPU 1983).

The idea of mutual aid — the exchange of ideas, expertise and resources, has been actively promoted by the Action Resource Centre (ARC). Established in England and Wales in 1973 with an autonomous Scottish ARC being added in 1976, this organisation has the aim of making business skills available to the wider community. It acts as a form of clearing house, matching resources (expertise, services, plant, manpower) available in the private sector with identifiable gaps in the voluntary and community sectors. ARC and SARC are both organised by the private sector, staffed by seconded managers and financed by private companies and a number of national foundations. 'SARC emphasises the interdependence of business and the community and attempts to create greater understanding between the business community and the community in general about social needs' (LEDIS, A9, 1982). SARC has recently widened its remit to assist in small business development in both the profit and in the not-for-profit sectors, with their involvement with the Goodwill organisations in Glasgow and Dundee combining the philosophies of mutual aid with the development of community business and youth training.

SARC has also promoted the concept of corporate social responsibility. Covering a bewildering range of objectives from charitable giving through philanthropy to enlightened self-interest, a number of the larger UK companies, for example, Shell, IBM, Ferranti have deliberately used limited sums, traditionally earmarked for charitable purposes, to finance schemes that assist with local economic development. Other companies, for example, United Biscuits and Marks and Spencer have actively pursued a policy of staff secondment, releasing staff for limited periods to work on or with local projects that impact on local economic circumstances. Other forms of corporate responsibility include the free disposal of redundant factory space, direct involvement with small firms, local purchasing policies, youth training and hiring policies and the financial support of a variety of business schemes.

The involvement by UK companies in social, community and increasingly economic affairs has been influenced, some might say inspired, by the tradition of corporate social responsibility in the USA (SRI 1982; Fosler and Berger 1983; Boyle and Rich 1984). Corporate involvement in community affairs by companies such as IBM, General Motors, Control Data and Dayton-Hudson has been actively encouraged by federal governments. President Reagan endorsed a Task Force on Private Sector Initiatives (1982) while policy developments in urban affairs (HUD 1982) and in local economic strategy have increasingly looked towards the private sector for new resources, ideas and organsational systems. What is new about this reliance on the private sector is that it is being encouraged as a replacement for and not as an addition to public investment, particularly federal spending, on local economic distress. Hence, corporate social responsibility in the USA has, at least temporarily, been elevated from charitable giving to a mechanism for generating local economic renewal in the absence of policy and resources coming from the public sector. Furthermore, the influence of private sector involvement with non-profit or not-for-profit community enterprise in the USA has not gone unnoticed in the UK (Newham 1980). The impression of successful Community Development Corporations, the impact of a number of Community Renewal Programmes and the widely reported activities of non-profit organisations such as the Local Initiatives Support Corporation in areas like the South Bronx presents an attractive model for collaboration between private investment, private philanthropy and local economic problems. This model proved attractive for the Conservative government committed to reducing local dependency on state support and supportive of programmes encouraging self-help through stimulating local private businesses.

Despite the scale of unemployment and the severity of the 1979–81 recession, assistance for small firms became the main component of government support for economic development (Lawless 1981), with the private sector being expected to play a key role in translating government policy in practice. Although the Labour government of 1974–79 had encouraged private sector involvement in local economic development and had actively supported small firm expansion, it is difficult to underestimate the impact of the Conservative election victory in 1979. Their manifesto commitment to assist small business was translated into policy through the (then) Department of Industry and through a succession of tax and regulation changes introduced in the first budgets of the Government. Ministers were eager to directly involve private companies in local economic development projects. Speaking just after the 1979 election, Michael Heseltine, then Secretary of State for the Environment, argued that public policies for depressed inner-city economies should 'encourage the private sector to come in, and to come in on a large scale'. Two years later he told the London Chamber of Commerce and Industry that:

> the flair, ambition and determination to succeed that were so much a part of developing local economies in the past are not traits that come easy to bureaucratic and institutionalised organisations. That impetus must come from the private sector. . . . I want to engender the belief that if the private sector takes on a more positive, assertive role in local affairs, the benefits to the community will be enormous.

This redirection and strengthening of policy in support of small firms resulted in a 'Minister for Small Firms', increased resources for the Small Firms Service operated by the Industry Department, a review of the numerous and confusing financial aids available to industry, the sponsorship of 'enterprise events' and significantly the direct involvement of private organisations in policy development and in certain cases the implementation of programmes. Richardson (1983) has argued that this merely represents the 'politicisation of business leadership over the past three decades (and) has resulted in the private sector seeking to secure its position for the future by becoming more sensitive to their local markets and the community they serve'. The 'privatisation' of local economic development was also in response to renewed pressures for increased deregulation, for a reduction in the scale of public expenditure and employment and for a realignment of policy in support of a market orientated economy that was being advocated by new influential organisations such as the Adam Smith Institute and the Institute of Directors. The private sector had therefore become the key actor in the development of local economic strategy.

Private sector concern about the recession coupled with positive support from the Conservative government resulted in two separate initiatives that prepared the organisational framework for the development of a network of local enterprise trusts. The first was the creation of 'Business in the Community' (BIC), whose origins can be traced back to the now legendary conference held at the Civil Services College at Sunningdale in April 1980 where representatives from British Industry and from government (DOE, DI and MSC) met to learn from the American experience of corporate social responsibility. This led to the formation of the 'Pilkington Group', a working party on 'Community Involvement' that was given the remit to explore ways in which, following the American model, major British companies could more directly and more effectively become involved in community affairs. The working party was chaired by Sir Alastair Pilkington who was personally committed to corporate social responsibility through the St Helen's Trust.

The outcome of the Pilkington Group's deliberations was the formation in 1982 of Business in the Community. As a company limited by guarantee, it was financed and governed by an impressive array of 'blue-chip' companies including GEC, Marks and Spencer, IBM, BAT and Pilkington Glass and was administered by an executive council that had the services originally of 7 full-time secondees from large firms and government, including a full-time chief executive, Stephen O'Brien.

By the end of 1983, some 89 organisations were members of BIC with up to 16 seconded staff. An autonomous Scottish BIC was formed under the chairmanship of Sir Hector Laing in 1982.

The stated objectives of BIC are suitably vague but nevertheless support Lord Sieff's assertion that, 'the leaders of the free enterprise sector must clearly demonstrate that they possess a sense of social responsibility':

> To encourage industry and commerce to become more involved on a local basis with the economic, social, training and environmental needs of the communities in which they operate;
>
> To bring together local authorities, organisations and business, to assist in the development of effective action;
>
> To collect and disseminate information about successful local initiatives so that others can learn rapidly and effectively; and to work through and support existing initiatives and organisations.

Although BIC encourages a variety of techniques – secondment, distribution of surplus plant and machinery, local training schemes, company involvement with schools and so forth – their principle activity is to encourage and assist in the development of local enterprise trusts. By the beginning of 1984, BIC listed 130 local enterprise agencies in operation throughout the UK, with 30 in formation and a further 37 at 'an early stage in discussion' (DHS 1984).

The success of BIC and the growth of the enterprise trust movement can be attributed to three factors. Although difficult to evaluate, the role played by certain key individuals would appear to have been crucial. Pilkington was obviously an important factor but the personal support of senior industrialists and financiers such as Lord Sieff from Marks and Spencer, John Raisman from Shell and Sir Hector Laing from United Biscuits was crucial in attracting the support of other companies.

BIC also began with Ministerial support from Tom King, then at the Department of the Environment, secured links with Industry Ministers responsible for small firms and has had the personal involvement of several senior civil servants seconded to the London and Edinburgh offices. But perhaps the key to the success of BIC and of enterprise trusts in general has been the continued financial involvement by a 'committed' group of companies. McAllister (1984) demonstrated that while over 1,000 separate firms sponsor enterprise trusts throughout the UK, the involvement by five or six companies has been crucial (table 7.1).

Table 7.1. Company involvement in U K enterprise trusts.

Rank	Company	No. of trusts
1	Marks and Spencer	54
2	ICI	14
3	Shell	14
4	BP	12
5	United Biscuits	10
6	IBM	8
7	ICFC	5
8	GEC	4
9	Thorn EMI	4
10	Rowntree Mackintosh	4

Source : MacAllister 1984, p.22.

The combination of individual commitment and the 'ear of Government' was equally apparent in the second initiative underpinning the enterprise trust movement. At the request of the Secretary of State for Employment and with the backing of the Manpower Services Commission (MSC), the CBI in conjunction with several member companies established its Special Programmes Unit in 1980. Under the chairmanship of Lord Carr, former Conservative Cabinet Minister and chairman of Prudential Assurance, and chief executive, James Cook, the SPU developed three objectives:

> to assist the MSC in enlisting the fullest co-operation of large companies in response to present and future employment policies (with special regard to youth employment);
>
> to provide an expert and direct critique and commentary to government on those policies from the experience of large employer contact and its own field work; and
>
> to provide a management support for the MSC in their efforts to move from one major policy to the next. (Special Programmes Unit 1983)

These objectives were to be achieved through a series of Community Action Programmes (CAP) in selected unemployment 'blackspots'. Using contacts in local firms, the SPU began a programme of marketing firstly the Youth Opportunities Programme then the Youth Training Scheme (YTS) on behalf of the MSC. Working with seconded managers responsible to a supervisory board in each CAP, the SPU selected 25 Travel to Work areas where unemployment was above 12 per cent (in 1982) and began to establish a network of employer contacts who could be used as the focus for the YTS programme. By the end of 1983, 7 of these CAPs has developed into fields of local promotion, work creation schemes and full involvement with YTS. In three specific areas this employer activity was developed in conjunction with local labour market studies, financed initially by the National Westminster Bank. The SPU envisaged that the CAPs would eventually extend into areas such as direct employment and training schemes, education and industry linkage and also examine ways of improving local economic performance.

Considering the philosophical and organisational similarities between BIC and the CBI's SPU it was not surprising that the two initiatives were merged in October 1984, under the overall chairmanship of Lord Carr. Business in the Community now links Government policy with the training schemes of the MSC and co-ordinates a network of CAPs and enterprise trusts in almost every major centre in the UK. Private sector strategy for local economic development had, by 1984, a firm foundation for implementation.

If mutual aid, the impact of the recession and the political climate supplied the conceptual framework and if the CBI/SPU initiative, the Sunningdale conference and the creation of BIC delivered the necessary financial and governmental impetus, the organisational origins of the enterprise trust movement can be traced to a range of local initiatives that emerged during the 1970s. Once again the influence of the US model of community development was apparent when in 1975 the charity 'Alternative Society' began to use the term 'local enterprise trust' (Initiatives 1982). And at the same time co-ordinating organisations in the voluntary sector were active in promoting community self-help, tapping into financial assistance on offer by local firms.

Perhaps the first recognisable trust was that of Enterprise North. Established in 1973 by a successful local businessman with the support of the Newcastle office of the DI, it offered help and advice to new companies through a panel of business councillors acting on a voluntary basis. These panels were originally co-ordinated through Newcastle Polytechnic but became part of the Durham Business School's New Enterprise Development Project (LEDIS 1982). Using a similar approach but focussing attention on employment opportunities for young people, the Small Industries Group, Somerset, founded in 1977, was also originally dependent on the enthusiasm of committed individuals but eventually secured financial assistance and the active involvement of local government. The concept of large firm support for enterprise trusts was first fully tested through the London Enterprise Agency (LEntA) established in 1979 by the London Chamber of Commerce and Industry. Twelve major UK companies, including some already committed to corporate social responsibility like BP, Marks and Spencer and Shell, donated cash and seconded staff to the trust working towards three goals: small firm assistance, private sector involvement in urban renewal and the development of the enterprise trust concept throughout the UK. This third aim was subsequently absorbed by BIC in 1982.

LEntA also demonstrated how an enterprise trust could successfully diversify into a range of different functions, reflecting local problems but also capturing available resources as well as attracting government support such as Urban Aid. This model of large firm support, direct involvement by the Chamber of Commerce and the support of the DI was repeated in the Leeds Business Venture started in 1980.

Approaching similar problems from opposite directions, the work of

British Steel Corporation (Industry) Ltd. or BSC(I) as it is commonly known, on Clydeside, in South Wales and in the North East of England and the widely publicised activities of the Community of St Helen's Trust in Lancashire are the most famous precedents for the contemporary enterprise trust. BSC(I) was formed in 1975 to assist in the creation of new employment for redundant steel workers, providing help across the whole range of business services: advice, support, premises and especially access to grants and loans. BSC(I) developed local strategies working closely with central and local government to minimise the socio-economic impact of plant closure (Lawless 1981). In Scotland, BSC(I) was particularly active in the steel closure areas of North Ayrshire at Glengarnock and in North Lanarkshire where they redeveloped part of Clyde Iron Works as small workshop units. As enterprise trusts have developed, BSC(I) have gradually merged their regional activities into local trusts, transferring staff, premises and financial assistance and intended to withdraw from direct involvement in small firm assistance by 1984 (Hood 1984, 86).

The Community of St Helen's Trust is certainly the best known enterprise trust in the UK. Founded in 1978 by the Pilkington Glass Company along with the support of local government, the banks and the Chamber of Commerce, it was conceived in response to redundancies in the glass industry as new technology replaced traditional labour intensive methods. The St Helen's Trust was, however, a working model of corporate social responsibility with the Pilkington Company supplying not only staff to run a business advice centre but also establishing a small venture capital fund with assistance from other private sector interests.

With the notable exception of BSC(I), Scotland lagged behind England in developing early examples of enterprise trusts. The first concrete initiative was launched in May 1981 around the towns of Ardrossan, Saltcoats and Stevenson in Ayrshire, better known as ASSET. Building on the experience of the St Helen's Trust and Business Link in Runcorn this new venture was the product of a working party set up in response to the closure of ICI's nylon plant at Stevenson. ASSET was originally financed and governed by five equal partners: ICI and Shell (UK) from the private sector and the SDA, Strathclyde Regional Council and Cunninghame District Council from the public sector. Up to 6 full-time employees, some salaried, some seconded, have worked on a variety of activities in the ASSET area covering business advice, assistance with premises, training, limited support with start-up finance and technical advice through an Innovation Panel. As was the case in St Helen's and in LEntA, ASSET had the advantage of handling factory space made available by ICI as well as managing other industrial units provided by the SDA and the local authorities. The operating budget of ASSET was £116,000 in 1983, divided between the remaining four sponsors. Cunninghame District withdrew in 1983 when the Governing Board chose to convert the Trust to a company limited by guarantee.

In a number of ways ASSET became the model for enterprise trusts in Scotland. In particular, the relatively high profile by public bodies, not least the SDA, has become commonplace while the 'one door' concept, vigorously marketed by ASSET has been adopted by almost all subsequent trusts. But as we argue later the scale of ASSET, in terms of finance and the range of activities, has not been repeated throughout Scotland.

Organisation and Management

The initial stimulus behind a local enterprise trust comes from a variety of sources, occasionally from a single source, more commonly from a combination of events and organisations. Acting on its own behalf, Scottish BIC has been involved in the early stages of almost all trusts in Scotland and has worked with a number of private companies to generate interest in the concept of mutual aid. Only very rarely, however, does the initial stimulus come from individual companies. Where this has occurred, as in areas such as Bathgate, Ardrossan and Stirling, the reason for the support is because of plant closure or major 'rationalisation of activities'. The main stimulus in Scotland now comes from the SDA who have, since 1981, increasingly looked towards enterprise trusts as an important vehicle for the implementation of local economic policies and considers a form of enterprise trust as the logical organisational development of their Area Projects:

> enterprise trusts mirror the Agency's corporate objectives of fostering entrepreneurial activity. They reflect in particular two main thrusts of the Agency's own development priorities. Firstly, the participation of the business community enhances the resources that can be deployed towards economic regeneration. . . . Secondly, trusts depend upon local interests assuming leadership: the Agency firmly believes this to be essential to long term success and is thus able confidently to undertake a catalytic role. (SDA 1984)

There is some evidence that as enterprise trusts began to emerge, local government was suspicious of this unfamiliar organisation. They expressed understandable concern about the motives, financing and accountability of trusts, perhaps foreseeing the day when their hard-fought role in local economic development might be usurped by the private sector. Such fears have largely, but not entirely, disappeared. Strathclyde Regional Council, for example, has a policy that now endorses the enterprise trust concept and has committed resources to an Enterprise Trust Development Fund. Elsewhere, as in the withdrawal of support from ASSET by Cunninghame District Council, some distance, if not actual hostility, still exists between local government and emerging trusts.

Enterprise trusts in Scotland receive financial support from three sources. The SDA has a financial commitment in all but two enterprise trusts (the exceptions being the Barrows in Glasgow whose running costs are provided by the local stall owners and traders and the Monklands Trust funded by

Urban Aid); local government is financially involved in the majority of trusts, particularly those operating in the Project Agreement areas. Private support comes from a variety of different firms, the range and scale of private sponsorship varying between location and type of initiative. Apart from the involvement by certain large firms committed to corporate social responsibility, banks and insurance companies figure prominently in the lists of supporting companies. Sponsorship comes in four forms: cash support; secondment of staff on a full-time or part-time basis; assistance with premises, plant and machinery; and help with business counselling schemes run through the trust.

One aspect of practical government support for enterprise trusts was introduced in Section 48 of the 1982 Finance Act. This provides for tax relief on contributions (be it in cash or kind) to an approved local enterprise agency by a company or unincorporated business. Approval is given by the Industry Department for Scotland on the condition that the trust should be concerned with 'the promotion or encouragement of industrial and commercial activity or enterprise . . . especially the formation and development of small companies'. (DHS 1984) The commercial significance of this tax allowance needs, however, to be seen in the context of the scale of commercial sponsorship that, even with the larger trusts, it will represent a very small percentage of the pre-tax profit. Nonetheless, the incentive exists.

It is important to appreciate the scale at which enterprise trusts operate. As our survey shows, outside the larger cities and the special initiative areas, trusts are normally staffed by one full-time director with the necessary secretarial support. He or she is therefore very dependent upon part-time or occasional support from business advisors provided by sponsoring companies and public bodies. The effectiveness of the lone trust director will be a crucial factor in determining the success or otherwise of the local initiative. On the other hand, the scale at which trusts operate does encourage personal contact, assists co-operation and co-ordination and prevents the development of bureaucratic structures.

Local Enterprise Trusts in Scotland

If one of the strengths of recent economic development has been a degree of policy inventiveness, experimentation and diversity then surely one of its weaknesses has been the evident lack of policy monitoring and evaluation and the associated impact analysis of initiatives on local areas and problems. Both sponsors (government and private companies) and practitioners argue that new programmes need to have completed at least two full years before any accurate measurement becomes valid. This is indeed a cogent argument when dealing with policy experimentation on a very limited scale. It is difficult, however, to use the same argument when, with an almost complete lack of data, an idea, an experiment is suddenly replicated throughout the country, applying the same model in areas widely different in economic, social and political structure. This is precisely what has happened with the development of local enterprise trusts in Scotland. It follows, that there is therefore very little published data available, other than publicity material issued by individual trusts. Table 7.2 attempts to fill this gap, illustrating, on a comparative basis, certain operational indicators of the enterprise trusts in Scotland at the end of 1984.

Count and Location. As of November 1984, there were 24 trusts operating in Scotland, with a further two, in Levenmouth (Fife) and Clackmannan, due to be launched. In addition, Scottish BIC were at various different stages in discussion with a further 8 embryonic organisations. The oldest, ASSET, has been in existence for 3.5 years. The distribution of trusts is confusing and illustrates a number of the policy contradictions that surround private sector involvement in local economic development. Scottish BIC, for example, encourage the formation of trusts only where there is evidence of support from an existing but perhaps badly organised local business community. They prefer not, however, to commit time and resources to areas that are already very well organised or to areas where there is no obvious business network. Operating alone, they would not have encouraged trusts in Leith (an existing network) nor Wigtown (rural). Furthermore, it is difficult to discern any geo-economic logic in the location of trusts. Some, such as ASSET and CADET in Ayrshire, LIFE, MET and Monklands in north Lanarkshire and BASE in West Lothian have a connection with economic decline, with some of the highest rates of unemployment in Scotland, and with the impact of plant closure. Others, ALERT, East Kilbride and GET, are located in areas that have relatively low rates of unemployment and are at the centre of the developing high technology industries. This application of trusts in areas of severe economic decline as well as in areas of 'opportunity' is supported by the attitude of the SDA, who are prepared to support trusts in widely different circumstances. In Wigtown, for example, the trust is to play a 'reactive' role, while plans for an initiative in north Perthshire will look towards an 'aggressive' enterprise trust that will 'look for new opportunities and strengths in the area'.

Leaving aside those trusts formed at the behest of the SDA, the pattern of distribution reflects connections between certain private companies, between sponsors of Scottish BIC, local Chambers of Commerce and between individuals committed to developing the 'movement'. Or put another way, opportunistic development through the 'old-boy network'. There is evidence that the trusts in Glasgow, Edinburgh, Aberdeen and Dumfries evolved through this route. But if this makes policy analysis difficult, it renders policy development virtually impossible.

Resources. Enterprise trusts in Scotland come cheap. Taking the available data for 1984, annual running costs amount to just over £2 million, averaging out at £94,000 per trust per annum. This figure is inflated by the higher running costs of selected trusts; LIFE, for example, accounts for 21 per cent

Table 7.2. Local enterprise trusts in Scotland.

Organisation	Launch date	Annual budget	% income from public sources	Staff		Principle functions	SDA designation	Notes
				F/T	P/T			
Aberdeen	Nov. 84	70,000	37%	2	—	B	—	Estimated income for 84/5
Arbroath Venture	July 84	49,000	88%	2	—	B(A,E,P)	S	£2.174m capital investment over 3 years
Ardrossan – Saltcoats–Stevenson (ASSET)	May 81	116,000	50%	6	2	A,B,G,P,T	S	
Ayr (ALERT)	Apr. 83	75,000	50%	4	—	B,T	—	
The Barrows	July 82	45,000	0%	2	—	E,P	C	
Bathgate Area Support for Enterprise (BASE)	Sept. 83	180,000	100%	5	—	B,T	L	Public contribution includes Leyland Vehicles
Cumnock and Doon (CADET)	Mar. 84	42,500	100%	4	—	A,B,G,P	—	Public contribution includes NCB
Clackmannan	Nov. 84	50,000	50%				—	
Dundee Industrial Assoc.	Aug. 83	62,000	N/A	2	—	A,B	I	Limited rental income
East Kilbride Business	Sept. 84	77,000	53%	3	1	B	—	
Edinburgh Venture (EVENT)	Nov. 83	100,000	20%	5	—	B	—	
Falkirk Enterprise (FEAT)	June 83	53,000	46%	1	—	A,B,T	—	Evolved from Falkirk Business Forum
Fraserburgh Ltd	Oct. 84	54,000	75%	2	—	B(A,E,G,T)	S	
Garnock Valley Development Executive	Mar. 84	100,000	50%	3	1	B(A,E,G,P)	T,S	£1.017m total capital investment over 3 years
Glasgow Opportunities (GO)	Sept. 83	240,000	12.5%	9	—	B,T,G	?	
Glenrothes (GET)	June 83	50,000	50%	2	—	B,T	—	
Inverclyde	Apr. 84	52,000	60%	2	—	B,T	?	

Organisation	Launch date	Annual budget	% income from public sources	Staff F/T	P/T	Principle functions	SDA designation	Notes
Kilmarnock Venture	Jan. 83	100,000	88%	3	–	B(A,E,P)	S	£250,000 capital investment per annum
Lanarkshire Industrial Field Executive (LIFE)	Mar. 83	433,000	100%	10	–	B,P	L	Includes contribution of £325,000 from BSC(I)
Leith	Apr. 84	70,000	50%	2	–	B	I	
Levenmouth	Mar. 83							
Monklands	Oct. 83	24,000	100%	2	–	B	I	Urban Aid funded; for Monklands Project
Motherwell (MET)	May 83	82,000	68%	3	–	B	I	Estimated income for 84/5
Nithsdale – Annandale – Eskdale and Stewartry	Aug. 84	40,000	50%	2	2	B,T		
Stirling Enterprise Park	late 83	N/A	N/A	2	1	A	–	Major contribution by Imperial Tobacco
Wigtown Rural Development Company	May 83	60,000	98%	4	–	B(A,E,G,T)	S	£880,000 capital investment over 3 years

Function Key: A – asset management; B – business counselling and support services; E – environmental activities; G – grants/loan finance or business; P – non-local promotion; T – training (direct involvement); ( ) – under project agreement.
SDA Designation Key (Gulliver 1984): C – Comprehensive Urban Renewal; T – Task Force; I – Integrated Project; L – Local Partnership Initiatives; S – Self-Help Project.
N/A – not available.
Source: *Publication and Telephone Survey* (Nov. 1984).

149

of total costs in Scotland. While any financial review of enterprise trusts is fraught with difficulty – confidentiality, incomplete data, incorporation or exclusion of secondment costs, etc. – the data in table 7.2 clearly demonstrate that 'private' enterprise trusts operate with substantial financial support from the public sector. Almost two-thirds of recorded enterprise costs are met by contributions provided by the SDA, local authorities and the nationalised industries. Even with the removal of LIFE and BASE from this analysis, the private sector still fails to match, pound for pound, support from public bodies. This data excludes support in the form of premises, goods or specific services. There is, however, good reason to suppose that 'payment in kind' comes in equal proportions from both private and public sectors.

Together, trusts employ 82 full-time, 7 part-time and an unstated number of occasional staff. Employment in three trusts: ASSET, LIFE and GO absorb over 30 per cent of this total. Average employment is about 3.5 persons per trust, falling to less than 3 when the 'bigger' trusts are excluded. The claim that enterprise trusts are only concerned in 'creating jobs for the job creators' does not bear careful inspection.

Functions. Table 7.2 attempts to compare enterprise trusts in terms of their principal functions. This is somewhat complicated by the functional differences between trusts connected with SDA Area Initiatives and those operating on their own. Leaving this difficulty aside, it is evident that the majority of trusts are, first and foremost, involved with business counselling and support services for small firms. Each trust has a different operational style but all tend to adopt standard approaches for new starts, for survival plans for ailing firms, and for filling management gaps and preparing expansion plans for existing companies. The use of counsellors from local firms is widespread as is occasional support from the professions: accountancy, finance and law. It is now almost standard practice to develop this business advice into 'panels', drawing together commercial/technical expertise to review individual business ideas. Such similarities can, however, obscure differences in the objectives of different trusts. Business advice is more commonly used to 'weed-out' the more eccentric ideas, selecting 'winners' to present to the banks, SDA Small Business Division (SBD) and other sources of finance. In other circumstances, BASE being one example, the objective is to generate any form of enterprise, then use the resources available to develop a commercially viable scheme. All trusts see themselves as purveyors of information, guiding prospective and existing firms towards more detailed knowledge and tangible assistance. The larger trusts, GO and ASSET, can provide specialist information in-house; others, like LIFE, do not wish to work too closely with their clients; the majority, however, act as a clearing house, passing clients on to other agencies.

Leaving aside trusts that have a wider remit through their involvement with the SDA, a number consider that the provision and management of premises for small businesses is a key function. Some, like the Stirling Enterprise Park and the Dundee Industrial Association, were established with asset management as their main role. Others, in addition to providing information on the availability and suitability of premises, are eager to expand into the development and letting of managed workspace, combining short-let premises with business advice for the small firm sector. The success of LEntA, BSC(I) and the St Helen's Trust is percolating through the system. However, this ambition can lead the enterprise trust into direct competition with the public agencies (SDA and local government) who have long experience in this sector of the market and with private developers and agents who are well aware of the profit to be made on small-units. It is clear that those trusts operating in parallel with or co-ordinating Area Initiatives have the advantage of being able to offer new starts and existing firms a 'package' that combines advice, premises and perhaps finance.

Few 'independent' trusts have the necessary resources to offer small firms any form of direct financial help. A large majority have, however, quickly established links with local and national grant/loan schemes. The Barrows Trust in the east-end operates a 'block-grant' of LEGUPs from the SDA; CADET in Ayrshire works closely with NCB(Ltd); BASE can call on support from Lothian Region's Employment Subsidy Scheme and a Small Business Enterprise Fund organised by West Lothian District Council. Perhaps the most significant development between trusts and financial aid, and a reflection of the importance of the trust 'movement', is the Enterprise Fund for Youth (EFFY) scheme. Funded by the SDA (£400,000 in 1984), three trusts: GO, ASSET and BASE have been allocated funds to support new business ventures by people aged 16 to 25 years. Soft-loans, up to £3,000, are available for 'imaginative and positive schemes' with business support and advice being provided by the trust concerned.

The other activities of enterprise trusts vary according to location, circumstances and objectives. LIFE, for example, is charged with promoting Lanarkshire, albeit in potential conflict with the SDA, and allocates a significant annual budget to that end.

Training is considered very important by all trusts, but few have the manpower and skills to progress beyond the occasional promotion, visit to local schools or business seminar. BASE has taken its role in this field more seriously than some other trusts, implementing a 'manpower development capacity' that looks beyond conventional approaches to unemployment and skill deficiencies. BASE has appointed a Training and Personal Development Officer whose activities combine mainstream education, MSC training, community business and the development of welfare skills to be applied in non-commercial enterprise. Finally, enterprise trusts use local knowledge and contacts to improve business networks, linking local markets with new or expanding suppliers.

Policy Framework. The review of enterprise trust functions illustrates the significance of a correlation between the area initiatives of the SDA and some 13 local trusts in Scotland. This policy connection is further developed in table 7.3 illustrating that the SDA is not only supportive of the concept of private sector involvement but now envisages the enterprise trust as a vehicle for implementation and for the continuation of initiatives that have reached their original termination dates. The Garnock Valley Development Executive was, for example, formed out of the original Garnock Valley Task Force that invested £18 million between 1979 and 1984. This support for enterprise trusts is in line with the emerging philosophy of SDA's Planning and Projects Directorate (PPD) that is encouraging a move away from the 'strait-jacket' of the Project Agreement. Using enterprise trusts, PPD is examining ways of developing a more flexible organisational style that will also reduce manpower commitments and encourage an emphasis on business development and less attention to land renewal and property. Such a shift will also, it is argued, lend itself to integration with a stronger 'sectoral' focus in the newer area projects. PPD envisage that some form of Project Agreement will need to continue, if only to commit local authority resources, but that in future initiatives the local business community will be asked to play a central role in terms of leadership, organisation and finance. This is evident in the new 'Self-Help Projects' such as the Arbroath Venture and Fraserburgh Ltd discussed in chapter 5.

The relationship between the SDA, Scottish BIC and individual enterprise trusts can also be examined in terms of policy and programme conflict. This can be best illustrated through a review of the activities of BASE and LIFE, both receiving considerable financial support from the SDA. BASE is critical of the Agency on three separate counts. Perhaps not surprisingly, those involved in West Lothian feel aggrieved that the economic decline of their area (Leyland Vehicles, Plessey and North British Foundries) that attracted considerable media and political support did not result in substantial IDS or Agency support for the area, be it in terms of an Area Project or Enterprise Zone. The presence of Livingston New Town has, they would argue, attracted the attention of LIS and the Electronics Division of the SDA leaving the other parts of the region to fend for themselves. They are also critical of the day-to-day contact with the property and small firms divisions of the SDA. West Lothian has therefore been caught by the redirection of policy within the SDA, with the lead being taken by PPD. Bathgate was a 'loser', Livingston New Town was a 'winner'; let BASE, with considerable support from the local authorities, manage the decline; steer new firms and government support to those locations that offer 'opportunity', not a legacy of economic decline. Michael Fass, Director of BASE, suggests that this approach relies upon an indigenous business community that can be encouraged to develop alternative forms of local enterprise. Unfortunately, West Lothian, like many parts of the industrial heartland of Scotland, does not possess this essential ingredient.

Table 7.3. Policy framework: SDA, area initiatives and enterprise trusts.

SDA area initiative designation[1]	Relationship between trust and the area initiative	Role of trust in area initiative (current)	Examples
1. Task Force	Developed from original initiative	To continue initiative; overall management; co-ordination of participants; provision of business services; promotion	Garnock Valley Development Executive
2. Integrated Project	In parallel with project team	Provision of specific services on behalf of the project team, e.g. business services, letting workshop units	Leith Enterprise Trust Dundee Industrial Assoc.
3. Self-Help Project	Fully integrated with area initiative	Project management; co-ordination of participants; fund raising; provision of business services; (possible involvement with provision of other services)	Arbroath Venture Fraserburgh Ltd (ASSET)
4. Local Partnership Initiative[2]	Policy and organisation separation; SDA retains financial and board connection	Provision of specialist services addressing particular issues	Bathgate Area Support Executive (BASE) Lanarkshire Industrial Field Executive (LIFE)

[1] Developed from Gulliver (1984) and SDA (1984).
[2] SDA *not* involved in policy development nor project implementation.

153

The relationship between LIFE and the other public agencies involved with economic development in north Lanarkshire reflects recent history and the resultant organisational complexity. As with BASE, LIFE receives financial support from the SDA (Headquarters) but the operational relationship between the SDA's Project Teams in Motherwell and Coatbridge and the LIFE office appears, at best, strained. There are differences between the objectives of promoting 'Lanarkshire' and marketing Motherwell and Coatbridge; between the nature of business advice given by the LIFE office and small firm counselling offered by the Project Teams and the Motherwell Enterprise Trust; between LIFE's attempts to attract mobile inward investment and the placement of LIS inquiries; and between the involvement of five local authorities in LIFE and the selective investment of the SDA in Motherwell (£37m) and in Coatbridge (£10.7m).

A third example of conflict within the policy network can be illustrated in the Dundee case study. The Dundee Industrial Association, charged with the objective of letting and developing managed workspace in refurbished jute mills in the Blackness Project area, may be disadvantaged by the emerging policies of the much larger Dundee Project. The objectives, direction and marketing of the city-wide Project are aimed at attracting high technology industry to new sites. This has created an organisational style that focusses attention beyond Dundee, away from the immediate problems of the local business community. And at a pedestrian level, even the location and image of the Project Office is perhaps at variance with the needs and aspirations of local business interests. When the temporary offices of the Blackness Project close, the SDA presence in Dundee, for all activities, will be among the pot-plants of the Nethergate Centre, some distance in spatial and psychological terms from the commercial reality facing the Dundee Industrial Association.

As raised earlier, while local government was originally very wary of enterprise trusts, they became generally supportive of the concept with COSLA represented on Scottish BIC's Governing and Executive Councils and Region/District Councils represented in some capacity on all trusts with the exception of Glenrothes. There is little evidence, however, that enterprise trusts are considered as key elements in local economic policy development and no evidence that they have been integrated with the local planning framework of the District Councils. In some areas, therefore, local economic development – premises, advice, grants – is delivered in a policy vacuum, duplicated by competing organisations. The theory of the 'one-door' approach for the small businessman or unemployed school-leaver is not always translated into practice.

Assessing Enterprise Trusts

As in many areas of policy evaluation, it is difficult to separate objective analysis from self-fulfilling prophesy. At the second annual meeting of

Scottish BIC, held in November 1984, its chairman, Sir Hector Laing, stated that:

> These are early days for the movement but it is our belief that through the trust network and their varied operations, we are well on the way to making a major contribution to a national economic recovery.

He may well be correct, but it is necessary to point out that Scottish BIC, the SDA and others involved in local economic development lack any form of rigorous measurement for evaluating initiatives. Moreover, Hood and Young (1984) suggest that 'one of the first priorities should . . . be to assess the effectiveness of what is already being done'. Hence our assessment concentrates on the wider policy framework, linking private strategy for economic development with the activities of the public sector. Comment on the performance of individual trusts is kept to a minimum, although some lessons are drawn from the experiences of enterprise trusts in general.

Turning first to the integration of enterprise trusts with the wider policy network, it is self-evident that the concept of corporate social responsibility, the idea of mutual-aid within the private sector and the evangelism of Scottish BIC has been translated from a 'good idea' to an ever-expanding network of 24 enterprise trusts through the support and good offices of the public sector in the guise of the SDA. In Scotland, trusts and the spatial policies of the Agency are inseparable: of the 10 trusts established in 1984, 7 were directly linked to Area Projects or were in areas under examination by the SDA, for example, Levenmouth and Inverclyde. And as we have already discussed, enterprise trusts have become a vehicle for the implementation of future area initiatives and for the continuation of existing projects. What is less than clear, and here there are contradictions between the SDA and Scottish BIC and also between different parts of the Agency, are the objectives, priorities and targets for enterprise trusts over the life-span of area initiatives. This is further complicated by the use of trusts in markedly different circumstances, in unemployment 'blackspots' as well as in 'areas of opportunity', suggesting that the enterprise trust, certainly in Scotland, will become *the* instrument for delivering SDA programmes to local areas. How to measure their impact is another matter altogether.

Although Scottish BIC suggest that they are only interested in supporting 'business-lead' trusts, the pace and location of new trust formation and their funding arrangements suggest that Scottish BIC are reacting to a lead given by the SDA and lack their own strategy for the development of trusts in Scotland. Furthermore, as the SDA develops, albeit in a post-hoc manner, a monitoring capability, Scottish BIC will come to depend more and more on policy development from the SDA. Exactly what role the enlarged Scottish BIC/SPU will have in terms of training and youth employment is difficult to foretell. However, the lack of experience in this field by most enterprise trust directors may well lead to manpower difficulties in the future.

These comments can be balanced against a number of more favourable policy developments. At an operational level, relations between trusts and other components of the economic development network are generally very good. The close involvement by local authorities, at political and officer level, has eased a number of the tensions that were evident at the outset of the enterprise trusts movement. There is, however, some evidence of territorial conflict; between LIFE and MET in Motherwell and between EVENT, Leith and the Edinburgh Chamber of Commerce. As was the case with overlapping functions in local government, enterprise trusts may well need to examine duplication of effort, complementarity and conflict. Nonetheless, the 24 trusts have been largely successful in getting help and advice direct to the public. Unlike some other areas of local economic development, enterprise trusts operate as a 'client-centred' system, operating limited functions tuned to user demand. And this success has been in no small part due to careful use of promotion and advertising. This contact with the public was perhaps the reason for the choice of enterprise trusts for the EFFY scheme, targeted at young people.

As for the claim that enterprise trusts are now 'making a major contribution . . .' to the Scottish economy, the measurement of effectiveness is an analytical minefield. On the one hand, it is difficult to compare different trusts, different functions, different results: one director's 'telephone enquiry' may be another director's 'firm proposal'; ten jobs 'safeguarded' in one area may turn out to be ten lost in another. On the other hand, and even more confusing, it the common attempt to assess trusts in terms of a nebulous development of 'awareness' or improvement of 'business morale'. Yet it is this activity, as much as numerical job creation, that is used to 'measure' success. A conclusion, taken from the Deloitte booklet, clearly illustrates this point:

> they (trusts) have done much to ensure that each community creates the wealth necessary for survival and prosperity. They have also done much to encourage all interested parties to work together to make the best collaborative use of locally available human resources, while at the same time, fostering individual initiative and drive, and avoiding unnecessary bureaucratic trammels. (DHS 1984)

Amen!

At the local level, individual trusts can certainly claim a measure of success: 1,800 jobs safeguarded by GO, 336 jobs involved in 324 'proposals' in Falkirk: 250 jobs in Kilmarnock; 1,000 enquiries, 157 completed projects, 581 jobs in ASSET and so forth. It is, of course, very difficult to evaluate job creation in such areas in the absence of the trust; as the jargon puts it, measuring the policy-off effect. What is undeniable, however, is that job creation and safeguarding has, in many areas, failed to keep pace with local redundancies. This is not the fault of the enterprise trust movement but it serves to put their impact on employment into perspective. And bearing in mind that Scottish industrial employment is concentrated in medium and large firms, enterprise trusts may well need to consider a different target if they wish to increase their impact on the national economy.

This limited success, particularly in terms of employment in small firms, may have been at the expense of the original concept underpinning local enterprise trusts. The origins – of corporate *social* responsibility, of support for the local community, of involvement in social and environmental affairs – have not surfaced as central activities of enterprise trusts in Scotland. The criticism that private sector support for trusts is merely enlightened self-interest is borne-out by the evidence. There is an almost myopic concern with a narrow definition of business activities, with stimulating 'enterprise' at the expense of other pursuits, with creating traditional jobs in the formal economy. While this emphasis is hardly surprising considering the composition of Scottish BIC and the background of most trust directors, it does represent only one interpretation of local economic development.

The weakness of this pre-occupation is that enterprise trusts do not appear willing or indeed able to respond to other issues in their local areas. If, as may well be the case, small firms do not produce sustained increases in local employment, can enterprise trusts, can their support systems, adjust to new objectives, different sectors in the economy? There is every reason to suggest that as their policy capacity is severely constrained, the ability to change direction, to adopt new approaches, to employ different measures of success, and, critically, to implement change is beyond the meagre resources and limited skills of most enterprise trusts in Scotland.

Finally, the most obvious broad conclusion that can be drawn is that if enterprise trusts represent private involvement in local economic development then they rely to a huge extent on the public sector. Scottish BIC and the individual trusts certainly attract goodwill and limited assistance from parts of the private sector but their approach, many of their basic resources, over half their finance and many of their contacts come from government and other public agencies. In the case of trusts operating in parallel with SDA Projects, the aura of corporate social responsibility, the company crest or logo, the promise of some private housing, merely adds political respectability to traditional public intervention.

Yet this limited 'expenditure' by the private sector has paid handsome political dividends. With the approval of government and through policy redirection within the SDA, there has been a marked shift in the focus of local policies in Scotland; the objective of urban renewal (be it small areas or across cities) has been replaced by a pursuit of commercial expansion; a consideration of social development has lost ground to direct support for private enterprise; success is narrowly defined in terms of leveraging investments, safeguarding employment, securing rates of return and profitability. This is private strategy but at public expense; yet the modest achievements of enterprise trusts in Scotland bear no relation to the scale of the problem nor to their projected future as the main vehicle of local economic development.

8

NEW DIRECTIONS

For some years past, a field trip to Scotland has been an obligatory part of the apprenticeship of aspiring urban and regional planners and social policy makers. From the regional plans and growth poles of the 1960s, through social work developments after 1968, area policies on deprivation, to the GEAR project of 1976, Scotland has pioneered a series of urban policy innovations. What was of particular interest to observers from south of the border was that, by the late 1970s, Scotland seemed to have gained the capacity for a coherent and co-ordinated attack on the syndrome of urban decline. Urban and regional economic priorities did not clash as they did in many parts of England; a single government department, the Scottish Office, dealt with most urban policy functions, bringing together social and economic aspects; and, in the Scottish Development Agency, there existed a powerful interventionist body combining environmental improvement functions and the provision of industrial sites and premises with investment finance and business advice.

The GEAR project represented perhaps the most ambitious attempt at integrated urban renewal in the United Kingdom, aimed simultaneously at the physical, economic and social aspects of inner city decline. Yet, far from being the harbinger of a new approach to urban policy, GEAR has turned out to be the last of the old comprehensive renewal schemes based initially on the notion of multiple deprivation, then subsequently adapted to meet the economic objectives of the SDA. Since then, the various elements of urban policy have been progressively disaggregated.

The SDA was never happy about being in GEAR, into which it was pushed within a year of its creation. GEAR pre-empted resource, time and effort which the Agency would rather have kept free for more selective interventions in projects of its own choosing. It also became increasingly unhappy about the social policy role, regarding this as a distraction from its prime role of stimulating economic development. The Labour Government had never been very precise about what the role of the SDA should be, apart from 'tackling industrial decay and unemployment' and giving 'special attention to those industrial areas which have suffered the worst effects of the decline and decay of our older industries' (October 1974 Scottish Manifesto). As the Agency translated its general brief into an operational strategy, it refined its role, to concentrate on economic and industrial activities and the promotion of viable industries. The hard-headed businesslike approach was further reinforced after 1979 under pressure from the new government. Social objectives were steadily downgraded and job creation became less important than 'value-added' through increased industrial output. The SDA, as it now itself constantly emphasises, is not part of an 'assisted areas' policy but is a regional development agency aiming to exploit the native potential and natural advantages of the Scottish economy.

The result, as we have seen, was a policy developed along two axes, the sectoral and the spatial. The former was about the promotion of internationally competitive industry at the 'sharp end' of the economy, with a particular emphasis on high technology. The latter took the form of a series of 'area projects', programmes for environmental and economic development in declining industrial areas negotiated with local authorities. These had been preceded by emergency 'task forces' in Clydebank and the Garnock Valley, where the SDA had been sent in by the Scottish Office in response to major closures. The initial projects were essentially Industrial Improvement Areas for small pockets of land but the policy was soon expanded to encompass larger projects such as those in Motherwell and Dundee.

A series of dilemmas resulted, which we have examined in the course of the book. What was the relationship between sectoral and area approaches? Would investment finance be channelled into area projects only if each item could be justified in terms of the sectoral strategy and the requirement for a rate of return on investment? If the Agency's industrial policy and sectoral strategies were aimed at the creation of internationally competitive industry, could this not threaten employment as industries modernised? How were areas for projects to be chosen? If, in accordance with the new hard-headed approach of backing winners, it was only to be areas of potential, then what was to be the fate of the declining urban areas? In other words, is a policy of maximising economic growth potential compatible with positive discrimination in favour of the older industrial areas?

In most of the area projects, this problem was glossed over. The formula that projects would be sited, not in the most needy areas, but in those where there was the greatest gap between 'performance' and 'potential' allowed the SDA to maintain its hard-headed business language while being nudged by central and local government into areas like Motherwell, hit by major closures and threatened with more. Job creation targets were inserted into project agreements, demonstrating a continuing concern with employment, though this fits uneasily with the emphasis on 'value-added'.

The area approaches have had their successes. At their best, they have represented positive development planning, with the co-ordination of local government planning and infrastructure powers with the SDA's powers over sites and premises, investment finance and attraction of industry. In Dundee and Clydebank, the enterprise zone policy, potentially a disturbing force in urban development planning, has been incorporated into highly planned and interventionist strategies.

Social policy objectives, it is true, had largely disappeared after GEAR but the spatial and inter-agency integration of development policies under public sector leadership was still a marked feature of the area projects. The main grouse of local authorities was that the SDA's inward investment effort, through the Locate in Scotland organisation, did little for the cities, continuing to point foreign investors in the direction of new town sites.

On the other hand, the potential of the Scottish administrative structure for forging and implementing coherent development strategies has never fully been realised. The distinction between 'urban' and 'regional' economic policies, while productive of less conflict than in England, has been maintained, even though both come within the purview of the Scottish Office. For Scotland as a whole, there is an absence of economic or physical planning, belatedly recognised by the change of name of the Scottish Economic Planning Department to Industry Department for Scotland. The rhetorical emphasis on the reindustrialisation of the older urban areas sits uneasily with the need to maintain support for the new towns and growth areas in the interests of the Scottish economy as a whole. The Scottish Office must increasingly content itself with whatever industry it is able to attract, while devoting a large part of its energies in the battle to retain what exists. So there is no clear pattern of spatial development priorities.

At the regional level, too, the planning system has been largely by-passed by the new initiatives. Structure plans have proved poor successors to the sub-regional plans of the pre-reorganisation period and have neither been integrated with corporate and financial planning mechanisms nor endowed with effective means for their implementation. The lack of a clear framework or priorities for spatial development is exacerbated by the increasing centralisation of government, with the Scottish Office obliged to pursue UK initiatives such as enterprise zones, irrespective of their applicability to Scottish conditions and local authorities unable to make their own spending decisions in response to their assessment of local needs. Only where political authority and financial resources are available can policy effectively be co-ordinated behind coherent objectives, at the Scottish as at the local level.

More recently, we have detected another change of emphasis heralding a further disintegration of urban policy. Under the influence of government thinking – made effective through appointments as well as the usual channel of informal discussion – the agency has begun to de-emphasise urban renewal as such in favour of a more limited view of 'business development'. As so often, it has been preceded by a change of rhetoric placing the role of private initiative to the fore and talking in terms of 'opportunities' rather than 'problems'. Language, indeed, has almost become a barrier to understanding what is happening in Scottish urban policy. As new language is introduced to legitimise intervention in terms of the ideological fashions of the moment, it is not always easy to tell whether policy itself has changed and to some extent it may be true that the rhetoric of non-intervention is merely being used to cover a continuation of the old interventionist line.

There is, though, some practical evidence emerging of the change of strategy in the ending of formal 'area projects' negotiated with local government and their replacement with more informal arrangements, with more input from private business. In areas chosen for intervention, there is more emphasis on sectoral opportunities and business development, less on physical renewal. One product of this has been a closer integration of the area and sectoral approaches within the SDA itself as the emphasis is placed on the creation of internationally competitive industry rather than on shifting resources into areas of need. But it seems that now spatial planning and integration in the context of urban renewal may be following social policy objectives out the window.

An early product of the new approach is the Glasgow City Centre Project. Funded by the SDA and conducted by a consortium of consultants, research and analysis for the Project sought to establish a new commercial focus for the city, with an emphasis on radically altering the city's image for the potential investor – be that an international corporation, a local business or an individual tourist. The 'Glasgow's Miles Better' campaign launched by an energetic Lord Provost in 1983 was to be the springboard for marketing a 'new' Glasgow.

In keeping with this new approach, the consultants' reports were presented to a select audience in the form of a dramatic video. With the help of commercial marketing techniques – expansive concepts, apparently simple goals, message and method repetition – the viewer was presented with a bundle of real estate opportunities in or near the city centre. These ranged from roofed-in street junctions to major physical redevelopment of the semi-derelict dock area of the Broomielaw, to the removal and reconstruction of a famous Victorian church tower from the Gorbals to the top of Buchanan Street.

The Glasgow Project is predicated on the basis that the economic base of the city has permanently shifted and that in order to compete for investment against other major centres in Britain and Europe, the city must project the image of being capable of supporting a successful service-based economy. Hence the proposals presented focus on 'opportunities' for expanding what are now known as 'business services', tourism, linking into the Garden Festival planned for 1989 and further development of market centre functions, including retailing.

The SDA has rejected the formal 'project agreement' model of collaboration with local government and has substituted the private sector as the key participant in the initiative. A group of prominent businessmen has been invited to form 'Glasgow Action' whose role will be to pursue the various development opportunities highlighted by the consultants' studies and advance the ideas towards realisation. While the District and Regional councils will be represented, Glasgow Action will be led, administered and eventually financed by the private sector, developing strategies that accord with the current philosophy that 'what's good for business is good for Glasgow'. Indeed, in a further downgrading of the publicly planned element of renewal, the infrastructure and urban design elements of the proposals were largely dropped as soon as the local authorities made a bid for a major say in their form, to tie them into their wider priorities.

The 'new' style of civic improvement has obvious Victorian precedents. Cities such as Birmingham, Liverpool and Glasgow itself all expanded under the guiding hands of 'enlightened' urban entrepreneurs with the streets, sewers, warehouses and parks all monuments to business leadership. 'Glasgow Action', however, is modelled more closely on contemporary developments in the United States, where corporate influence is the fundamental component of urban change. Organisations such as the Allegheny Conference in Pittsburgh and the Greater Baltimore Committee have been instrumental in determining the scope and direction of urban renewal in these cities. Indeed, the tangible achievements in downtown areas of Philadelphia, Boston, Norfolk and even the Renaissance Center in Detroit have become the very model for the 'new' Glasgow.

American experience shows, however, that urban renewal based on private sector leadership, finance and control – particularly through corporate influences – is not without economic, social and political costs. The mirror-glass hotels and convention centres in downtown Boston and Baltimore are underwritten by massive public support, notably in the form of Federal grants in the 1950s and again in the late 1970s. While the publicity material talks of the private sector rebuilding the city, statistics reveal that instead of every public dollar 'leveraging' four private dollars or more, the reality is closer to 1:1. The figures for the Inner-Harbor development in Baltimore demonstrate that between 1960 and 1982 the private sector invested some $375m in new projects, matched by $330m from the City, State and Federal governments. Moreover, the targeting of public moneys in a relatively small area resulted in public disinvestment elsewhere.

The 'Urban Renewal' programme in the 1950s – the initial stimulus for downtown redevelopment – inflicted social costs on a number of US cities. While originally meant to contain a proportion of low-cost housing, redevelopment led to neighbourhood dislocation, increased suburban drift and further reductions in limited stocks of low-cost housing. Downtown renewal in the late 1970s may not have had the same direct social consequences but the indirect effects may be just as severe. The use of increasingly scarce public funds to bolster an entrepreneurial environment sits uncomfortably alongside a withdrawal of public expenditure across a range of essential welfare activities. It is instructive that the neon lights of the Renaissance Center and Baltimore's Harbor Place are surrounded by acres of blackened, semi-derelict tenement housing, home to an increasingly alienated under-class who benefit little from the corporate offices and tourist toy shops. Islands of prosperity surrounded by a sea of despair!

Perhaps the most sobering implication of transferring responsibility for urban revitalisation on to the private sector is that the objectives of urban reconstruction will, by necessity, become commercial objectives. What is good for the business community becomes the goal of the city. What is necessary for residential neighbourhoods may not figure at all on the agenda of corporate executives determining the shape and direction of urban invest-ment over the long term. If the private sector can see some form of com-mercial benefit from direct involvement in urban governance, they will retain their interest; if not, they will withdraw, leaving a political, organisa-tional and fiscal vacuum.

Private sector-led regeneration in any case depends on the entrepreneurs being present or coming forward. We are very sceptical of this. In Glasgow City Centre, there may be the business leadership to regenerate the service sector, given public sector support. In the industrial towns of north Lanarkshire, there is precious little evidence of a healthy native capitalism. In the Glasgow peripheral estates of Easterhouse and Drumchapel, the idea is utterly fanciful.

Present government policies are predicated on the oft-repeated distinc-tion between a 'wealth-creating' sector identified with privately owned manufacturing industry and traded services, and a 'wealth-consuming' sector including public services. Aid and support is to be given to the former which is said to support the latter. We find this distinction both naive and danger-ous. It rests at various times and in various formulations on three quite different criteria. At one time, wealth-creation will be identified with the ownership of the means of production, the private sector being 'productive' and the public sector a consumer of privately-created wealth. At other times the distinction rests of the nature of the activity, with material goods being 'productive' but services not. Most commonly these days, the distinction rests on the means of distribution, with traded goods and services being 'productive' and those free at the point of use not. In many instances, all three criteria are confusedly run together. The resulting implication that a job teaching the young or improving the environment is 'wealth consuming' while manufacturing tobacco or weapons is 'wealth creating' can lead to a decidedly distorted view of social priorities.

The fact is that the goals of urban economic policies are complex and often conflicting and cannot be reduced to simple formulae such as the need to promote the 'wealth creating sector'. The Government are no doubt correct to argue that industrial modernisation and the creation of internationally competitive industry and services must be a goal of national industrial policies (though there is, paradoxically, little evidence that they have been since 1979). Given modern technology, however, they will not produce large numbers of jobs. The distribution of work and of the social product generally, must therefore be a separate policy objective. Concentration of resources in encouraging entrepreneurs in favoured locations may in itself produce development which passes large numbers of disadvantaged city-dwellers by.

In practice, what seems to be developing is a 'dual' approach to urban economic regeneration. On the one hand, there is the business activity at the 'sharp end' of economic policy, led by the market and responding to profit considerations. The locational implications of this increasingly dominant approach may be to move capital yet further from the deprived areas. On the other, there are initiatives with a more 'social' purpose in places such as Easterhouse and Drumchapel, aimed at helping the casualties of economic change rather than seeking to control the pace and direction of that change itself. Both types of policy, however, are being pushed towards the same 'bootstrap' philosophy of self-reliance and private sector leadership. It is likely that the Easterhouse and Drumchapel initiatives will develop along the lines of the community-based strategies we discussed in chapter 6. In contrast to the profit-seeking approach of development officers in the SDA and to the entrepreneurial evangelism of the enterprise trust movement, this form of local development will be more social than economic. Furthermore, in the absence of a private sector and the necessary commercial structures, we believe that regeneration in the peripheral estates will, first and fore-most, be targetted at community development, planned and largely imple-mented by the public sector. In the absence of a large public expenditure commitment, and particularly in view of the cuts in housing support which we have chronicled, they are likely to become the poor relations of urban regeneration policy.

Our researches have shown that successful urban development has been the result of public leadership, intervention, investment and planning. Certainly, there is a role for public-private partnership in economic regeneration and in housing, but public planning is necessary to reconcile the varied goals of urban renewal and ensure accountability for decisions taken on urban futures. We suggest that to rely on the private sector to take the lead in urban economic regeneration is misguided. First, there is no evidence that the enterprise trusts or other parts of the private sector have the necessary resources seriously to address economic dislocation. Moreover, Inner City Enterprises, a private company seeking new investment opportunities in the inner city, has been largely unsuccessful in attracting new private funds into the deprived sections of English cities. Despite the encouragement of the Financial Initiatives Group formed by Michael Hesletine in the aftermath of the 1981 riots, pension funds, assurance companies and other investors have been reluctant to risk their capital in the inner city or in other less profitable locations. There is no reason to expect that, apart from selective private housing development reflecting local housing market conditions, the de-prived areas of Scottish cities will prove any more attractive to investment capital. Secondly, to replace public planning with the market is to replace public objectives with the profit motive that may, in the long run, prove of little benefit to distressed communities.

Of vital importance to urban regeneration remains public expenditure. Cuts in capital spending have both hampered the infrastructure renewal which is part of urban regeneration and damaged economic prospects for urban Scotland. The prospect of channelling what remains or urban public expenditure through the SDA may result in yet further disinvestment in localities which do not play host to an area 'project'. Furthermore, the political and organisational demands on the Agency may result in an increasing proportion of resources being directed towards prestige projects, while basic urban needs are neglected.

There is a marked transatlantic imitation effect in urban policy, with American initiatives reflected in developments in Scotland and regular visits by SDA officials to see the latest developments in the USA (Boyle and Rich 1984). Yet some of the lessons of American experience are cautionary. The history of the Urban Development Action Grant in the USA shows that public funds earmarked for schemes that must generate or lever extensive private investment can all too easily become isolated from the original objectives chosen for the programme. Instead of addressing problems of urban stress, public money is used as a direct subsidy, frequently supporting projects, often in city centre locations, which would have gone ahead in any case without public assistance. Scarce public urban resources are used to finance property development which has, at best, a marginal impact on the problems of the urban economy. The use of private agencies, be they enterprise trusts, 'action' committees or private companies, as the vehicles for project selection and implementation can only encourage further selectivity in the employment of public funds, with commercial criteria dominant.

We are also concerned that the direction of recent urban policy and, in particular, the focus of public expenditure, may weaken the social fabric of Scotland's cities. While we recognise the importance of assisting private sector investment in profitable locations, we suggest that of equal importance is the continuation of economic, social and physical renewal in the less attractive parts of urban Scotland. Without this parallel expenditure, urban policy is in danger of creating, as we have already implied, two separate urban places. On the one hand, parts of the city centres, specific greenfield industrial sites and selective suburban housing areas will continue to attract private funds and public subsidies. The other urban Scotland, particularly the peripheral housing schemes and the industrial towns of the central belt, will become increasingly isolated from the mainstream of the Scottish economy, forced to adapt to the rigours of declining public support. The consequences of directing urban policy towards 'picking commercial winners' are thus very serious indeed.

Of particular importance here is the reduction in capital spending on housing, in both the public and, following the cuts of 1984–85, private sectors. Housing investment is a vital spatial policy instrument as it can be targetted spatially by local authorities and its direct and multiplier effects can provide employment, often in locally-based firms. It also has a vital role to play in environment and social policy, so impinging on all three strands of 'urban policy'. Renewal of the outdated water and sewerage infrastructure is another means of combining essential physical works with employment creation. Current expenditure cuts have reduced both services to the needy and employment opportunities. If industrial modernisation is not going to be a large creator of jobs, then public service employment becomes all the more vital as an instrument of distribution. Much play has been made by government of the need to provide jobs in the service industries yet, for many of the areas we have examined, private service industries are virtually non-existent. So dogmatic objections to public service employment will have to be overcome.

As unrepentant Keynesians, we believe that a solution to Scotland's urban crisis will require, first and foremost, a macro-economic reflation. Cuts in large areas of public expenditure, the depression of aggregate demand and exchange rate policies have served to exacerbate the condition of vulnerable sectors and areas, with devastating effects on employment in Scottish cities. Without a change in national economic policies, supply side measures of the sort considered here will, at best, shift the location of economic activity in favour of the urban areas. Yet, a reflation of the type recommended by the Opposition parties could all too easily pass urban Scotland by, without spatial targetting of investment and a coherent approach to physical, economic and social regeneration. Spatial planning, combining the planning and infrastructure powers of local government with the investment resources and financial expertise of the SDA, must be a vital part of this. Scotland in the last twenty years has accumulated a great deal of experience and wisdom about planning and urban regeneration. It is vital that these are put to good use and not cast aside in the pursuit of Victorian economic virtues or a belief that simply turning on the public expenditure tap will automatically bring sustenance to needy city areas.

REFERENCES

Boddy, M. and Fudge, C. (eds) (1984) *Local Socialism? Labour Councils and New Left Alternatives* (London: Macmillan).

Berger, P. L. and Neuhaus, R. J. (1977) *To Empower People; The Role of Mediating Structures in Public Policy* (Washington, DC: American Enterprise Institute).

Birdseye, P. and Webb, A. (1984) 'Why the rate burden on business is a cause for concern', *National Westminster Bank Quarterly Review*, February.

Booth, S. and Moore, C. (1985) 'Urban Economic Adjustment and Regeneration: The Role of the Scottish Development Agency', working paper no.10, *Inner City in Context*, ESRC.

Booth, S. A. S., Pitt, D. C. and Money, W. J. (1982) 'Organisational Redundancy? A Critical Appraisal of the GEAR Project', *Public Administration*, 60.1.

Boyle, R. (1983) 'Privatising Urban Problems: A Commentary on Anglo-American Urban Policy', *Studies in Public Policy*, 117, University of Strathclyde.

Boyle, R. and Rich, D. (1984) 'In Pursuit of the Private City: A Comparative Assessment of Urban Policy Orientations in Britain and the United States', *Strathclyde Papers on Planning*, 3, University of Strathclyde.

Campbell, C. (1983) 'Cooperatives in Scotland: The Role of the Scottish Cooperative's Development Committee', *Regional Studies*, 17 (4), pp.281-3.

Carter, C. (1980) *The Development of Regional Planning in Scotland* (Dundee: Duncan of Jordanstone College of Art).

Coon, A. G. (1981) 'Local Plans', *Scottish Planning Law and Practice*, 3, May.

—— (1982) 'Structure Plans: Approved in Parts', *Scottish Planning Law and Practice*, 5, February.

—— (1983) 'Local Plans', *Scottish Planning Law and Practice*, 9, June.

Crawford, P., Fothergill, S. and Monk, S. (1985) *The Effect of Rates on the Location of Employment. Final Report.* Department of Land Economy, University of Cambridge.

Cullingworth, J. B. (1976) *Town and Country Planning in Britain,* sixth edition (London: George Allen and Unwin).

Deloitte, Haskins and Sells (1984) *Local Enterprise Agencies: A New and Growing Feature of the Economy* (London).

DOE (1985) *Enterprise Zone Information, 1983-4* (London: Department of the Environment).

DTI (1983) *Regional Industrial Incentives. Some Economic Issues* (London: Department of Trade and Industry).

Fisher, J. (1984) 'The SDA and Community Business', *Community Business News*, 11.

Fosler, R. S. and Berger, R. A. (1983) *Public-Private Parnerships in American Cities: Seven Case Studies* (Aldershot: Gower).

Foster, N. (1983) *Chambers of Commerce: A Comparative Study of Their Role in the UK and other EEC Countries* (London: Industrial Aids Ltd).

Freeman, J. D. (1984) *Community-Based Economic Development Organisations in Minnesota* (Minneapolis: Center for Urban and Regional Affairs, University of Minnesota).

Grieve, R. (1980) in *The Planner,* 66.3.

Gulliver, S. (1984) 'The Area Projects of the Scottish Development Agency, *Town Planning Review,* 55 (3), 322-34.

Hayton, K. (1983a) 'Employment Creation in Deprived Areas: The Local Authority Role in Promoting Community Business', *Local Government Studies,* 17 (3), p.208.

Heal, A. R. (1983) 'BP's Corporate Responsibility Programme', Proceedings, PTRC Conference, University of Sussex.

Heald, D. (1980) 'Territorial Equity and Public Finance. Concepts and Confusions', *Studies in Public Policy,* no.75, University of Strathclyde.

—— (1983) *Public Expenditure* (Oxford: Martin Robertson).

Henderson, R. (1974) 'Industrial Overspill from Glasgow 1958-68, *Urban Studies,* 11.1.

Higgins, J., Deakin, N., Edwards, J. and Wicks, M. (1983) *Government and Urban Poverty* (Oxford: Blackwell).

Hood, N. (1984) 'The Small Firm Sector', in N. Hood and S. Young (eds), *Industry, Policy and the Scottish Economy* (Edinburgh University Press).

Hood, N. and Young, S. (1984) 'Conclusions: The Way Ahead', in N. Hood and S. Young (eds), *Industry, Policy and the Scottish Economy* (Edinburgh University Press).

HUD (1983) *Partnerships for Community Self-Reliance* (draft) (Washington, DC: Department of Housing and Urban Development).

Initiatives (1982) 'Can Enterprise Trusts be Trusted?', May.

Jolliffe, C. (n.d.) 'Bending Main Line Programmes: The Utilisation of Main Programmes for Urban Regeneration', working paper no.8, *The Inner City in Context,* ESRC.

Jordan, G. and Reilly, G. (1981) 'Enterprise Zones. The Clydebank EZ and Policy Substitution', in H. M. Drucker and N. L. Drucker (eds), *The Scottish Government Yearbook, 1982* (Edinburgh: Paul Harris).

Keating, M. (1982) 'The Stodart Committee and Planning in Scotland', *The Planner,* 68.1.

Keating, M. and Midwinter, A. (1983a) *The Government of Scotland* (Edinburgh: Mainstream).

—— (1983b) 'Region-District Relationships: Lessons from Glasgow', in D. McCrone (ed.), *The Scottish Government Yearbook, 1983* (Edinburgh: Unit for the Study of Government in Scotland).

Keating, M. and Waters, N. (1985) 'Scotland in the European Community', in M. Keating and J. B. Jones (eds), *Regions in the European Community* (Oxford University Press).

Labour Party (1973) 'Scotland and the National Enterprises Board' (Glasgow: Labour Party, Scottish Council).

Lawless, P. (1981) *Britain's Inner Cities – Problems and Policies* (London: Harper and Row).

Leclerc, R. and Draffan, D. (1984) 'The Glasgow Eastern Area Renewal Project', *Town Planning Review,* 55 (3).

Lock, D. (1977) 'Silent Voice of Experience', *Town and Country Planning,* 45.2.

Lythe, C. and Majmudar, M. (1982) *The Renaissance of the Scottish Economy?* (London: George Allen and Unwin).

McAllister, E. (1984) *Local Enterprise Trusts –A Growth Industry,* unpublished MSc dissertation, University of Strathclyde.

References

McArthur, A. A. (1984) 'The Community Business Movement in Scotland: Contributions, Public Sector Responses and Possibilities', *Discussion Paper 17*, Centre for Urban and Regional Research, University of Glasgow.

MacDonald, S. (1983) 'How Grows the Thistle?', *The Planner*, 69.4.

McKinnon, R. V., Samars, P. W. and Sullivan, S. (1982) 'Business Initiatives in the Private Sector', in J. A. Meyer (ed.), *Meeting Human Needs* (Washington, DC: American Enterprise Institute).

Mawson, J., Martins, M. and Gibney, J. (1985) 'The Development of the European Community Regional Policy', in M. Keating and J. B. Jones (eds), *Regions in the European Community* (Oxford University Press).

Meyer, J. A. (1982) 'Private Sector Initiatives and Public Policy: A New Agenda', in J. A. Meyer (ed.), *Meeting Human Needs* (Washington, DC: American Enterprise Institute).

Midwinter, A., Keating, M. and Taylor, P. (1983) 'Excessive and Unreasonable. The Politics of the Scottish Hit List', *Political Studies*, XXXI, 394-417.

—— (1984) 'The Politics of Scottish Housing Plans', *Policy and Politics*, 12.2, 145-66.

Mier, R. and Wiewel, W. (1983) 'Business Activities for Not-for-Profit Organisations', *APA Journal*, 49 (3), pp.316-25.

Monopolies and Mergers Commission (1982) *The Hongkong and Shanghai Banking Corporation, Standard Chartered Bank Limited, The Royal Bank of Scotland Group Limited: A Report on the Proposed Mergers*, Cmd 8472 (London: HMSO).

Moore, B. and Rhodes, J. (1973) 'Evaluating the Effects of British Regional Policy', *The Economic Journal*, 83, pp.87-110.

Nairn, A. G. M. (1983) 'GEAR – Comprehensive Redevelopment or Confidence Trick?', *Fraser of Allander Economic Commentary*, Vol.2.

Newnham, R. (1980) 'Community Enterprise: British Potential and American Experience', *Occasional Paper 3*, School of Planning Studies, University of Reading.

Pearce, J. (1983) 'LEAP into Action', *Initiatives*, pp.24-6.

—— (1982) 'Forget Them! This is the Us Solution', *Guardian*, Jan. 11.

President's Task Force on Private Sector Initiatives (1982) *Investing in America: Initiatives for Community and Economic Development* (Washington, DC).

Randall, J. (1980) 'Central Clydeside – A Case Study of One Conurbation', in G. C. Cameron (ed.), *The Future of the British Conurbation* (London: Longman).

Richardson, J. J. (1983) 'The Development of Corporate Responsibility in the UK, *Strathclyde Papers on Government and Politics*, 1, University of Strathclyde.

Rodrigues, D. and Bruinvels, P. (1982) *Zoning in on Enterprise. A Businessman's Guide to the Enterprise Zones* (London: Kogan Page).

Roger Tym (1984) *Monitoring Enterprise Zones. Three Year Report* (London: Roger Tym and Partners).

Ross, J. (1981) 'The Secretary of State for Scotland and the Scottish Office', *Studies in Public Policy*, University of Strathclyde, no.87.

RSA (1983) Regional Studies Association, *Report of an Inquiry into Regional Problems in the United Kingdom* (Norwich: GEO).

Saloman, L. M. (1984) 'Nonprofit Organisations; The Lost Opportunity', in J. L. Palmer and I. V. Sawhill (eds), *The Reagan Record* (Cambridge, Mass.: Ballinger).

Scottish BIC 1982) *Local Enterprise Agencies: An Outline Prospectus* (Edinburgh).

SDA (1980) *GEAR Strategy and Programme* (Glasgow: Scottish Development Agency).

—— (1984) *Annual Report, 1984 – The Agency in Partnership* (Glasgow).

SEPD (1975) *New Towns in Scotland: A Consultation Document* (Edinburgh: Scottish Economic Planning Department).

—— (1978) 'Annual Gross Changes in Manufacturing Employment in the Scottish New Towns and the Rest of Scotland, 1950-70', *Scottish Economic Bulletin,* 14.
—— (1981) *New Towns in Scotland. A Policy Statement* (Edinburgh: Scottish Economic Planning Department).
SRI (International) (1981) *Developing Public-Private Approaches to Community Problem-Solving* (Washington, DC).
SPU (1983) *The Community Action Programmes Report* (London: CBI).
Taylor, S. (1981) 'The Politics of Enterprise Zones', *Public Administration,* 59, 421-41.
Thomson, S. (1983) *An Evaluation of Local Plan Production and Performance* (Glasgow: Planning Exchange).
Thornley, J. (1981) *Workers' Cooperatives: Jobs and Dreams* (London: Heinemann).
Tyler, P., Moore, B. and Rhodes, J. (1980) 'New Developments in the Evaluation of Regional Policy', SSRC Urban and Regional Studies Group.
Wannop, U. (1981) 'The Future for Development Plans', *The Planner,* 67.1.
—— (1983) *The Future Management of GEAR: A Report to the SDA* (Glasgow: University of Strathclyde).
Wheatley (1969) Royal Commission on Local Government in Scotland 1966-69, chairman Lord Wheatley, *Report,* Cmd 4150 (London: HMSO).
Woodson, R. L. (1982) 'The Impact of Neighbourhood Organisations in Meeting Human Needs', in J. A. Meyer (ed.), *Meeting Human Needs* (Washington, DC: American Enterprise Institute).

INDEX

Abercrombie, Sir Patrick, 31
Aberdeen, 8, 25, 26, 70, 78, 108
Action Resource Centre, 138
Anderson Strathclyde, 17
Angus District, 60, 62
area development, 24
Arbroath, 61, 62, 88
Arbroath Venture, 62
Area Development Directorate, 4, 45
Areas of Priority Treatment, 6
ASSET, 144, 145

BSC (Industries), 80, 144
Ball, Colin, 119
Barlow Committee, 33, 34
Barnett formula, 18, 19
Bank of Scotland, 58
BASE, 152-4
Bathgate, 19, 32, 50, 145, 152
Blackness, 87, 88, 103, 105, 110, 154
Borders Region, 51
branch plants, 58
British Leyland, 50
British Shipbuilders, 20
Business in the Community (BIC), 140

'call-in' powers, 39, 40
capital allocations, 69, 73, 78
Central Region, 5, 51, 78
chambers of commerce, 137-8
Chrysler Corporation, 19
Churchill, Winston, 16
CIPFA, 73
'clawback', 74
Clydebank, 11, 20, 41, 45, 56-8, 59, 62, 64, 85, 86, 88, 109, 110, 159
City Action Teams, 11
Clyde Valley Plan, 31, 32
Coatbridge Project, 79, 88
Commissioners for Special Areas, 47

Community Action Programme, 3
Community Development Project
    (CDP), 3-4
Community Programme, 15, 80
Comprehensive Community Programme
    (CCP), 4
Confederation of British Industry (CBI),
    16, 38, 51, 142-3
corporate planning, 40
cooperatives, 116-18
Corby, 63, 64
corporate responsibility, 137, 157
COSLA, 79
Craigneuk, 4
Cromarty Firth, 59
'crowding out', 71-2
Cumbernauld, 32, 34, 35, 38
Cunninghame District, 144-5

Denny and Bonnybridge, 88
Department of Agriculture and Fisheries
    for Scotland (DAFS), 13
Department of Employment, 56, 109
Department of the Environment (DOE),
    4, 9, 15, 56, 60, 70, 86, 122
Department of Health and Social
    Security (DHSS), 12
Department of Trade and Industry
    (DTI), 12, 15, 23, 39, 48, 50, 122,
    140-1
Development Areas, 48, 52
development control, 28, 29, 40, 84
development plans, 28
devolution, 17, 20
Drumchapel, 163-4
Dundee, 8, 9, 32, 48, 53, 60-2, 64, 87, 88,
    92, 103-9, 159
Dundee Project, 60, 64, 78, 87-8, 91,
    103-9 *passim*

171

Economic Priority Areas, 83
East Kilbride, 31, 32, 34, 35, 37, 38 ←
Easterhouse, 163-4
Edinburgh, 48, 73, 92, 98, 99
Education Priority Area, 2, 3
employment, 8, 12
Employment Protection Act, 55, 58
enterprise trusts in Scotland, 146-52
enterprise zones, 11, 20, 53, 55-64, 85,
    100
ethnic minorities, 2
European Commission, 20, 66, 67
European Community, 18, 47, 65-7, 80
European Coal and Steel Community,
    65, 80
European initiatives, 65-8
European Investment Bank, 65, 66
European Regional Development Fund,
    65-8
European Social Fund, 65, 66, 80, 82
evaluation, 109-110
Examination in Public, 29

Fife Region, 36, 51
Ferguslie Park, 3, 125
'fire brigade' interventions, 20, 24
Forth and Clyde Canal, 29, 31
Fraserburgh, 137
free market policies, 41, 55, 56

Garnock Valley, 85, 86, 88, 109, 110, 152
General Improvement Areas, 2
Gilmour Committee, 15
Glasgow, 4, 5, 25, 31, 32, 33, 34, 36, 40,
    41, 44, 47, 57, 58, 67, 68, 92, 99-100,
    112, 161
Glasgow Action, 161-2
Glasgow Corporation, 31
Glasgow District Council, 25, 39, 40, 43,
    46, 67, 77, 78, 81, 82
Glasgow Eastern Area Renewal (GEAR),
    4, 9, 21, 24, 36, 41-6, 106, 158, 160
'Glasgow's Miles Better' campaign, 81
Glengarnock, 11, 20
Glenrothes, 35, 38, 52
Goodwill, 138
Goodyear, 41
Goschen formula, 17
Govan, 41, 129
Grampian Region, 5, 8, 25, 51, 77, 82
Grangemouth, 51
Greater London Council, 26, 76, 83

Gray, Sir William, 41
green belt, 61
growth poles, 48, 50

Hall, Peter, 55
Heseltine, Michael, 140, 164
Highlands and Islands Development
    Board, 14, 15, 59, 63, 66, 118
Highland Region, 31, 59
Home Office, 3, 4
Howard, Ebenezer, 33
House of Lords, 83
housing expenditure, 106
housing associations, 2
Housing Corporation, 2, 43
housing policy, 1, 2
Housing Support Grant, 69, 75, 99-100

Industrial Development Certificates, 48
Industrial Improvement Areas, 79, 159
industrial promotion, 21, 36
industrial policy, 32, 76
'Industrial Strategy', 19
Industry Department for Scotland, 13,
    14, 21, 30, 48, 146, 160
Inner Area Studies, 4
inner cities, 4, 19, 38
inner city partnerships, 106
Inner Urban Areas Act, 4, 79
Integrated Development Operation, 47,
    67, 68
Intermediate Areas, 48, 51
International Monetary Fund, 71
Inverclyde, 113, 132, 155
Invergordon, 19, 20, 50, 58-9, 63, 64
Invest In Britain Bureau, 23
Irvine, 34, 35, 37, 38

Johnston, Tom, 16, 17
joint ventures, 80-1

Kilmarnock, 88, 103

Labour Party, 4, 21, 25
Laing, Sir Hector, 141, 155
'lame duck' industries, 21
LEGUP, 151
Layfield Committee, 70
Leith, 45, 48, 88, 110
LIFE, 154
Linwood, 19, 28, 32, 40, 50, 89
Liverpool, 11

Livingston, 32, 34, 35, 36, 38
local economic development policies, 76-84
Local Enterprise Advisory Project (LEAP), 125, 134
local government, 25-7, 68-84
local government aid to firms, 81-2
Local Government and Planning (Scotland) Act, 76, 81
local government expenditure, 69-76
local government reorganisation, 6, 25, 30, 71
Local Government (Scotland) Act, 26, 81
local planning, 28-31, 78
local plans, 28, 29, 30, 40, 44
Locate In Scotland, 14, 23, 104, 111
Location of Offices Bureau, 4
London, 9, 50, 55, 81
London Docklands, 11
Lothian Region, 36, 77, 78

Manpower Services Commission, 15, 18, 44, 66, 80, 109, 122, 142
manufacturing employment, 8, 9, 35, 42, 49
Maryhill, 41
Merseyside Task Force, 11
migration, 35, 36
Mondragon, 117
Monklands District, 79
Monopolies Commission, 17
Moss Morran, 51
Motherwell, 4, 20, 87, 92, 98, 103, 104, 109, 110, 111, 156, 159
multiple deprivation, 2, 47
multiplier effect, 50

National Enterprise Board, 21, 24, 118
National Plan, 33
National Planning Guidelines, 30
new towns, 5, 31, 33-8
New Towns Acts, 34
'new urban left', 76
'non-additionality', 65-7
North East of Scotland Development Association, 77, 81, 82
North Sea oil, 24, 51, 77

overspill, 31, 32, 34, 35

Paisley, 3

Pearce, John, 119, 125-6
pension funds, 82
peripheral estates, 163
Plan for Central and South East Scotland, 32
Planning Advisory Group, 28
Plowden Committee, 2, 80
policy autonomy, 14-15
Port Dundas, 88, 103, 105, 109
Port Glasgow, 132, 136
Post Office Savings Bank, 19
Powell, Enoch, 3
private rental, 2
project agreements, 103
public expenditure, 17, 18, 19, 71-6, 165-6
Public Sector Borrowing Requirement, 71-2

racial tension, 3
rates, 55, 63, 69, 70, 73
Rate Support Grant, 3, 65, 69, 74, 75, 76, 92, 99-100
Radio Cyde, 58
Ravenscraig, 4, 19, 20, 32, 40, 50, 80
Regional Development Grants, 48, 51, 81
Regional Employment Premium, 48, 50, 51
regional growth centres, 34
regional planning, 31-3, 39, 48, 50
regional policy, 9-11, 19, 20, 47-55
Regional Reports, 6, 30, 33, 36, 78
Regional Studies Association, 11
Reith Committee, 34
Ronan Point, 2
Rootes, 28
Ross, William, 16, 17
Royal Bank, 17

Scott Lithgow, 20
Scottish Business in the Community, 154, 155
Scottish Cooperative Development Committee, 118
Scottish Council (Development and Industry), 16, 17, 21, 23, 32
Scottish Council Research Institute, 21
Scottish Development Agency, 11, 13, 14, 15, 19, 21-5, 30, 36, 41, 45, 52, 57, 58, 60, 61, 62, 66, 79, 80, 82, 83, 84, 85-114, 124, 125, 126, 158

Scottish Development Department, 13, 14, 21, 30, 57
Scottish Development Finance Ltd, 13
Scottish Economic Council, 16
Scottish Economic Planning Board, 33
Scottish Economic Planning Council, 33
Scottish Economic Planning Department, 13, 30, 32, 36, 56, 57
Scottish Education Department, 13
Scottish Home and Health Department, 13
Scottish Industrial Estates Corporation, 21
Scottish Office, 3, 6, 12, 13-21, 30, 31, 32, 39, 41, 46, 51, 57, 58, 59, 60, 65, 72, 86, 88-9, 90, 92, 113, 160
Scottish Special Housing Association, 41, 43
Scottish Trades Union Congress, 16
Secretary of State for Scotland, 16, 17, 18, 21, 28, 29, 37, 48, 51, 58, 72, 75
'Section 50' agreement, 61
'Section 83', 81
sectoral policies, 159
Seiff, Lord, 141
Select Committee on Scottish Affairs, 19, 23, 30
selective financial assistance, 48, 52
Silicon Glen, 55
Singer works, 41, 54
small firms, 52
Small Industries Council for Rural Areas in Scotland, 21
social balance, 34, 35
social deprivation, 6
Solicitor-General for Scotland, 60
South of Scotland Electricity Board, 59
Special Development Areas, 48
Special Programmes Unit (of CBI), 142-3
Springburn, 41
Stonehouse, 4, 6, 34, 36
Strathclyde Community Business, 124, 126, 134
Strathclyde Region, 5, 8, 25, 30, 31, 35, 48, 66, 100
Strathclyde Regional Council, 6, 33, 36, 39, 57, 67, 77, 78, 80, 107
structure plans, 14, 28, 29, 30, 31, 33, 36, 38, 40, 61, 78
Stuart, James, 16

subject plans, 31
sub-regional plans, 25, 33
Sullom Voe, 51

Task Forces (England), 11
Task Forces (Scotland), 57, 58, 59, 159
Tayside Region, 9, 51, 60, 62, 66, 77, 78, 80
Tayside Regional Industrial Office, 77
Technical and Vocational Education Initiative, 14, 80
Technology Parks, 60, 61, 91, 105
Toothill Report, 52
Town and Country Planning Act, 28
Town and Country Planning Association, 33, 34, 36
Trades Union Congress, 16, 51
transport policies and programmes, 14, 78
Treasury, 14, 18, 19, 56, 65, 72

USA experience, 119-20, 139, 162, 165
unemployment, 6, 8, 42, 45, 48, 50, 54, 78
Urban Aid, 122, 125, 133
urban deprivation, 3, 5, 9, 33, 78
Urban Development Corporations, 11, 46
urban economic policy, 11
urban policy, 1, 2-13, 44, 45
urban planning, 5, 28-46
urban priority areas, 24
Urban Programme, 3-6, 12, 79
urban renewal, 41, 44, 45, 46
Urban Renewal Directorate, 41, 45
Urban Renewal Unit, 6, 57

voluntary organisations, 3

Walker, Peter, 4
West Central Scotland Plan, 5, 6, 21, 33, 36
West Midlands, 9, 11, 19, 20, 50, 81
Western Isles, 118
Wheatley Commission, 25, 33, 34, 38, 76
Wigtown, 88
Wilson, Harold, 3, 16, 17

Youth Training Scheme, 15, 142